For Tom Faulkner

Creating and Consuming Culture in North-East England, 1660–1830

Edited by

HELEN BERRY
University of Newcastle

JEREMY GREGORY
University of Manchester

ASHGATE

Published by
Ashgate Publishing Limited
Gower House
Croft Road
Aldershot
Hants GU11 3HR
England

Ashgate Publishing Company
Suite 420
101 Cherry Street
Burlington, VT 05401-4405
USA

Ashgate website: http://www.ashgate.com

British Library Cataloguing in Publication Data
Creating and consuming culture in North-East England, 1660-1830. - (The history of retailing and consumption)
1.Popular culture - England, North East - History - 17th century 2.Popular culture - England, North East - History -18th century 3.Popular culture - England, North East - History - 19th century 4.Consumption (Economics) - England, North East - History - 17th century 5.Consumption (Economics) - England, North East - History - 18th century 6.Consumption (Economics) - England, North East - History - 19th century 7.Regionalism - England, North East - History - 17th century 8.Regionalism - England, North East - History - 18th century 9.Regionalism - England, North East - History - 19th century 10.England, North East - Social life and customs
I.Berry, Helen II.Gregory, Jeremy
306'.09428

Library of Congress Cataloging-in-Publication Data
Creating and consuming culture in North-East England, 1660-1830 / edited by Helen Berry, and Jeremy Gregory.
p. cm. -- (The history of retailing and consumption)
Includes bibliographical references and index.
ISBN 0-7546-0603-1 (cloth : alk. paper)
1. Consumers--England, North East--History. 2. Consumption (Economics)--England, North East--History. 3. England, North East--Civilization--18th century. 4. England, North East--Civilization--17th century. 5. National characteristics, British--History. 6. England, North East--Social life and customs--History. 7. England, North East--History. I. Berry, Helen M., 1969- II. Gregory, Jeremy. III. Series.

HC254.5.C74 2003
339.4'7'094280903--dc21

2003052348

ISBN 0 7546 0603 1

Printed and bound in Great Britain by MPG Books Ltd, Bodmin, Cornwall

Contents

List of Illustrations

Found between pages 90 and 98

List of Tables

Notes on Contributors

RICHARD C. ALLEN is Lecturer in History at the University of Newcastle and Visiting Fellow at the University of Northumbria, Newcastle. He has published extensively on the history of the Society of Friends, including '"Taking Up Her Daily Cross": Women and the Early Quaker Movement in Wales', in Michael Roberts and Simone Clark (eds), *Women and Gender in Early Modern Wales* (Cardiff, 2000); '"Mocked, Scoffed, Persecuted, and Made a Gazeing Stock": The Resistance of the Religious Society of Friends (Quakers) to the Religious and Civil Authorities in Post-Toleration South-East Wales c.1689-1836', in Gilbert Bonifas (ed.), *Resistances* (Nice, 2003); and '"A Most Industrious Well-Disposed People", Milford Haven Quakers and the Pembrokeshire Whaling Industry c.1791-1821', in Pamela O'Neill (ed.), *Nation and Federation* (Sydney, 2003). His current research focuses upon the emigration and settlement patterns of Quaker communities in America and in the Caribbean.

HELEN BERRY is Lecturer in History at the University of Newcastle, and is the author of *Gender, Society and Print Culture in Late-Stuart England. The Cultural World of the Athenian Mercury* (Ashgate, 2003). She has published several articles on culture and society in early modern England, including '"Prudent Luxury": the Metropolitan Tastes of Judith Baker, Durham Gentlewoman', in Rosemary Sweet and Penelope Lane (eds), *Women and Urban Life in Eighteenth-Century England* (Ashgate, 2003), and 'Promoting Taste in the Provincial Press: National and Local Culture in Eighteenth-Century Newcastle Upon Tyne', *British Journal for Eighteenth-Century Studies*, 25 (2002). She is currently writing a history of eighteenth-century coffee houses.

J. A. CHARTRES is Professor of Social and Economic History at the University of Leeds and former Editor of the *Agricultural History Review*. Among recent publications have been 'Country Trades, Crafts and Professions' and 'Industries in the Countryside' in the *Agrarian History of England and Wales, VII, 1850-1914* (Cambridge University Press, 2000); 'Leeds, Regional Distributive Centre of Luxuries in the Eighteenth Century', *Northern History*, XXXVI (2000); and 'The Eighteenth-Century English Inn: a Transient "Golden Age"?', in Beat Kümin and B. Ann Tlusty (eds), *The World of the Tavern: Public Houses in Early Modern Europe*, (Ashgate, 2002).

ADRIAN GREEN is Lecturer in History at the University of Durham. His publications include research into houses and social relations in North-East England: 'Tudhoe Hall and Byers Green Hall: Houses and Social Change in Lowland County Durham in the Seventeenth and Early Eighteenth Century', *Vernacular Architecture*, 29 (1998); 'Houses in North-Eastern England: Regionality and the British Beyond, c.1600-1750', in Susan Lawrence (ed.), *Archaeologies of the British* (Routledge, 2002) and 'Durham City 1550-1750', in Adrian Green and Roger Leech (eds), *Cities in the World, 1500-2000* (Society for Post-Medieval Archaeology, forthcoming). He is currently writing *Dwelling in England: Houses and Society 1550-1750.*

JEREMY GREGORY was Principal Lecturer and Head of History at the University of Northumbria and is now Senior Lecturer in the History of Modern Christianity at the University of Manchester. He has written extensively on the long eighteenth century and his publications include: *Restoration, Reformation, and Reform, 1660-1828* (Oxford University Press, 2000); with Jeremy Black (eds), *Culture, Society and Politics in Britain, 1660-1800* (Manchester University Press, 1991); with John Stevenson (eds), *The Longman Companion to Britain in the Eighteenth Century* (Longman, 2000). He is currently working on the links between the Church of England and North America, 1680-1790.

REBECCA KING was awarded her doctorate by the University of Durham in 2001 for a thesis entitled 'Aspects of Sociability in the North-East of England, 1600-1750', which examines the experience of sociability in the 'long seventeenth century'. While studying for her doctorate she taught and lectured part-time at the University of Durham. Her University of Durham MA thesis, 'Rape in England, 1600-1800: Trials, Narratives and the Question of Consent', was on the law of rape, the conduct of rape trials, and attitudes to sexual violence in the early modern period. She gained a Postgraduate Diploma in Law from BPP Law School in 2002, during which she researched the development of corporate criminal liability and won the Criminal Law Prize. She is currently a trainee solicitor.

LORNA SCAMMELL, formerly WEATHERILL, has had an eclectic career. Her main historical work was done in the 1970s and 1980s on industrial development, especially in the pottery industry and then on consumer behaviour. Her widely-cited book *Consumer Behaviour and Material Culture in Britain, 1660-1760* (1988) has now entered its second edition (Routledge, 1996). Since then, she has been attracted by technology and is now the University database adviser in the University of Newcastle upon Tyne, where she has developed particular interest in displaying research data on the Internet.

PAUL USHERWOOD is an art critic and historian teaching at Northumbria University. He has written extensively on aspects of northern culture and on nineteenth-century and late twentieth-century British art, especially public art. His publications include *Lady Butler, Battle Artist, 1846-1933* (Allan Sutton and the National Army Museum, 1987) and *Public Sculpture of North-East England* (Liverpool University Press, 2000).

KATIE WALES, FRSA, FEA, is currently Dean of Learning and Teaching in the Faculty of Arts, University of Leeds, and Chair of English Language. She is Editor of the journal *Language and Literature*, and author of over 50 articles on English language and literature from Old English to the present-day. Books include *A Dictionary of Stylistics* (second edition) (Pearson 2001); and *Personal Pronouns in Present-day English* (Cambridge University Press, 1996); also co-editor of *Shakespeare's Dramatic Language* (Thomson Learning, 2001). She is currently working on a book on the cultural history of Northern English for Mouton.

Acknowledgements

The editors would like to thank the University of Northumbria for its generous support in funding the research project 'Nationalising Taste: Cultural Value and National Identity in Eighteenth-Century Britain, with Special Reference to the North-East of England', the inspiration behind this collection. Thomas Faulkner and Allan Ingram gave much time and helpful advice in the course of the project. Helen Berry would also like to thank the University of Newcastle for an Internal Research Fellowship in 2002 that allowed her to complete the final editing of this book, and Victoria Gardner, who compiled the Index.

General Editor's Preface

The History of Retailing and Consumption
Series Editor: Gareth Shaw, University of Exeter, UK

It is increasingly recognised that retail systems and changes in the patterns of consumption play crucial roles in the development and societal structure of economies. Such recognition has led to renewed interest in the changing nature of retail distribution and the rise of consumer society from a wide range of academic disciplines. The aim of this multidisciplinary series is to provide a forum of publications that explore the history of retailing and consumption.

Chapter 1

Introduction

HELEN BERRY and JEREMY GREGORY

As befitted a decade which saw a huge amount of discussion about modern-day consumerism, nationalism and regionalism, two topics dominated the agenda of historians who were writing on eighteenth-century England during the 1990s: cultural consumption and diffusion, and national and regional identity. The first topic had it roots in the early 1980s, with the publication of the now-classic collection of essays written by Neil McKendrick, John Brewer and J. H. Plumb, *The Birth of Consumer Society: the Commercialisation of Eighteenth-Century England* (1982). This became one of the key texts in highlighting the importance of the eighteenth century in the development of a consumerist society, and it alerted historians of the need to turn away from studying changes in production to studying changes in consumption to understand the hallmarks of modern society and its culture. McKendrick's text has been highly influential but it has not gone unchallenged. In particular, its emphasis on an urban 'middling class' which effectively drove the consumer revolution has been queried by those historians who have been concerned that as an explanatory device it had many flaws; for example, it ignored the question of incomes (unless people had more disposable income, how could they purchase these extra goods?). It also marginalised the role of the aristocracy and landed gentry, as well as the role of those below 'middling' ranks, in shaping and buying into the new consumer culture. Some have argued that it is impossible to separate out aristocratic culture from that of the middling sort, preferring to see 'élite culture' as increasingly widely diffused, and that this, in some accounts, helps explain the so-called 'stability' of the mid-eighteenth century. But others have derided the concept of cultural emulation, which this criticism implies, and have explored cultural tensions, which to some extent map on to class differences. Above all, for our purposes, McKendrick's consumer revolution is supposed to have created a national culture and market, which eroded and transcended regional and local cultural forms.

Some of the criticisms noted above, as well as amplifications and workings out of the 'McKendrick thesis', were aired in the monumental trilogy edited by John Brewer, Roy Porter, Ann Bermingham, and Susan Staves,[1] as well as being more directly challenged in the work of Carol Shammas, Beverly Lemire,

---

1 John Brewer and Roy Porter (eds), *Consumption and the World of Goods* (London, 1993); John Brewer and Ann Bermingham (eds), *The Consumption of Culture, 1660-1800: Image, Object, Text* (London, 1995); John Brewer and Susan Staves (eds), *Early Modern Conceptions of Property* (London, 1995).

Lorna Weatherill, and Peter Borsay.[2] But despite these objections, the 'McKendrick thesis' has had a wide impact; for instance, many of its insights and assumptions about the importance of the middling sorts helped shape the broader social and political narrative of Paul Langford's *A Polite and Commerical People: England, 1727-1782* (Oxford, 1989) and no collection of essays which aims to explore how culture was consumed, such as this, can ignore it.

The second topic that riveted historians writing in the 1990s was the issue of national and regional identity, which developed in tandem but to a surprisingly large degree independently of the work on cultural consumption. How far contemporary developments such as the collapse of Communism in Eastern Europe in 1989 and debates over devolution within the United Kingdom (which to a large extent dominated the domestic political agenda in the 1990s) affected historians working on the eighteenth century is a matter of conjecture, although Linda Colley acknowledges the influence of these events in her thinking while penning her seminal *Britons. Forging the Nation, 1710-1837* (1992). The significance of Colley's work, which explored how and when people living in England, Scotland and Wales (although frustratingly she did not turn her attention to Ireland) began to see themselves as 'British' opened up a new and fruitful topic for historians of the period. Her study initiated some interesting debates: how far was national identity the same as 'nationalism' (which has usually been seen as the preserve of the post-1789 era), and how far did loyalty to Britain subvert and overtake existing loyalties? The 'Colley thesis' was explored and to some extent challenged from two main directions. First, there were those who thought that one of her primary mechanisms for the creation of national identity, Protestantism, was in fact a very unstable basis for nationhood.[3] Secondly, there were those who argued that her concentration of the development of a single national identity minimised other 'Scottish', 'Welsh' and 'Irish' identities.[4] Certainly, Colley's work begged a number of salient questions, the most pressing for the present authors being; who precisely participated in this national culture?

It is interesting that the limits to Colley's Britishness were usually seen as coming from that of rival 'nations'. A few notable works, especially C. Harvie's, *Scotland and Nationalism: Scottish Society and Politics, 1707-1994* (1994), Murray Pittock's *The Invention of Scotland: the Stuart Myth and Scottish Identity* (1991), his *Inventing and Resisting Britain: Cultural Identities in Britain and Ireland, 1685-1789*, and Colin Kidd's, *Subverting Scotland's Past: Scottish Historians and the Creation of an Anglo-British Identity, 1689-1930* (1993) are

---

[2] Carol Shammas, *The Preindustrial Consumer in England and America* (Oxford, 1990); Beverly Lemire, *Fashion's Favourite: the Cotton Trade and the Consumer in Britain, 1660-1800* (Oxford, 1991); Lorna Weatherill, *Consumer Behaviour and Material Culture* (London, 1988; 2nd edn, 1996); and Peter Borsay, *The English Urban Renaissance: Culture and Society in the Provincial Town, 1660-1700* (London, 1989).

[3] See the essays in Tony Claydon and Ian McBride (eds), *Protestantism and National Identity: Britain and Ireland, 1650-1850* (Cambridge, 1998).

[4] See Lawrence Brockliss and David Eastwood (eds), A *Union of Multiple Identities. The British Isles, 1750-1850* (Manchester, 1997); and Alexander Murdoch, *British History, 1660-1832. National Identity and Local Culture* (Basingstoke, 1998) for forceful explorations of the attractions of other and competing loyalties.

particularly illuminating in this regard. But given that the contemporary political debate in the late twentieth and early twenty-first century has not only been about the creation of a Scottish Parliament and a Welsh National Assembly, but also about more devolved regional government and assemblies *within* England (such as that proposed for the North-East, Cornwall, and with less conviction for the North-West), it is noteworthy that few have explored how far those living within eighteenth-century *England* came to see themselves as part of a British, or even as part of an English, national culture. Colley's book begins from the assumption that that battle had already been won, and that the crucial concern in the period after 1707 was how to integrate Scotland and Wales into Britain: she is less concerned with how the English regions were or were not integrated into that English and British whole.

To this extent, Colley's work implicitly mirrors the emphasis of one of the greatest of eighteenth-century travelogues: Daniel Defoe's, *A Tour Thro' the Whole Island of Great Britain* (1724-6). Defoe's *Tour* provides us with a mine of local and regional detail so that it is almost obligatory for historians writing about a particular town or region to begin their study with a quotation from Defoe. But the thrust of his work is to offer an upbeat account of the integrated nature of British economy and society; those regions which do not fit into what he considers to be that march of history are marginalised. Regions and localities within Britain are applauded to the extent that they help the 'national' purpose, and those that do not do this are deemed backward. It is noticeable how in his work (as there was in some of the discussion on identity in the 1990s) there is a constant slippage in the use of the terms 'England', 'Britain', 'English' and 'British'. In large measure, of course, Defoe and Colley may have been right. Those historians who in the 1970s and early 1980s made a vogue for 'county studies' for the period before 1660, and maintained that loyalty to the 'county' was more compelling than loyalty to the 'nation', have been challenged by those who have convincingly argued that county leaders were fully integrated into a national agenda and frame of reference.[5] If concepts of 'Englishness' were well entrenched, and if loyalty to nation was something which overrode regional loyalties in the period before 1660, then (it could sensibly be suggested) there is not much point worrying about the case after 1660. But county studies usually centred on the attitudes of the county élite. Can we be sure that other social groups felt the hegemonic sense of national identity? In any case, some historians of the nineteenth and even twentieth centuries have demonstrated the persistence of regional and local loyalties which might challenge

[5] One of the earliest landmarks in the post-war revival of county history writing was W. G. Hoskins, *Devon. A New Survey of England, No. 2* (1954). The publication of county-based works that were especially concerned with the period between the Reformation and Civil War in England gathered pace in subsequent decades, with works such as A. Everitt's *The Community of Kent and the Great Rebellion* (Leicester, 1966); J. T. Cliffe, *The Yorkshire Gentry from the Reformation to the Civil War* (London, 1969); J. S. Morrill, *Cheshire, 1630-1660: County Government and Society During the English Revolution* (Oxford, 1974); A. J. Fletcher, *A County Community in Peace and War. Sussex 1600-1660*, and *idem, The Outbreak of the English Civil War* (London, 1981); Clive Holmes, *Seventeenth-Century Lincolnshire* (Lincoln, 1980). County history writing continues in the formidable project of the *Victoria History of the Counties of England* (see www.englandpast.net). For an over-view of historiographical trends in this area, see Charles Phythian Adams, *Re-Thinking English Local History* (Leicester, 1987).

loyalty to the nation, and so it might be premature to discount the importance of regional identity.[6] There may therefore be some mileage in thinking about the English regions in the eighteenth century and the issue of their integration into the wider national picture.

Taken together, the essays in this collection address both the topics of cultural consumption and national and regional identity by focusing on the creation and consumption of culture in the North-East of England between 1660 and 1830. They can be seen as the fruits of the first year of an interdisciplinary research project funded by the University of Northumbria, 'Nationalising Taste: Cultural Value and National Identity in Eighteenth-Century Britain, with Special Reference to the North-East of England'. That project, directed by Jeremy Gregory, working with Allan Ingram and Thomas Faulkner, with Helen Berry as its first Research Fellow, and Richard Allen as her successor, sought to bring together these two areas of interest. By focusing on a specific region, the project aimed to explore how far identity was bound up with cultural consumption, but also wanted to ask how far the culture created and consumed in the North-East exhibited what might be called 'national' or 'regional' trends, tropes and themes. It is true that, at the general level, some interdisciplinary studies had previously been written which attempted to engage with the question of the interrelationship between culture and national identity. John Lucas, *England and Englishness: Ideas of Nationhood in English Poetry, 1688-1900* (1990), Michael Dobson, *The Making of a National Poet: Shakespeare, Adaptation and Authorship, 1660-1760* (1992) and Howard Weinbrot, *Britannia's Issue: The Rise of British Literature from Dryden to Ossian* (1993), were important explorations of this theme in literature. Meanwhile, art historians such as John Barrell and David Solkin engaged with similar issues.[7] Giles Worsley's *Classical Architecture in Britain: the Heroic Age* (1995) and Tom Williamson's *Polite Landscapes: Gardens and Society in Eighteenth-Century England* (1995) did much the same for design. But none of these studies was regionally focused, and many were concerned with the interests of a national and metropolitan élite.

The choice of the North-East as a site to test and explore the above literature was not merely one of convenience (although the fact that we were both living and working there at the time certainly helped). Rather, we felt that an exploration of cultural consumption and national identity with reference to the North-East might be useful because the location of the region at the extremity of England, and its position as a border region (providing both a buffer zone and a liminal space between England and Scotland) made it a geographical location particularly well-suited to this task. If McKendrick's and Colley's theses hold true, then they ought to work here. We were also impressed by the range and quality of the hitherto largely untapped primary source materials. Indeed, one of the aims of

---

[6] A case in point is made by the contributors to R. Colls and W. Lancaster (eds), *Geordies. The Roots of Regionalism* (Edinburgh, 1992).

[7] John Barrell, *Painting and the Politics of Culture: New Essays on British Art, 1700-1850* (Oxford, 1992), and David Solkin, *Painting for Money. The Visual Arts and the Public Sphere in Eighteenth-Century England* (New Haven, 1993).

the current collection is to make the diversity and richness of this material more apparent to those working outside the North-East.

But, it might be fairly asked, what do we mean by the 'North-East'? As the historian Alan Everitt pointed out some time ago, 'the North-East', just like 'Tyneside' and 'Merseyside', 'the West Midlands' and 'Home Counties', are expressions that do not go back very far, and caution must therefore be exercised when applying them retrospectively.[8] Contemporary political debates about a North-East regional assembly have revealed tensions on this point, not only between Newcastle and Teesside, but also between Newcastle and Northumberland. If we are still unclear about the definition of the North-East today, where was the 'North-East' in the eighteenth century and how strong and coherent a region was it, if at all?

Our intention was never to prescribe a single definition of 'the North-East' for our contributors, who would no doubt have rebelled at any attempt to limit their academic freedom. Rather, we aimed to highlight how the shifting boundaries and definitions of 'North-East' in themselves present new challenges to our modes of thinking about what constitutes regional identity, past and present.

This is not to say that the project of pursuing a region-based approach to historical study ought to be abandoned: quite the opposite. As Joyce Ellis has reminded us, it would be illogical to isolate eighteenth-century towns from their hinterlands, since this would fail to take into account the broader social and economic transformations that were taking place during this period.[9] If we thus accept the value of a wider, regional approach to historical study, for our purposes, Charles Phythian Adams' definition of a 'cultural region' is a useful starting point.[10] Phythian Adams eschews the 'endless sterile agonizings over the impossibility of comprehensive definition [of regions]'. Instead, he proposes that a region, by definition, ought to have 'a meaningful context for its inhabitants, and with which may be associated a set of distinguishable cultural traits, not the least of which will be the shared susceptibility to the same outside influences'.[11] For this reason, he identifies the North-East, which he calls the province of the 'North ('Scandinavian') Sea', as one of fourteen distinct English cultural provinces, a territory linked by a 'broad underlying axis of activity' (including Baltic trade) centring on the Tyne and its tributaries between the Tees and Tweed.

Many eighteenth-century commentators, and several of the essays that follow, have been broadly in accord with the idea of a 'North Sea' cultural province, that is, the geographical territory between the Tees in the South, to the Tweed in the North, with the Pennines forming a western boundary. Katie Wales'

---

8 Alan Everitt, 'Country, County and Town: Patterns of Regional Evolution in England', *Transactions of the Royal Historical Society*, 5th ser., 29 (1979), 79. Prof. Everitt dates the term 'Home Counties', for example, only to the 1870s.

9 Joyce Ellis, 'Regional and County Centres, 1700-1840', in P. Clark (ed.), *Cambridge Urban History of England, II, 1540-1840* (Cambridge, 2001), pp. 681, 684, 697 and *passim.*

10 Charles Phythian Adams (ed.), *Societies Cultures and Kinship, 1580-1850. Cultural Provinces and English Local History* (Leicester, 1993). See in particular his 'Introduction: an Agenda for English Local History', pp. 1-23.

11 Ibid., pp. 9-10, 14-16.

essay, however, notes that from the perspective of many eighteenth-century southerners there was in fact an undifferentiated 'North'. She therefore takes the boundaries of the ancient kingdom of Northumbria (extending to the Mersey, Trent and Humber) as the geographical focus of her illuminating study of dialect, poetry and language. Other contributors deploy county divisions to define the North-East, which is usually taken in this case to encompass present-day Northumberland, Country Durham and Tyne and Wear. The historian's problem here is that modern county boundaries are different from their historical antecedents (County Durham, as one local aristocratic landowner has recently lamented, has been 'shrinking' for the past 50 years).[12] Moreover, this approach is not without its limitations since county boundaries are often transcended by other ancient administrative and legal divisions. Depending upon the topic in hand, it may be more meaningful to study the patterns of land tenure (shaped by powerful local families such as the dukes of Northumberland), or the distinct civic and ecclesiastical jurisdictions of the Corporation of Newcastle and the bishops of Durham.[13]

If we accept the need for flexibility in defining the North-East for the moment, another critical issue arises, one that is highlighted by the question posed in the very first essay in this collection: how distinctive was the North-East? Did it just replicate much of what went on in other regions? Lorna Scammell's[14] succinct and provocative essay addresses this challenge head-on. Her comparative data, using probate records from a number of dioceses, concludes that the diocese of Durham was indeed different. Here, it needs to be emphasised that the diocese of Durham until the 1880s encompassed the counties of Durham *and* Northumberland, so that the implications of her findings are even more significant than might appear at first sight to the modern reader.

In choosing to explore the North-East as a test case, we were working on a region that has had its own lively historiography, although, until recently, most of the work has been done on periods before the early modern period and after the eighteenth century. Perhaps because of the North-East's role in an industrialising economy, it is not surprising that historians have analysed an industrial culture and that most work has concentrated on the nineteenth and twentieth centuries. Where the eighteenth century has been studied it has usually been seen as a precursor to this period, and those aspects of it that can be labelled as 'modern' have been emphasised. We note that studies which include the eighteenth century often begin

[12] Lord Durham of Lambton Castle, interviewed in *The Independent on Sunday* ('Revival of Old Shires Could Redraw the Map of Great Britain', 5/1/03).

[13] The complex interaction of competing power-bases at the civic, county and regional level are highlighted by Carl B. Estabrook, *Urban and Rustic England. Cultural Ties and Social Spheres in the Provinces, 1660-1780* (Manchester, 1998); Jonathan Barry, 'Provincial Town Culture, 1640-1780: Urban or Civic?', in J. H. Pittock and A. Wear (eds) *Interpretation and Cultural History* (1991); Ellis, 'Regional and County Centres', p. 684; Jon Stobart, 'County, Town and Country: Three Histories of Urban Development in Eighteenth-Century Chester', in Peter Borsay and Lindsay Proudfoot (eds), *Provincial Towns in Early Modern England and Ireland*, Proceedings of the British Academy, 108 (Oxford, 2002).

[14] The author of one of the most frequently-cited works on the history of eighteenth-century consumption, published under her former name; Lorna Weatherill, *Consumer Behaviour and Material Culture in Britain, 1660-1760* (1988, 2nd edn, London, 1996).

circa 1780, or 1760, with neglect of those aspects that do not fit easily into the modern agenda.[15] This collection, on the other hand, aims to understand eighteenth-century culture on its own terms, and not simply as a precursor to what came after, however important those future developments may have been. For this reason, the present volume has as its time frame the now widely-recognised 'long eighteenth century' (1660-1830) which acknowledges the historical continuities between the Restoration and early eighteenth century. An end date that trespasses into the nineteenth century also gives scope for considering long-term continuity and change. Although this chronology has been most often used by historians of high politics, this collection suggests that it is surprisingly useful for cultural historians as well.

In preparing this collection, we have been fortunate that in the past years a growing interest has been discerned in the North-East between 1660 and 1830. The political history of the region has been partly explored in Kathleen Wilson's, *The Sense of the People. Politics, Culture and Imperialism in England, 1715-1785* (1995). On electioneering, economic and social history, we have several articles by W. A. Speck, the pioneering work of Joyce Ellis, and the later chapters of Keith Wrightson and David Levine's *The Making of an Industrial Society, Whickham, 1560-1765* (1991).[16] Religious denominations have been explored by J. C. Shuler, Françoise Deconinck-Brossard, Ruth Sansbury, and Geoffrey Milburn;[17] the press has been examined by Maurice Milne and Peter Isaac;[18] and the social history of crime has been uncovered by Gwenda Morgan and Peter Rushton's, *Rogues, Thieves and the Rule of Law. The Problem of Law Enforcement in North-East England, 1718-1800* (1998). Architectural history has been expertly dealt with by Thomas Faulkner and Phoebe Lowery.[19] The reader may be surprised to find little in this volume on Thomas Bewick, arguably the North-East's greatest artist in the period covered here. This is in part because Bewick has already been examined

---

[15] Norman McCord, *North East England: an Economic and Social History* (London, 1979); *idem* (ed.) *Essays in Tyneside Labour History* (Newcastle, 1977); R. Colls and W. Lancaster (eds), *Newcastle upon Tyne: a Modern History* (Chichester, 2001).

[16] W. A. Speck, 'Northumberland Elections in the Eighteenth Century', *Northern History* 28 (1992), 164-77; Joyce Ellis, 'A Dynamic Society: Social Relations in Newcastle upon Tyne, 1660-1760', in P. Clark (ed.), *The Transformation of English Provincial Towns, 1660-1770* (Oxford, 1989); *idem*, 'The "Black Indies": the Economic Development of Newcastle upon Tyne, c.1700-1840' in W. Lancaster and R. Colls (eds), *Newcastle upon Tyne. A Modern History* (Chichester, 2000).

[17] J. C. Shuler, 'The Pastoral and Ecclesiastical Administration of the Diocese of Durham, 1721-71, with Particular Reference to the Archdeaconry of Northumberland', unpublished University of Durham Ph.D. thesis (1975); Françoise Deconinck-Brossard, '"We live so far North": the Church in the North-East of England', in J. Gregory and J. S. Chamberlain (eds), *The National Church in Local Perspective. The Church of England and the Regions* (Woodbridge, 2003), pp. 223-42; Ruth Sansbury, *Beyond the Blew Stone. 300 years of Quakers in Newcastle* (Newcastle, 1998); Geoffrey E. Milburn, *The Travelling Preacher: John Wesley in the North-East, 1742-90* (Sunderland, 1987).

[18] Maurice Milne, *The Newspapers of Northumberland and Durham* (Newcastle, 1971), and Peter Isaac (ed.), *The 'Fourth Estate' at Work in Northumberland and Durham* (Richmond, 1999).

[19] Thomas Faulkner and Phoebe Lowery, *The Lost Houses of Newcastle and Northumberland* (York, 1996); T. E. Faulkner (ed), *Northumbrian Panorama: Studies in the History and Culture of North East England* (London, 1996).

extensively elsewhere, most notably in John Brewer's, *The Pleasures of the Imagination. English Culture in the Eighteenth Century* (1997). Our present endeavour is less about polishing existing icons, and more about showing how much of the North-East's history remains to be explored.

If the 'North-East' remains a problematic category, what does this collection mean by 'culture'? Again, we have opted for an inclusive definition. Many think of culture in terms of fine art; one imagines the lone painter, musician or sculptor engaged in imaginative creativity. But this is a post-Romantic definition, and for most of the eighteenth century much cultural production was collaborative. The scope of this volume includes, but goes beyond, the 'high' culture of the fine art world to a broader definition favoured by anthropologists and historians alike. The production and consumption of a wide range of goods and services, from alcoholic beverages, to luxury consumer items such as china, books, curtains and clocks, the construction and use of domestic and public buildings and spaces, social gatherings, and the ways in which people behaved and dressed, all fall within the remit of cultural activity and are explored in the essays below. Words - written, heard, spoken and sung - are another form of cultural production and consumption considered here, as are the leisure activities of the middling sort. The social parameters of North-East society are explored, from powerful patrons (nobility and gentry) to those lower down the social scale, who have left us far fewer written records (such as Quakers and keelmen).

So what do the essays below reveal about the creation and consumption of culture in the North-East of England from 1660 to 1830? All of them, in their various ways, acknowledge the importance of the coal trade as a contextual factor behind the culture created and consumed in the region. Defoe, writing in the 1720s, observed that 'the road to Newcastle gives a view of the inexhausted store of coal and coal pits, from whence not London only, but all the south part of England is continually supplied'.[20] That trade explains why, for Lorna Scammell, the North-East was different from other regions. The communication and distribution networks on which the coal trade depended also provided an infrastructure for the distribution of alcoholic spirits, which, as John Chartres has found, meant that there was no need to manufacture or produce spirits locally. The coal trade forms both the subject matter and the cultural context for Katie Wales' dialect poetry; it provided the staple work for some of the guilds such as the Hostmen and Shipwrights detailed by Rebecca King, and provided the income that furnished Adrian Green's Betty Bowes with the lifestyle and leisure to read and collect books. Richard Allen's Quakers tried to find a counter-culture in the midst of mining communities; coal money funded much of the construction of the Newcastle Assembly Rooms studied by Helen Berry, and gave local standing to the intelligentsia who had taken control of Newcastle's art institutions by the early 1830s as described by Paul Usherwood.

Within this general framework, some preliminary signs emerge that some aspects of the region did mark it off from elsewhere. Lorna Scammell's essay

[20] Daniel Defoe, *A Tour Through the Whole Island of Great Britain* (1724-6), Penguin edition (Harmondsworth, 1971), p. 535.

intriguingly shows that (at least as revealed by inventories) up until the 1730s the North-East lagged behind other regions in its ownership of books. There may of course be reasons why private ownership of books was not recorded in wills (but these would have applied to other regions as well). It may be that the public availability of books through lending libraries (such as the Thomlinson collection in St Nicholas's Newcastle, the Dean and Chapter library at Durham, and, towards the end of our period, Newcastle's Literary and Philosophical Society) and a culture of book borrowing made private ownership less necessary in the North-East than elsewhere. Nevertheless, the discrepancy between the North-East and the North-West in this regard needs further investigation. Adrian Green's study of Betty Bowes's library makes an intriguing contrast to Scammell's findings, suggesting that by mid-century, there were notable examples of bibliophiles among the gentry in the North-East. If the region possessed fewer book-owners than elsewhere, this is not necessarily indicative of a moribund literary scene. Katie Wales's research suggests a vibrant local tradition of storytelling, poetry and writing across the social spectrum. Records also demonstrate that the region's inhabitants were more precocious in their consumption of other goods than elsewhere, especially of china-ware. John Chartres, following Peter Clark, argues that gin-drinking was a vice of prosperity, not an index of depravity, and he concludes that the North-East as an industrialising economy may have had advanced tastes in comparison to other regions. Scammell's second finding that, as far as ownership of goods is concerned, there was a greater discrepancy between urban and rural contexts than in any other English region, is again suggestive of the importance of the urban base to North-East culture, although it must be admitted that inventories only record certain material goods and that culture should be by no means be limited to these alone.

Another general finding of these essays is revealed in the addition of another 'c' which we did not use in the title: continuity. There is a tendency for cultural historians to concentrate on what is new. The model put forward by McKendrick has encouraged historians to examine the new world of goods, and indeed it has been argued that the most distinctive contribution of the eighteenth century to culture was the invention of the novel. But it is too easy to assume that changes in the socio-economic sphere brought about cultural changes. The relationship may be more nuanced, and against this model some of the essays highlight cultural persistence and the ways in which tradition could dominate the assumptions and cultural practices of those living in the North-East. There were of course new developments, such as the building of smart new assembly rooms. But Rebecca King's essay challenges the view that the eighteenth century witnessed the demise of the guild, which had been so central to social and communal gatherings and with the creation of cultural activity in the middle ages and in the early modern period. In Newcastle and Durham at least (and here comparative work on other regions would be interesting) what is more striking is the flexibility and adaptability of the guild to accommodate new social and economic circumstances. In her analysis, guilds in the North-East did not die out to be replaced by the newly-fashionable clubs, rather they provided the context for the emergence of clubbable behaviour.

Similarly, Adrian Green's analysis of Betty Bowes' reading matter is evidence not of eighteenth-century individualism, but rather represents more traditional patterns of familial solidarity. The inventory of her reading material is also significant; as a single, comfortably-off woman, she might have looked like a prime candidate for devouring the novel. But in fact Betty owned surprisingly little imaginative literature (and, he notes, no regional histories). At the end of the collection, Paul Usherwood's essay focuses on the battles between artists and the intelligentsia for control over the Newcastle art institutions in the 1820s. What is particularly interesting here is the context of civic humanism into which he places the victorious intelligentsia. Again this is an example of the persistence of another cultural tradition which, in Usherwood's analysis, links the intelligentsia of the early nineteenth century with that of the late seventeenth and early eighteenth centuries. But again there is adaptability and flexibility: a creed for a landed gentry class has been transmuted into an ideal for an early nineteenth-century urban élite.

Another general finding of this collection might be that some of the literature which has assumed a binary polarity between 'nation' and 'region' and between 'metropolitan' and 'provincial' may, at least for the eighteenth century, be a little misplaced. Although often seen as binary opposites, in fact these polarities were not mutually exclusive. Katie Wales' analysis of dialect poetry suggests that, in practice, regionalism was not incompatible with nationalism; rather, the North-East, as reflected in the poems she studies, was against *metropolitan* values and vices, not 'national' ones. The Newcastle Assembly Rooms discussed by Helen Berry showed evidence of 'national' taste in their style and formal use, but were designed by a local architect, and attracted a distinctive social mix of people who did not shy away from discussing coal profits on the dance floor. Adrian Green also reminds us that contrasting 'regional' with 'national' may be problematic since the region itself produced, or at least gave periods of sustained residence to a number of writers of national importance in the period such as Mary Astell, Elizabeth Carter, Elizabeth Montagu and Mary Wortley Montagu. We might also add Mark Akenside and John Brown.

But this collection does not claim to be comprehensive. There is no coverage given specifically to the culture of mining communities (despite the all pervasive influence of the coal-trade on the essays).[21] There is less than there might be on the architectural activity on the gentry estates in rural County Durham and Northumberland, although some of that has been covered recently elsewhere, notably by Thomas Faulkner and Phoebe Lowery.[22] Similarly, there is no consideration of the cultural impact of the Church of England, although again a recent essay by Françoise Deconinck-Brossard suggests something of the cultural hold of the Church in the region, which, as an agent of national culture and values, had to deal with and accommodate North-East variants.[23] And what about the

---

[21] Although there is much work on this subject for the nineteenth century, less research has been done on the eighteenth century in this area. One notable study is R. Colls, *The Collier's Rant: Song and Culture in the Industrial Village* (London, 1977).

[22] Faulkner and Lowery, *Lost Houses*, *passim*.

[23] Deconinck-Brossard, '"We live so far North"'.

culture of the other minority groups in the North-East apart from the Quakers, notably the strong influences of Scottish and Irish settlers in the region who were sometimes accommodated, but also in other cases operated as a distinct sub-culture? These omissions indicate that the essays that follow should be read as a spur to further investigations, as a starting point rather than a conclusion for those interested in the cultural diversity and distinctiveness of the North-East. Given the ways that some modern North-Easterners were at first suspicious of cultural intrusions such as Antony Gormley's Angel of the North and the Gateshead Millenium Bridge, but then quickly came to regard them as their own, and as debates continue about the need for a North-East regional assembly, the essays that follow may be of use in thinking about the historical strengths and limitations of cultural regionalism, which might even offer some insights for those living in the twenty-first century.

Chapter 2

Was the North-East Different from Other Areas? The Property of Everyday Consumption in the Late Seventeenth and Early Eighteenth Centuries

LORNA SCAMMELL

Introduction

Was the North-East significantly different from other areas of England in patterns of consumption and consumer behaviour? This chapter reviews patterns of ownership of key goods between 1675 and 1725 in the North-East and elsewhere.[1] It argues that mechanisms influencing ownership of movable property in other parts of the country are valid for an understanding of the North-East, so the North-East was similar to other places in England. However, there were some specific differences, mostly to do with urban areas, trade and wealth, which throw light on the economy of the region.

Ownership of household goods

In a national survey of the ownership of a selection of household goods in the late seventeenth and early eighteenth centuries it was evident that ownership was more likely in some areas than others, as Table 2.1 illustrates. England did have distinctive economic and social landscapes and the North-East itself had a distinctive economy in the late seventeenth and early eighteenth centuries, an economy based on the mining of coal and other primary activities, as well as contacts with London through the coal trade. At the same time there were contrasts between the somewhat backward agriculture of the Pennines and coastal plain and the commercial elements in the economy. One way to measure ownership of property is to examine influences on ownership using listings of

---

[1] This chapter is based on research published in Lorna Weatherill, *Consumer Behaviour and Material Culture, 1660-1760* (London, 1988 and 1996). The original data can be roughly searched on the World Wide Web at http://seastorm.ncl.ac.uk/invs/. For further background see John Brewer and Roy Porter (eds), *Consumption and the World of Goods,* (London, 1993); David Levine and Keith Wrightson, *The Making of an Industrial Society* (Oxford, 1991).

household goods in probate inventories. The whole sample was taken from eight dioceses in England at ten-year intervals between 1675 and 1725. The sample was not stratified to include particular types of household, so there are tradesmen, farmers and urban dwellers from all the areas covered, although the proportion of urban inventories was rather higher than elsewhere in the diocese of Durham, which covered the North-East.

The inventories give a fair comparison of domestic material culture over different areas because they were drawn up in similar ways in all the dioceses. Attention here is focused here on a few goods with varying characteristics, namely books, clocks, earthenware, curtains and china. These represent different usage and supply conditions and are therefore revealing of different influences over ownership. Books were associated with literacy and a wider culture. Clocks were associated with keeping time and they also had a high intrinsic value. China was a new, decorative but useful item imported from the Far East with specific supply conditions. Curtains were decorative and enhanced comfort and privacy. Earthenware was associated with cookery and meals and was modest in cost at less than one penny a piece. For each item cross-tabulations were produced (along with the Chi-squared statistics) from which were calculated the probabilities that an item would be owned.[2]

Table 2.1 provides an overview from which to gauge similarities and differences between the North-East and other parts of the country. It shows the proportion of households with selected items of movable property from eight parts of England, including the North-East (the diocese of Durham). It also shows the median values of household goods (used later in the chapter as a proxy for wealth) and the median values of the total inventory for each diocese. These values illustrate that valuations in the North-East were somewhere in the middle of the range from the highest (Kent) and the lowest (Cumbria). The date range for the North-East is a decade less than for most of the other areas. This was because the documents become rare after 1715, some years earlier than elsewhere. Books, for example, were much less commonly recorded in this area than in other parts of the north and they were recorded in London and the southern dioceses two to three times more often. On the other hand, ownership of china was notably higher here than anywhere else but London. This is important because china was a new commodity, and yet, even by 1715, was well represented in the North-East. Earthenware was not as frequently listed here as in the North-West of England, another area with plentiful fuel and clay. For the other items, representing novelty and increased comfort, ownership was behind Kent, London and South Lancashire, which suggests some consumer-orientation

[2] Details about the sample are fully described in Weatherill, *Consumer Behaviour*, pp. 201-207. The tables were constructed using cross-tabulations in SPSS and especially the chi-square statistic. I am grateful to Martin Charlton of the Geography dept in Newcastle University for introducing me to SPSS and chi-square. There are many recent books on these methods but I found the following most helpful: A. Walsh, *Statistics for the Social Sciences* (London, 1990). The odds ratio is a calculation based on the probabilities of ownership in town and country. If it is around 1, then the probabilities in town and country are equal and so the conclusion that location has no influence on ownership is a reasonable one. Higher figures suggest relationships between ownership and location.

in this area and thus some similarity with the 'advanced' commercial areas elsewhere.

Table 2.1 Ownership of selected goods in eight parts of England, 1675 to 1725

The percentages of inventories with these goods:

Diocese	No: invs	Earth/ ware	Books	Clocks	China	Window curtains
London	367	41%	30%	29%	12%	40%
Durham	325	26%	10%	15%	10%	14%
Carlisle	390	23%	17%	7%	2%	1%
Winchester	260	13%	24%	7%	0%	7%
S. Lancs	390	75%	20%	33%	1%	8%
Kent	390	58%	26%	36%	3%	19%
Ely	390	32%	12%	14%	3%	9%
Staff/Shrop	390	17%	15%	7%	0%	3%

Some details about the inventories:

Diocese	Median h/hold	Median total	Date range
London	£20	£57	1675-1725
Durham	£13	£34	1675-1715
Carlisle	£7	£44	1675-1725
Winchester	£19	£110	1675-1705
S. Lancs	£17	£74	1675-1725
Kent	£26	£98	1675-1725
Ely	£13	£63	1675-1725
Staff/Shrop	£11	£48	1675-1725

Sources: Probate inventories from eight dioceses in England: see full detail in Weatherill, *Consumer Behaviour*, Appendix 1.

The inventories also give useful information on a number of variables that influenced ownership both in the North-East and elsewhere, specifically wealth, social position and urban/rural location. Table 2.2, and the other tabulations concerning the association between the variables and ownership, were constructed using cross-tabulations in SPSS and especially the chi-square statistic. The chi-square test of independence is a test of significance that is used for data in the form of frequencies, percentages or proportions. It can be used to determine the dependence or otherwise of two categorical variables. The p-value is the probability of error and thus is a measure of significance. The higher the p-value, the more likely it is that we should accept the null hypothesis that the variables are independent. Accepting the null hypothesis means that we conclude that the variable (such as location in town or country) was not a factor in ownership. If the p-value is less than 0.05 the null hypothesis is rejected and the conclusion made that the variables are dependent and thus that a variable such as location and ownership were associated. Note that even if we show that a variable and ownership were associated, this does not mean that the relationship was one of cause and effect.

Table 2.2 is an overview of the discussion presented in the rest of this chapter. It compares the North-East with three other area groupings in terms of whether the ownership of the key goods was associated with the three variables. If all the areas are taken together, there was an association between social position and ownership, between wealth and ownership and between location in town or country and ownership. However, there are some contrasts when individual areas are grouped together and seen separately. In the North-East the general associations between the variables and ownership remain, with the exception of china. Yet in the other areas there is some indication that different mechanisms were at work. For example, there was no association between ownership and urban/rural location in the North-West and (to some extent) in the South-East. This difference might point to differences in the economy of the North-East and will be further explored later in the chapter. Wealth was normally associated with ownership in all areas. Social position was associated with ownership in all areas for some of the goods (curtains, books and clocks), but less often for the new commodity, china, and for the established earthenware.

Table 2.2 Summary of influences over ownership of five key goods in the North-East and other parts of England

		curtains	china	e/ware	books	clocks
All areas	social	●	●	●	●	●
	wealth	●	●	●	●	●
	urban/rural	●	●	+	●	●

		curtains	china	e/ware	books	clocks
Area 1 N.E.	social	●	+	●	●	●
	wealth	●	●	●	●	●
	urban/rural	●	●	●	●	●
Area 2 Midlands	social	●	+	+	●	●
	wealth	●	●	+	●	●
	urban/rural	●	●	●	●	+
Area 3 N.W.	social	●	+	+	●	●
	wealth	●	+	●	●	●
	urban/rural	+	+	+	+	+
Area 4 S.E.	social	●	●	●	●	●
	wealth	●	●	●	●	●
	urban/rural	●	+	+	●	+

+ no association

● a significant association between ownership and the variable.

Area 2 - Cumbria and parts of Staffordshire / Shropshire
Area 3 - North-West = South Lancashire
Area 4 - South-East - Kent and Cambridgeshire

Sources: see Table 2.1.

Differences between town and country are notable in this region, although there was not a strong association between urban living and ownership of goods in England as a whole.[3] Table 2.3 shows the percentages of the key goods in rural and urban inventories in the North-East and elsewhere. There were notable contrasts in the North-East between the rural and urban areas; clocks, for example, were three times more likely in towns than in country areas, whereas elsewhere they were equally likely. Indeed this is the only area where the towns contrasted with the countryside in the manner that text-books imply should be the case. The

[3] Lorna Scammell, 'Town vs. Country: the Property of Everyday Consumption in the Late Seventeeth and Early Eighteenth Centuries', in J. Stobart and A. Owens (eds), *Property and Inheritance in Towns, c.1700 to 1900* (London, 2000).

area does have larger geographical/economic contrasts than some of the others, with the urban areas representing the more advanced parts of the economy, with trading contacts with London.

Table 2.3 Percentages of the key goods in inventories from the North-East and elsewhere, in town and country

Key goods	Both		Town		Country	
	NE n=325	Other n=2210	NE n=193	Other n=308	NE n=132	Other n=1902
clocks	15%	18%	21%	18%	7%	18%
books	11%	19%	14%	27%	5%	17%
curtains	15%	8%	21%	19%	5%	6%
e/ware	26%	8%	34%	46%	14%	36%
china	10%	2%	15%	3%	3%	1%

Sources: see Table 2.1. The figures exclude the Diocese of London.

The first two columns of Table 2.4 show that the differences between location in town or country and the ownership of the selected goods were significant. Table 2.4 also extends the argument by considering the differences between town and country in two broad wealth groups, high and low. Wealth is hard to define from inventories for there are major problems in using the valuation of the whole inventory as a 'proxy'. For example, inventories can contain different capital items for different groups of people; the capital stock of farmers (crops and livestock) was included and at some times in the year could be substantial. On the other hand thc working capital of tradesmen was not valued in the same way and tools of the trade were often of more modest value than the farm equipment. Here the valuation of the total household element, although this does not indicate wealth, merely the value of household items left after death.[4] The median was used as a measure of central tendency rather than the mean because the distribution was skewed, with a long tail of high values. For the purposes of this exploration the inventories were divided into two groups, 'high' and 'low' in order to investigate the hypothesis that wealth influenced ownership. The 'high' group contained the inventories that had valuations for household goods above the median for the whole sample. The 'low' group contained all those equal to or below the median.

---

[4] Shammas has used different approaches for her economic account of similar data; see Carole Shammas, *The Pre-industrial Consumer in England and America* (Oxford, 1990), pp. 100-112, especially Table 4.11; and pp. 169-188, Tables 6.5 to 6.9.

Table 2.4 Association between location and ownership of five goods in the North-East and elsewhere

	Location in town or country					
	All levels of wealth		Upper wealth		Lower wealth	
	NE n=325	Other n=2577	NE n=145	Other n=1351	NE n=180	Other n=1226
clocks	●	●		●	●	●
books	●	●		●	●	●
curtains	●	●	●	●		●
e/ware	●	●			●	●
china	●	●	●			●

● a significant association between the variables and ownership of the goods.

Sources and methods: see Table 2.1 and footnote 2.

The patterns shown here for the North-East were different from elsewhere; clocks and books were not associated with location in town or country in the upper wealth group, although they were elsewhere. Only earthenware and china in the upper wealth groups in other areas were not associated with urban/rural location.

Table 2.5 Association between social position and location and ownership of five goods in the North-East and elsewhere

	Social position / occupation					
	Both		Town		Country	
	NE n=325	Other n=2577	NE n=193	Other n=326	NE n=132	Other n=1169
clocks	●	●	●			●
books	●	●		●		●
curtains	●	●			●	●
e/ware	●	●			●	●
china	●	●				

● association between the variables and ownership of the goods.

Sources and methods: see Table 2.1 and footnote 2.

Table 2.5 similarly suggests that social position was more important than urban/rural location, although here the distinction between the North-East and elsewhere is less, whilst clocks and books in country areas and in towns were different. This again points to the conclusion that town/country was more important in the North-East than elsewhere, regardless of wealth or social position. Urban/rural contrasts were partly a result of wealth differences.

Social position appears easy to define from inventories because occupations or status designations are frequently given. After experimenting it was decided to group the occupations and status designations in much the same way that I have done in previous work but with a few simplifications.[5] In order to be able to work with as few groups as possible the trades have all been combined. Widows are included if it was obvious what their occupation or status had been, otherwise they are 'unknown'; labourers and husbandmen are combined with yeomen to give a 'farming' group.

Table 2.6 Percentages of inventories in the North-East and elsewhere with the key goods, according to social position

Key goods	1 – gentry etc		2 - trades		3 - farming		4 – not known	
	NE	Other	NE	Other	NE	Other	NE	Other
clocks	45%	54%	19%	24%	2%	16%	9%	14%
books	26%	54%	12%	25%	2%	15%	9%	19%
curtains	24%	25%	21%	21%	3%	4%	12%	17%
e/ware	34%	45%	35%	48%	11%	34%	24%	31%
china	13%	4%	15%	6%	4%	1%	6%	4%

1 = gentry/professional
2 = trades
3 = yeomen/husbandmen/labourer
4 = not known

Source: See text for further detail and footnote 6 for the methods and sources.

[5] Weatherill, *Consumer Behaviour*, chapter 8; also by the same author, 'Consumer Behaviour and Social Status in England, 1660-1750', *Continuity and Change*, ii (1986), 191-216; Michael Mascuch, 'Social Mobility and Middling Self-Identity: the Ethos of British Autobiographers, 1600-1750', *Social History*, 20 (1995), 45-61; Jonathan Barry and Christopher Brooks (eds), *The Middling Sort of People: Culture, Society and Politics in England, 1550-1800* (London, 1994).

Table 2.6 focuses on social position and simply shows the percentages of key goods recorded in the inventories in the North-East and elsewhere. The percentage of households owning the key goods was less in all social groups in the North-East than in other areas taken together. The exception, as might be expected from Table 2.1, was china, which was more commonly recorded in the North-East. Curtains were similar. To that extent, Table 2.6 shows the differences, but it also hints at similarities in that the patterns of difference between these four groupings are not different; for example the gentry/professional groups normally owned goods like clocks and curtains more often than the tradespeople, who, in turn, owned more frequently than the yeomen/husbandman group. China was slightly more frequent in the trades group in both the North-East and elsewhere.

Table 2.7 Association between wealth/social position and ownership of five goods in the North-East and elsewhere

Key goods	social status / occupation					
	All		Upper wealth		Lower wealth	
	NE n=325	Other n=2577	NE n=145	Other n=1351	NE n=180	Other n=1226
clocks	●	●	●	●		●
books	●	●		●		●
curtains	●	●		●	●	●
e/ware	●	●		●		●
china	●	●		●		

● a significant association between the variables and ownership of the goods.

Sources and methods: see Table 2.1 and footnote 2.

The first two columns of Table 2.7 show that there was a general association between status and ownership. When social position is looked at, taking account of the two wealth groups, there is less often an association; in other words wealth and social position are themselves related and some of the observations in Tables 2.6 and 2.7 are also observations about wealth and social position. However, this is much stronger in the North-East, so that in the upper wealth group there is no association with social position, whereas there is an association in the other areas, a pattern that is similar, but less marked, in the lower wealth group. Therefore social position was not as important in the North-East as elsewhere as a factor in the ownership of goods.

Table 2.8 Percentages of inventories in two wealth groups in the North-East and elsewhere with key goods

Key goods	Both groups		Low wealth group		High wealth group	
	NE n=325	Other n=2577	NE n=180	Other n=1226	NE n=145	Other n=1351
clocks	15%	20%	6%	6%	26%	32%
books	11%	20%	6%	9%	16%	30%
curtains	15%	13%	6%	5%	26%	20%
e/ware	26%	38%	17%	30%	37%	45%
china	9%	3%	4%	1%	17%	5%

Source: The wealth groups are explained in the text. Other methods are outlined in footnote 2.

As already pointed out, wealth is measured here by the values of the household goods but wealth can also be measured in other ways. For example, the median value of clock-owners' household goods was £32, whereas that of non-owners was £12. Table 2.8 makes the point that higher proportions of inventories in the high wealth group recorded the goods in the North-East and elsewhere, emphasising similarities in the mechanisms in all parts of England.

Why would the North-East be similar to other areas?

The cross-tabulations suggest that many of the influences on ownership of goods (and thus on consumer behaviour) were similar in the North-East and other areas. This is to be expected, for choices were made on the basis of general domestic behaviour.[6] Food, mealtimes and drinking were important and many of the possessions listed in probate inventories were everywhere used for these parts of life. Meals were, as they still are, important social events at which people sat down together, ate and talked. The 'traditional' way of serving any meal was that all dishes of food were placed on the table at once and each person had their own plate or trencher onto which they carved or helped themselves from the serving dishes. New ways of serving gradually became apparent, especially in London and the households of the upper gentry from the late seventeenth century with the table carefully laid and food served in a series of courses. There were no real differences between mealtime behaviour in the North-East and elsewhere at this time and so there was unlikely to be massive differences in ownership of mealtime goods. Likewise, drinking was a social activity and drinking at home with friends and family was important, the more so when tea became available and a visit could be described as 'taking tea' or 'drinking tea' with someone. From the late seventeenth

[6] Scammell, 'Town vs Country', has a longer account of behaviour based on contemporary descriptions.

century, drinking tea and coffee became more frequent and both tea and coffee were familiar to many people of middle rank by the early eighteenth century, even if it did not enter daily routines until later in the century. Middling households provided the time and occasion for leisure, even if it were no more than talking to friends or reading, drawing, writing, studying or religious devotions. There was an active material culture associated with this social side of peoples' lives, represented in inventories by a range of goods serving different practical functions: books, clocks, and decorative items like mirrors and curtains. Books, well known and popular for some long time before the seventeenth century, were not equally likely everywhere and they were less common in the North-East than elsewhere. Decorative items were again less likely in the North-East and they were especially unlikely amongst the lower social and wealth groups. Nonetheless the impression from the overview given in Table 2.1 is that the North-East shared much consumer behaviour and material culture with the rest of the country.

The differences

In examining the behaviour of households, some differences have been noticed. First, the impact of towns seems stronger as people in towns more often owned the key goods, notably china and curtains. Was there something about the North-East that led to different supply conditions for some goods? This is likely to have been the case for china, which is a good example of an imported household item. It was distributed in a way that tended to focus supply in some areas before others. Chinaware was entirely imported in very large quantities from the later seventeenth century.[7] For example, five million pieces were imported in a peak year of 1715 alone and a total of about forty million pieces before 1725, enough to provide very household in the country with numerous pieces, although they were not evenly distributed. Most of the pieces were relatively modest; the supra-cargoes diaries in Canton show that the main items in the earlier eighteenth century were saucers, cups and small plates. They were not ornate and were distributed along a sophisticated network of dealers, which began in London, where it was auctioned in large lots from the East India Company warehouses. Provincial dealers and shop-keepers got supplies through one of the chinaware merchants, who were already in business as 'chinamen' by the early eighteenth century. This concentrated the sales network on London and provided a mechanism by which china quickly became available in places with ready trading routes to London, such as the North-East. So some of the differences were connected with goods being available in the North-East due to trading contacts with London, where merchant goods featured as part of the return trade of colliers.

---

[7] Lorna Weatherill, 'The Growth of the Pottery Industry in England, 1660 to 1815' (Ph.D. dissertation, University of London, 1982), pp. 125-129 and 197; see also India Office Library, East India Company Records, Home Miscellaneous series, 10-14 (1710-24) for auction sales; Lorna Weatherill, 'The Business of Middleman in the English Pottery Trade before 1780', *Business History,* xxviii (1986), 51-76.

On the other hand, there may have been other mechanisms at work. Could there have been different attitudes to the consumption of household goods in this part of the country. The towns would then be seen as 'advanced' parts of the economy, accustomed to consumption, with people in the more rural areas behaving in a 'traditional' way. In lowland Scotland, for example, there is evidence that farmers were inclined to use surplus resources for feasts and special occasions until the later eighteenth century and to be 'frugal' in spending on ordinary domestic items. There is no similar evidence for the North-East and the patterns of ownership shown in the tables do not suggest that the situation was that extreme. One study of consumption in a local community in the coalfield area found that patterns of ownership were much as would be expected in any English parish. There is no evidence that domestic aspirations were much different here than in other parts of England. Many in the rural areas were not as well off as those in other parts of the country and as wealth was an important determinant of ownership, we do not need to look for 'traditional' attitudes so much as limited resources.

There were sufficient differences between the North-East and elsewhere to be worth concluding that the area was different. If the area is seen as one in which there was mixed economic development, then the patterns make more sense. Economic activity was mostly the production of raw materials and metal-working. And there was not a wealthy agricultural sector as in some other parts of the country. Most of the new goods were not made locally but were traded from London – much as the colonies of the West Indies and North America imported china, textiles, ceramics and household goods at this time and later. Seen in this light the patterns of ownership of goods say something about the local economy as much as they do about domestic life and material culture.

Chapter 3

North of the Trent: Images of Northern-ness and Northern English in the Eighteenth Century

KATIE WALES

Old Tyne shall listen to my Tale,
And echo, down the bordering vale,
The liquid melody prolong… [1]

The period 1660-1830 has been seen as a crucial span of time in the history of the English language, since there is witnessed a significant ideological shift in relation to the 'standardization' of English in Britain, with serious implications for perceptions of and attitudes towards regional dialects. In general terms the rise of Standard English and its codification have been well documented in cultural and political histories of English, so I shall not be reproducing the evidence and discussions here. However, what I do want to highlight are the very particular issues relating to the perceptions of 'Northern English' by the contemporary writers on the English language, the grammarians and dictionary-makers, which are usually either ignored or cursorily dealt with in present-day historiography. I also want to examine these views in the broader context of images of the 'North' in general, the mental landscapes, as it were, of travellers, essayists, ballad-makers and poets, in order to stress that the North is as much a cultural and discursive formation as it is geographical and social.[2]

In discussing representations of the North, my own map will cover not only the North-East as strictly circumscribed 'twixt Tweed and Tees, but also (although in less detail) regions south to the Trent and Humber and 'over the top', the Pennines, to the Lake District. In the period 1660-1830 the Border regions were certainly a salient region from a literary point of view, since they were crucial to the development of the popular ballad tradition in the North. The 'Border ballads' hint at the vestiges of a deeply-rooted political conflict between the Scots and the

---

1 Epigraph to Joseph Ritson, *The Northumberland Garland* (Newcastle, 1793), collected in *The Northern Garlands* (London 1810; repr. Danby PA, 1973).

2 Some of the issues raised here are more broadly discussed in K. Wales, 'North of Watford Gap: A Cultural History of Northern English (from 1700)', in R. J. Watts and P. Trudgill (eds), *Alternative Histories of English* (London, 2002), pp. 45-66. For help on particular points in this chapter I am grateful to Joan Beal, David Bovey, Malcolm Chase, David Fairer, Vic Gammon and John Widdowson.

English and representing an ancient 'North-South' divide. Even as late as 1640 the Scots had invaded England and occupied Northumberland and Durham for a year.[3] The Act of Union in 1707 signified that Scotland and England were now politically united; but over many centuries for 'southerners' the North of England had been seen as inextricably associated with Scotland and hence different from other 'peripheral' regions, such as the South-West of England. In linguistic terms also Lowland Scottish English and Northumbrian English were descended from the same, English, roots of Old Northumbrian in the Old English period. So *mickle* 'much', *gang* 'walk', *bairn* 'child', *bonny* 'pretty', *sic* 'such', *twa* 'two', *ken* 'know', *sark* 'shirt' are found in the dialect and ballads both sides of the border. The Scottish educated and literati, however, throughout the eighteenth century imposed their own cultural and ideological border, despite attempts to bring Scots in line with London English: Lowland Scottish English had been the national language of literature since the Middle Ages, and was upheld in the work of Robert Burns and Allan Ramsay.

For the purposes of this chapter, my southern boundary corresponds to the ancient boundary of Northumberland, 'north [of the] Humber': roughly the Mersey-Trent-Humber confluences. In the eighteenth century, for Daniel Defoe, the Trent and Humber not only 'may be said to cut the Island across the middle', but they seem to have been a particularly significant threshold. In his *Tour Thro' the Whole Island of Great Britain* (1724-6) not once but several times he refers to having had to make what is clearly a dreaded crossing. In a passage evoking the trepidation of some Polar explorer we can note his first striking image, revitalising the etymological meaning (the river dividing Italy from Cisalpine Gaul), at the same time as confirming the significance of the event:

> Having thus passed the Rubicon [i.e. the Trent] and set my face Northward, I scarce knew which way to set forward, in a country so full of wonders... and yet to leave nothing behind me to call on as I came back, at least not to lead me out of my way on my return...

He finds the river at the Humber estuary a 'dangerous passage', which he crossed with 15 horses, 10 or 12 cows and 17 or 18 passengers 'called Christians' (p. 493). He is sea-sick, but once in West Yorkshire he is surprised at how wealthy and healthy the people are, a fact he has not seen noted by other travel-writers. Unfortunately it is August, and snowing.[4]

Ideas of the 'alien' country that is the North were prevalent in the eighteenth century, and persist even to this day. Then as now Manchester, for example, was the butt of jokes. Beau Brummell (1778-1840), on learning his regiment was being sent from Brighton to Manchester, is reputed to have said that he had not reckoned on foreign service when he joined up.[5] Images of the North by

---

[3] See H. Jewell, *The North-South Divide* (Manchester, 1994), p. 64.

[4] Daniel Defoe, *A Tour thro' the Whole Island of Great Britain* (London, 1927), pp. 493, 552.

[5] Jewell, *North-South Divide*, p. 3.

'outsiders', by travellers and writers, were coloured by Metropolitan values, and the North unfavourably contrasted with the South and with London, even before the growth of the Northern industrial centres at the end of the eighteenth century. John Ray has the proverb 'Cold weather and knaves come out of the North'.[6] Many commentators and 'explorers' noted the harsh climate and huge tracts of open land: the uncultivated moorlands and the hills of the Lakes. Areas seemed 'wilder' than they were because, in comparison with the South, the North was certainly much less populated and the housing of the labourers was very poor. In an anonymous letter 'A Tour to the Caves in the W. Riding of Yorkshire', attached to Thomas West's *A Guide to the Lakes* discussed below the author says:

> We could not but lament, that instead of peopling the wilds and deserts of North America, our fellow subjects had not peopled the fertile wastes of the North of England.[7]

This author at least recognises the farming potential; Defoe, however, on his same tour found Westmorland 'the wildest, most barren, and frightful of any [region] that I have passed over in England'.[8]

But the wild North, from travellers' accounts, laid the foundations in this period for 'Romanticism' and the 'Gothic'; as a result, the discourse of Northern-ness was also positively inscribed to encompass images of natural, untamed beauty and solitude. The object of attention then, like Homi Bhabha's idea of the fetish was both desired and feared, attractive and repellent.[9] This duality was also the basis of eighteenth-century ideas of the 'sublime', aptly defined by the Yorkshireman Joseph Priestley in his *Course of Lectures on Oratory and Criticism* as represented by 'large rivers, high mountains... storms, thunder, lightning'.[10] This image of the sublime is well illustrated in J. M. W. Turner's paintings following his own tour of the North in 1797. His painting of Buttermere Lake in Cumberland, for example, is entirely dominated by dark jagged peaks, grey clouds and mist, with the palest of rainbows in the centre of the picture. It resembles the verbal 'paintings' of Elizabeth Smith's poem 'Calm after a Hurricane at Patterdale' (d. 1803); and of Mrs Radcliffe's 'picturesque' account of 'The Scenery in a Ride over Skiddaw, 1794', Article XI, attached to the seventh edition of Thomas West's *Guide to the Lakes*. West's *Guide* reveals the same admiration as the poet Thomas Gray, who in 1765 kept a journal of his tour, but who had already by the 1750s become intensely preoccupied with the history of the North, including Scotland.[11] Northerners too

---

6 John Ray, *A Collection of English Proverbs* (Cambridge, 1670).

7 Thomas West, *A Guide to the Lakes* (London, 1778, 7th edn., 1799), p. 246.

8 Defoe, *Tour*, p. 679.

9 H. Bhabha, 'The Other Question: The Stereotype and Colonial Discourse', *Screen* (24 January 1983); see also K. Wales, 'North and South: An English Linguistic Divide?', *English Today*, 61, vol. 16, no. 1 (2000), pp. 4-15.

10 Joseph Priestley, *Course of Lectures on Oratory and Criticism* (London, 1777; Scolar Press facsimile no. 126, Menston, 1968).

11 See further J. Lucas, *Ideas of Nationhood in English Poetry 1688-1900* (London, 1990), p. 50.

themselves contributed to an early Romantic view of their own countryside. My opening epigraph, taken from Ritson's *The Northumberland Garland* and also John Bell is actually itself a quotation from the poet Mark Akenside, born in Newcastle in 1721, who has several references to the Tyne in his poetry, and also the Wansbeck at Morpeth, his river 'Muses'.[12]

For modern critics like Raymond Williams the vogue for travels to the North and to the Lake District in particular as the eighteenth century progressed testifies to 'conspicuous aesthetic consumption' on the part of the fashionable and the prosperous, who lived comfortably off the profits of improving agriculture and trade, and who were more used to areas of land reclamation and drainage.[13] Yet en route to the solace of the wilds of the North such tourists found oases of civilisation to entertain them, often much to their surprise. York is consistently praised, and indeed there are many rhymes and *blasons populaires,* songs of local rivalry, through the ages comparing it favourably with London. Harrogate, Scarborough and Knaresborough between the Tees and the Humber were fashionable spa towns for those eager to spend money on a different kind of tour, of the sort parodied by Smollett in his novel *The Expedition of Humphry Clinker* (1771). The young man Jery Melford thinks Harrogate 'treads on the heels of Bath, in the articles of gaiety and dissipation'; but his uncle Matthew Bramble dislikes it:

> Harrigate is a wild common, bare and bleak, without tree or shrub, or the least signs of cultivation...One might expect, indeed, that there would be no occasion for a fire at Midsummer; but here the climate is so backward, that an ash tree... is just beginning to put forth its leaves... [14]

The fictional Bramble's disappointment matches Defoe's, on reaching Knaresborough: he is surprised to find so many people there in such a 'desolate out-of-the-world place where men would go only for religious mortifications'. Arthur Young (1770) in Scarborough thinks the 'rendez-vous of pleasure, the long rooms, paltry holes'.[15]

Nonetheless, as hinted above, strangers or 'foreigners' like Defoe and Young found themselves admiring parts of the North, almost against their will; and, like Defoe and Young, who both had a distinct economic agenda rather than simply pleasure-seeking, were struck by regions of prosperity, especially in the cloth-market towns, well established since Elizabethan times. Defoe thought Leeds 'a noble scene of industry and application', and it appears a 'pop'lous Leeds' in John Dyer's Arcadian and patriotic poem *The Fleece* (1757), which traces the process of wool production from the fields of Herefordshire out to the towns and the trade routes beyond. Further North, on the Tees border of the North-East, Defoe commented on Stockton and Yarm shipping lead and butter to London. Local pride

---

[12] Epigraph to Ritson, *Garland*; John Bell, *Rhymes of Northern Bards* (Newcastle, 1812).

[13] R. Williams, *The Country and the City* (London, 1985) p. 127f.

[14] Tobias Smollett, *The Expedition of Humphry Clinker* (New York, 1960), pp. 165, 167.

[15] Daniel Defoe, cited in Jewell, *North-South Divide,* p. 145; Arthur Young, *A Six Months Tour though the North of England*, vol. 2 (London, 1770), p. 10.

on Teesside, and a perception of the region's affluence, is revealed in local verses collected in Joseph Ritson's *The Bishopric Garland*, which first appeared in Stockton in 1784, where Ritson himself was born (1752). Song number three, an account of an historic football match in 1635, begins:

> Upon the stately river Tees
> A goodly castle there was placed...
> Affording rich commodities,
> With corn and lead unto our nation...

Song number five, *The New Way of Stockton's Commendation*, by Benjamin Pye, Archdeacon of Durham, celebrates the fairs and lead trade; and song number six opens with an address to 'ye freeholders of Stockton-town', and praises the orchards, spacious streets, merchants, ships, wool and lead trade. Just across the Tees from Stockton lies Yarm, and in Ritson's *Yorkshire Garland* first published in York in 1788 there is a song in praise of the town, which compares life in Yarm with that of London: 'At Yarm all is peaceful, health breathes in the air'; on the 'sweet winding Tees'

> Here plentiful prospects are seen all around,
> Rich merchants dispensing the fruits of the ground...[16]

In such locally patriotic poems, versions of the *blazon populaire*, there is a strong sense of a prosperous North-East, wealthy from agriculture, lead-mining and trade: a rose-tinted view perhaps, and the use of 'standard' English rather than local dialect reinforcing the self-advertising message to a wider public. Such songs also add a striking pastoral element to the discourse of Northern-ness, also obvious in the many local verses about shepherds. So *Tarry Woo*, sung at the sheep-shearing, compares the life of a shepherd favourably with that of a king.[17] As historians point out, in the 1760s there were still many agricultural areas surrounding the towns in Durham and Yorkshire, although these were growing in size. So Middlesbrough was still a hamlet in 1821 with a population of just 40 people.[18] Industrial conurbations had still to develop, and so too the popular now stereotypical image of the North with smoking chimneys and grimy mills, confirmed in the mid-nineteenth century in the novels of writers like Gaskell and Dickens.

Not that the Industrial Revolution had not already begun. The first steam engine in Northumberland was working at Byker colliery by 1714. The 'flying shuttle' was invented by John Kay, a Lancastrian. Defoe on his tour noted the 'black houses' in Sheffield, as a result of the pollution from the steel works. Samuel

---

[16] Joseph Ritson, *The Bishopric Garland* (Stockton, 1784); *The Yorkshire Garland* (York, 1788): both also in *The Northern Garlands* (1810).

[17] Allan Ramsey, *The Tea-table Miscellany* (Glasgow, 1740, 15th edn., 1768).

[18] M. Chase, 'The Irish in British Labour History', in P. Buckland and J. Belchem (eds), *Conference Proceedings in Irish Studies*, Institute of Irish Studies, University of Liverpool, and Society for the Study of Labour History, no. 1 (1992), pp. 47-58.

Johnson, allegedly, thought Gateshead 'a dirty lane leading to Newcastle'.[19] Even before industrialisation reached its peak, both George III (1802) and William IV (1833) introduced 'factory acts' in the interests of health and morals.

One major industry in the North-East in the eighteenth century was coal-mining, and it still presents a potent stereotype of Northumberland and Durham today. It is also the focus in the period under review of popular local literary representations. 'Carrying coals to Newcastle' is a proverb at least as old as the seventeenth century.[20] John Collier of Newcastle (1777) describes how Henry III gave Newcastle men licence to dig coals and stones in the thirteenth century, and how Elizabeth I obtained a lease from the Bishop of Durham for all the coal-mines and coal-pits in the manor of Gateshead.[21] Popular collections of songs and ballads collected around the turn of the century contain many about the 'colliers' or 'pit-men', several still known and sung today, nationally as well as locally: such as *Weel May the Keel Row*; *Bonny Keel Laddie; The Collier's Rant*; *The Pitman's Revenge against Buonaparte*; *The Collier's Pay Week*, and a song about the opening of Jarrow colliery in 1803. *The New Keel Row* refers to the 'keel lads o' coaly Tyne', and begs 'Long may the Coal Trade flourish/Upon the dingy Tyne'. The popular conception of miners may well have been similar to Arthur Young's (1770), who, on reaching Swinton colliery in North Yorkshire writes:

> Miners in general, I might always say universally, are a most tumultuous, sturdy set of people, greatly impatient of control, very insolent, and much void of common industry.[22]

These poems, however, present a composite image of the pit-men as a jolly, patriotic set of fellows, bringing home their pay to their families once a week, enjoying dancing and drinking at the *hoppings*, although this often turns to brawling. Only *The Sandgate Girl's Lamentation* paints a darker picture: she has married a keelman, 'an ugly body', who kicks her down the stairs. Terms specific to the North-East coal industry are prominent: *keel* itself, a flat-bottomed boat; *keel-bullies*, who carried coals to and from the ships; *tram*, a coal-truck in the mine; *hoggars* (a kind of pump: pre-dating the *OED* [1850]); *huddock,* the cabin of the keel;[23] *duddies*, workclothes (still heard as *duds* in the North-East today); *motty*, metal tally on coal-tub, and *marrows*, for 'mates' down the pit (as in *The Bonny Geatsiders*, 1805), still used in the 1950s. *The Collier's Rant* has successive verses beginning 'As me and my marrow…'. John Ray's collection of 'North Country' words gives it the meaning of 'one of a pair', e.g. shoes or gloves, and so it is

---

19 H. L. Honeyman, *Northumberland* (London, 1949), p. 227.

20 It is noted by Francis Grose in his *Provincial Glossary* (London, 1787; Scolar Press facsimile no.130, Menston, 1968).

21 John Collier, *An Essay on Charters* (Newcastle, 1777).

22 Young, *Six Months Tour,* p. 288.

23 Noted by Joseph Wright, *The English Dialect Dictionary,* 6 vols (Oxford, 1896-1905).

defined in Bailey's *Universal Etymological English Dictionary.*[24] Its origin is unknown, although it is also found in Scots.

Allied to this sub-genre of 'pitmen poems' or 'collier songs' is perhaps a long mock-epic poem of about 700 lines by Edward Chicken, called *The Collier's Wedding*, probably first written around 1730.[25] Not a lot is known about Chicken (1698-1747), except that he was at first a weaver in Newcastle and then a schoolmaster, and he also wrote a satirical poem on the 1741 election (*No! This is the Truth*). A Rabelaisian, bucolic poem, *The Collier's Wedding* pictures a 'golden age' when 'Colliers and their wives/Liv'd drunken, honest, working Lives'. It is written in 'standard' written English, with just the occasional use of what must be Northern rhymes: e.g. *House/Choose; Disaster/Master; down/soon.* In the dialogue there is some sparse attempt at representing Northumbrian speech: *thou's beat them all*; *thou's dry*; *get Hame*; *Hinny* ('honey', term of endearment); *dee* ('die').

On the whole, however, Northern poetry, especially the anonymous popular ballads and songs, are important sources of evidence for Northern dialect in the eighteenth and early nineteenth centuries. Not that all of them were consistently written down in dialect: many are in standard English; others have just a smattering of local words for colour; some switch to dialect for dialogue, or for the refrain. John Lucas suggests that dialect in anthologies such as Bell's was not likely to be taken seriously, with a shift to standard English for patriotic poems; but this I believe is far too simplistic.[26] The songs collected in the anthologies of the period were written versions of mostly oral originals, so 'translation' to the literary standard was clearly probable; the sung versions would undoubtedly retain the accents of their local singers. Many ballads did move from one area of the country to another, from one ballad-singer or hawker to another (e.g. *Elsie Marley*, still known on Tyneside, a variant of *Alice Marley*, describing an ale-wife of Chester) with modifications to make them more local in colour. It is probable that rendering them in standard English made this transference easier. The fact that the collections of the turn of the eighteenth century were intended for a middle-class reading public (see below) undoubtedly also influenced editors to 'tidy up' the language in some cases, an accusation, for example, levelled at Bell (1812); although Ramsay (1740) carefully provided a glossary of 'Scots Words' for his readers. It is certainly the case that some dialect words and phrases recur almost formulaically from ballad to ballad, like the formulaic themes and tropes themselves (*canny; bonny; gannin*); but the local exclamations and endearments add liveliness (*howay pet; hinny*); particular regional characteristics of speech are revealed (*seun* for 'soon' with Northern 'oo'-fronting; *fyess* 'face'; *wo(u)r* 'our'; *claiths* 'cloth(e)s'; *divent* 'don't', *intiv* 'into'; *doon* 'down'); and localised lexis (*thropple* 'throat'; *gobbin* 'talking'; *fash* 'bothered'; *hoy* 'throw'). Only on Tyneside would it be possible to picture

---

[24] John Ray, *A Collection of English Words* (London, 1674; Scolar Press facsimile no. 145, Menston, 1969); Nathan Bailey, *An Universal Etymological English Dictionary* (London, 1721).

[25] Edward Chicken, *The Collier's Wedding* (2nd edn., Newcastle, 1764).

[26] Lucas, *Ideas of Nationhood*, p. 136f.

lasses thronging round as 'Thick as curns [currants] in a spice *singin hinnie*', i.e. bun (*Canny Newcassell,* in Bell, 1812).

What is also interesting about these ballads and songs is their occasional metalinguistic commentary on Northumbrian speech. The notorious 'Northumbrian Burr' or uvular 'r' comes in for particular comment. In the *Flight of the Young Crows from Newcastle Exchange* (in Bell, 1812), an event recorded in several such poems, it is prophesied that 1783 will be a remarkable year:

> The keelmen will stop cursing and drinking…
> Refining in language, improving in notes,
> Letter R will run smoother, and glib through their throats…
> Ralphs, Richardsons, Rogersons, uttered with ease…

In *Croakum Redivivus* a raven returns to find 'nought as 'twas before': she would not have known the town 'Had I not heard the Burr'. In *Canny Newcassell* cited above, by 'T. T.' of Newcastle, the lads of the town on their visit to London have 'wor bur' made game of in 'rum-gum-shus chimes' (i.e. sharp, witty, according to Joseph Wright). The Burr is famously commented on by Defoe (1724-6), which he calls a 'Shibboleth upon their Tongues'; '[the Natives] cannot deliver [the letter R]… without a hollow Jarring in the Throat'.[27] Francis Grose, commenting on the Northumberland proverb 'He has the Newcastle burr in his throat' which he localises to 'Newcastle, Morpeth and their environs' adds: 'Few if any of the natives of these places are ever able to get rid of this peculiarity'. John Collier of Newcastle, himself a 'native', graphically describes it a 'choaking guggle of a sound'.[28] Its origin is still a mystery to dialectologists: in this period Hugh Jones (an American), ascribes it to Scottish influence; John Collier to problems in articulation faced by Danish and Norwegian settlers; James Adams to the influence of Norman [French].[29]

Clearly commentators were mostly disparaging: for those 'outsiders' the Northumbrian Burr's 'harshness' accorded with general ideas about the harshness of Northern life and roughness of manners; and accorded well also with an increasingly critical and condescending attitude to 'provincial' speech, as the eighteenth century progressed, in contrast with the 'standard' for emulation as used in London amongst the educated, courtly and 'polite'. The Northumbrian Burr, like the South-West 'r', was to become an obvious symbol of rusticity and 'vulgarity' to outsiders, especially since rhoticity in general disappears the soonest in the South in this period. The Northern short vowel 'u' became a similar symbol, noted as a Northern feature by John Walker in his pronouncing dictionary.[30]

---

[27] Defoe, *Tour,* p. 662.

[28] John Collier, *An Alphabet for the Grown-up Grammarians of Great Britain* (Newcastle, 1778), pp. 18-19.

[29] Hugh Jones, *Accidence of the English Tongue* (London, 1724; Scolar Press facsimile no. 22, Menston 1967); Collier, *Alphabet*; James Adams, *The Pronunciation of the English Language Vindicated: Appendix on the Dialects of All Languages* (Edinburgh 1799; Scolar Press facsimile no. 72, Menston, 1968).

[30] John Walker, *A Critical Pronouncing Dictionary and Expositor of the English Language* (London, 1791; Scolar Press facsimile no.117, Menston, 1968). See also J. Beal, 'The Jocks and the Geordies:

There is plenty of well-documented evidence generally, in this period so crucial for the emergence of ideas about language which still persist today, of a felt need and desire for a standardised writing and grammar based on London English, a 'standard' believed to be 'rational' and 'logical'. This idea was propounded and declaimed by school-teachers even of Northern extraction, no doubt sensitive to socio-(linguistic) 'marginalisation'. There was Ann Fisher, for example, married to a Newcastle printer, whose *New Grammar* reached 35 editions by 1800.[31] In fact, outside London, Newcastle published more grammars than anywhere else.[32] Deriding the Northumbrian Burr suggests that accent too should be levelled in favour of a southern, educated London accent, provincial accents seen as 'vicious' (i.e. impaired, corrupt):[33] note also the vogue from the 1760s onwards for 'pronouncing dictionaries'.[34] However, it is difficult to estimate the extent to which educated Northerners actually modified their accents: presumably preachers, teachers and actors were more likely to do so, as today. Walker (1791) firmly believed that even the best educated people in the provinces were 'sure to be strongly tinctured with the dialect of the county in which they live'.[35] Ann Fisher's own *Grammar*, for example, has short 'a' for *blast*, *past*, *ant*, *aunt.*[36] Still, Francis Drake, a York surgeon, writes in 1736 that

> the better sort talk the English language in perfection at York without the affected tone and mincing speech of the Southern people, as well as the broad open accent and twang of the more northern.[37]

John Collier of Urmston in his 'observations' on Lancashire pronunciation, notes changes that have taken place:

> ... the Inhabitants not only Travel, but encourage all Sorts of useful Learning; so that among Hills and Places formerly unfrequented by Strangers, the People begin within the few years of the Author's Observations to speak much better English. If I can properly be called so....[38]

Modified Standards in Eighteenth-Century Pronouncing Dictionaries', in D. Britton (ed.), *English Historical Linguistics 1994* (Amsterdam, 1996) pp. 363-82.

31 Ann Fisher, *A New Grammar* (Newcastle, 1750; Scolar Press facsimile no. 130, Menston, 1968).

32 Beal, 'Jocks and Geordies', p. 364.

33 See T. Crowley, (ed.), *Proper English* (London, 1991) p. 75f.

34 For example William Johnston, *A Pronouncing and Spelling Dictionary* (London, 1764; Scolar Press facsimile no. 95, Menston, 1968); Walker, *Dictionary and Expositor*; Thomas Sheridan, *A Pronouncing Dictionary of the English Language* (London, 1796; Scolar Press facsimile no. 144, Menston, 1969).

35 Cited in Crowley, *Proper English*, p. 209.

36 For a discussion of the Newcastle-born educationist Thomas Spence's pronunciation, see A. F. Shields, 'Thomas Spence and the English Language', *Transactions of the Philological Society* (1974) pp. 33-64.

37 Cited in W. E. Bennett, 'The Blason Populaire of England' (unpublished dissertation, University of Sheffield, 1982).

38 John Collier, *The Miscellaneous Works of Tim Bobbin, Esq., Containing his View of the Lancashire Dialect* (Manchester, 1775), p. iv.

Nonetheless, despite the growth of good Northern grammar schools in this period (so Dame Eleanor Allan founded a school for St. Nicholas's parish in Newcastle in 1705), wealthy *nouveau riche* business men, colliery owners and what Crowley has dubbed the 'millocracy' tended to send their sons southwards to acquire education and fashionable tastes; and this would certainly mean ridding their language of Northernisms and also the Northern rising intonation.[39] As Mugglestone underlines, then as now, a Northern accent could impede social progress and professional advancement.[40]

The problem is, as literary historians and linguists have argued,[41] that no matter how earnestly elocutionists and educationists like Thomas Sheridan or the radical Thomas Spence advocated London English in the interests of equality, what this really brought about was an increased awareness of social difference: those who were educated/sophisticated/ Metropolitan and those who were not: 'provincial' synonymous with illiteracy, 'vulgarity' and even immorality.[42] Northerners in particular were associated with 'barbarism' of manners. It is not surprising, therefore, that by the nineteenth century and the rise of industrialisation proper, 'working-class' connotations should supersede those of the peasant or labouring class, and the political implications of the provincial-metropolitan divide become more significant and sinister. Linguistic 'disadvantage' went hand in hand with political disadvantage, the lack of a vote;[43] and regionalism became emotively associated with anarchy and radicalism. The class-tying of the vernacular becomes particularly associated with Northern English, regretfully remaining so to this day.

Having said all this, there was another, more positive, image of the Northern dialects in particular that emerged in this period, and which came to figure strongly in Romanticism and beyond. Defoe (1724-6) at least acknowledged that the Northumbrians valued their 'Imperfection' of speech because it showed 'the Antiquity of their Blood'. This is also stressed by Samuel Johnson, in the *Grammar* appended to his *Dictionary* (1755):

> The language of the northern counties retains many words now out of use, but which are commonly of the genuine Teutonic race, and is uttered with a pronunciation which now seems harsh and rough, but was probably used by our ancestors. The northern speech is therefore not barbarous but obsolete.[44]

Already in the late seventeenth century there were antiquarians and local historians who helped John Ray, for example, in collecting regional words and proverbs, his

---

[39] T. Crowley, *Standard English and the Politics of Discourse* (London, 1989), p. 153; Jewell, *North-South Divide*, pp. 122f, 136.

[40] L. Mugglestone, *Talking Proper* (Oxford, 1995), pp. 42-3.

[41] For example J. Barrell, *English Literature in History 1730-80* (London, 1983); Crowley, *Proper English*.

[42] Thomas Sheridan, *A Course of Lectures on Elocution* (London, 1768; Scolar Press facsimile no. 129, Menston, 1968); Thomas Spence, *The Grand Repository of the English Language* (Newcastle, 1775; Scolar Press facsimile no. 155, Menston, 1969).

[43] Lucas, *Ideas of Nationhood*, p. 134.

[44] Cited in Barrell, *English Literature*, p. 138.

list of 'Northern Words' being considerably longer than the Southern and Eastern lists; and these were incorporated in turn into dictionaries like Elisha Coles' and later Bailey's.[45] Francis Grose, himself an antiquary and artist, compiled his *Provincial Glossary* to help readers understand 'our ancient poets' (Preface). Travellers to the Lake District like Thomas West referred to at the beginning of this chapter helped to draw wider public attention to local speech, by providing 'specimens' in appendices, in West's case, of the Cumberland dialect. He notes:

> In parts so sequestered from the world, the vulgar language ...may be supposed to continue very little altered from what it has been for many ages...

And so there was constructed an image of Northern English as a respectable antiquarian curiosity, and of the labourer or peasant himself, as uncorrupted, close to 'primitive' Nature. In Lucas's words the Northern countryside for the literati was a valuable 'regenerative alternative to the decadence of the society of the city'.[46]

It is against this background that local poets flourished like Robert Anderson (1770-1833), a calico-printer from Carlisle. Born in the same year as Wordsworth, his *Cumberland Ballads* composed to be sung appeared in 1805. In introducing himself as the 'Cumberland Bard' he evokes the spirit of Robert Burns over the Border as well as the genre of 'peasant poetry'; and constructs a friendly but proud image of his region for local literary consumption. In his poem *Canny Cumerlan'* there is an interesting comment on the tourist industry: he notes how 'thousands on thousands' have come to the Lakes to wonder at them. His message is: 'We help yen anudder; we welcome the stranger'.[47] His poems were popular in the region well into the nineteenth century and eventually were published in London, but again as antiquarian 'specimens'. West himself took his own specimens of Cumberland dialect from the pastoral poems of 'the ingenious and modest Relph, an author of some estimation in those parts'.[48]

The eighteenth century had witnessed also, of course, a strong interest nationally in ancient Northern and particularly Scottish ballads, as a result of the antiquarian taste and zeal of men like Allan Ramsay, himself a poet, and particularly Thomas Percy (1765) (an edition of the *Reliques* being published in Frankfurt in 1803); and thus inspiring the more localised North-Eastern collections such as Bell's (1812). A land-surveyor by profession, his explicit aim, he says, is to

> rescue from the yawning jaws of oblivion the production of the *Bards of the Tyne*; and by so doing, hand them down to future ages as *Reliques of Provincial Poetry*.[49]

---

45 Elisha Coles, *An English Dictionary* (London, 1676; Scolar Press facsimile no. 268, Menston, 1971); Bailey, *Universal English Dictionary* (1721).

46 Lucas, *Ideas of Nationhood*, p. 9.

47 Robert Anderson, *Cumberland Ballads* (Carlisle, 1805).

48 Thomas West, *Guide to the Lakes*, Article X, addenda.

49 Thomas Percy, *Reliques of Ancient English Poetry*, 3 vols. (London, 1768, 3rd edn., 1775), Preface [his italics].

Joseph Ritson, like Percy, was fascinated by the Middle Ages, publishing collections of metrical romances, stories of Robin Hood, fairy tales and legends of King Arthur.

There was undoubtedly a readership (middle class) for what Ramsay himself called 'Tea-Table Miscellanies': Jewell argues for a 'disproportionate' improvement in literacy levels in the North of England, particularly the North-East.[50] By the 1770s, literacy rates were 100% for gentry, 76% for yeomen and 72% for craftsmen and tradesmen. Ritson's *Garlands* sold for 6 shillings each: not a cheap price.[51] However, the geographical spread of the readership outside the North-East is difficult to determine. Certainly Ritson's four collections were later published in one volume in London in 1810, in 500 copies. Nonetheless, mainstream written literature was so decidedly standardised and pro-Metropolitan in taste and values by the end of the eighteenth century that even Wordsworth's radical vision for his own 'ballads' in 1798 , so obviously inspired by the Northern bards and balladeers, was inevitably to result in a compromise: the 'real language of men' from a community he clearly admired 'purified' of dialectalisms for a sophisticated Establishment readership.[52]

If for 'outsiders' dialect and dialect poetry generally excited antiquarian interest, for 'insiders' they were living and flourishing. For this chapter I have concentrated on collections like Ritson's and Bell's, but they are testimonies to a vibrant, continuing tradition of local poetry in the North-East that is still popular today. Many of the poems in these collections, as in numerous collections published later in the nineteenth century, would have been recited in the Theatre Royal in Newcastle, printed in the local newspapers, and later sung in the Victorian music-halls to working-class audiences. Ballad presses were active until the twentieth century, for consumption in music-hall and parlour.[53] Popular Tyneside song-writers like Joe Wilson (1841-5) and Ned Corvan (1830-65) dealt with homely issues; dialect verse, in imitation of the old oral ballads, continued to be composed: the famous comic narrative song *The Lambton Worm*, with its chorus of 'Whisht, lads, haad yer gobs,/Ah'll tell yer all an aaful story…' dates from the 1860s.

Lucas makes the general point about the nineteenth century that 'regional commitments and identification came more readily to those who had no good reason to think of themselves as primarily belonging to a nation'.[54] This may be so, but between 1660 and 1830 at least there is evidence from the popular literature

---

[50] Jewell, *North-South Divide*, p. 143.

[51] Lucas, *Ideas of Nationhood*, p. 136.

[52] See further Wales, 'North of Watford Gap'. It has to be said, however, that Wordsworth did know the work of Cumberland poets who did not always write in dialect: e.g. John Brown (1715-66). As Melvyn Bragg says in his introduction to *Cumbria in Verse* (London, 1984, p. xi), Brown likewise appreciated the 'awesome and emotionally perturbing power of the district' in picturesque poems like *The Vale of Keswick*, reprinted in Wordsworth's own *Guide through the District of the Lakes* (Kendal, 1835). He may also have known the work of John Dalton (17-0963).

[53] R. Palmer (ed.), *Everyman's Book of English Country Songs* (London, 1979), Introduction.

[54] Lucas, *Ideas of Nationhood*, p. 134.

that regionalism was not incompatible with patriotism, and not just local patriotism either (although this is very evident). There are many songs and ballads about the Keelmen Volunteers and the Wallsend Rifle Corps, for example, involved in the Napoleonic Wars. Northerners clearly felt themselves to be part of a United Kingdom, but at the same time proud of their own region. 'Oursels and our country we'll iver defend', sings Robert Anderson in *Canny Cumerlan'*. Regionalism is not in opposition to nationalism in this period, but included within it: or, as the Romantics like Wordsworth saw it, the 'root' of it.[55] However, regionalism is clearly in opposition to 'Metropolitanism'. Lucas also believes that regionalism is 'a form of false consciousness', but operating as a very powerful one.[56] I doubt whether it is different from patriotism in this respect; but the idea that regionalism is a construct, that a region is a cultural formation, I would certainly stress. What emerges in this period are diverse overlapping and also conflicting mental landscapes of the North and images of Northerners and Northern speech:

> To drink good ale to clear my throat,
> To hear the bagpipes spritely note,
> To ramble round the North Country,
> This is the life that pleaseth me.[57]

[55] See further K. D. M. Snell, 'The Regional Novel: Themes for Inter-disciplinary Research', in Snell (ed.), *The Regional Novel in Britain and Ireland 1890-1990* (Cambridge, 1998), pp. 1-53.
[56] Lucas, *Ideas of Nationhood,* p. 7.
[57] Epigraph to Joseph Ritson, *The North-Country Chorister* (Durham, 1802; also published London, 1810).

Chapter 4

Spirits in the North-East? Gin and Other Vices in the Long Eighteenth Century[*]

J. A. CHARTRES

The 'Reign of Queen Gin' between the mid-1720s and the late 1740s is a familiar symbol of excess consumption. Hogarth's *Gin Lane* (1742) gave its social costs iconic form, and framed perceptions for the majority of subsequent historians and others looking at the period. Home-produced spirits, above all gin, have thus been set into a fundamentally metropolitan frame of reference, and seen as affecting the lowest orders of society. Excess consumption of spirits was seen by both contemporaries and subsequent observers as a drug of despair, affecting those without ambitions or hope, and was a gendered vice, displaying particularly damaging effects upon women, and by transference, their children.[1] For the second quarter of the century, public anxiety over this vice was sharpened by apparently clear evidence of wild excesses, although policy makers and medical authorities retained concern for much longer.

Modern work has significantly revised this picture, while leaving the purely metropolitan aspect unchallenged. Peter Clark's work suggested that spirits may have been the drugs of affluence, not despair. He expressed clear doubts as to the extent to which the 'gin mania' was quite so destructive of effort as the traditional imagery indicated. There appeared to be some association between spirit retailing and artisan districts in London, and this raised a conflict between the traditional historiography and the hard evidence of likely

[*] Some of the material of this chapter was the result of ESRC Project Grant R000222612, and this support is acknowledged with pleasure, as is the contribution of Dr Christine Garwood, Research Fellow on that project, who contributed so much on London archives.

[1] M. Dorothy George, *London Life in the Eighteenth Century* (London, 1925), pp. 41-55; G. Rudé, '"Mother Gin" and the London Riots of 1736', *Guildhall Miscellany*, I (1959), 53-62, reprinted in idem, *Paris and London in the 18th Century: Studies in Popular Protest* (London 1970), pp. 201-21; John Burnett, *Liquid Pleasures: a Social History of Drinks in Modern Britain* (London, 1999), pp. 162-5; Jessica Warner, 'In Another City, in Another Time: Rhetoric and the Creation of a Drug Scare in Eighteenth-Century London', *Contemporary Drug Problems* (1994), 485-511; and Lee Davison, 'Experiments in the Social Regulation of Industry: Gin Legislation, 1729-1751', in Tim Hitchcock, Tim Keirn, and Robert B. Shoemaker (eds), *Stilling the Grumbling Hive: the Response to Social and Economic Problems in England, 1689-1750* (Stroud, 1992), pp. 25-48.

consumers.[2] Since others have suggested comparatively high levels for the real wages of early eighteenth-century London, by comparison with the surrounding counties, gin may have been consumed in dangerous binges, but by the affluent, not the poverty-stricken worker. Its passing as a perceived threat to the social order came through change in this position, London's real wages probably falling from mid-century, by the arrival of other attractive goods in the shop windows, and by successful regulation.[3]

None of this has touched upon the position of spirits in provincial England, of which very little is currently known. If affluence could explain much of the excess of London in the second quarter of the century, perhaps the model could apply to other major towns and industrialising districts and to other parts of the century. At the least, there should be some relationship between the development of relatively mature markets for consumer goods and the presence of spirits among the basket of other indicative luxuries. Along with crockery, tea, coffee, cutlery, clocks, wines, and cotton goods, spirits in provincial England signified a changing material culture from the later seventeenth century.[4] In following their trail through the long eighteenth century, we may thus learn more of the comparative standing of English regions and towns during the period in which consumer goods have been seen as key elements inducing the 'industrious revolution', now widely preferred as the explanatory model of England's economic growth over most of the period.[5]

This chapter follows spirits in the context of the North-East to explore some of these issues. After presenting an overall picture of the distilling industry and its products in the period, it explores the onset of spirit consumption from the middle of the seventeenth century, and its regional incidence. North-Eastern spirit consumption cannot be directly measured, but some comparisons are drawn with other consumer goods and changes over the course of the eighteenth century, before focusing upon the local market and its supply systems in the final quarter of the century. These developments are followed to a conclusion, by exploring the supply network for distilled liquors in the North-East in the early decades of the nineteenth century, when the impact of urban and industrial growth had matured. Proximity to the North Sea and to Scotland also opened the regional market to potential penetration by invaders, first the smugglers, and then the large Scottish distilleries that came to enter the English market from the 1770s, and the final section explores these threats to legitimate trade.

---

2 Peter Clark, 'The "Mother Gin" Controversy in the Early Eighteenth Century', *Transactions of the Royal Historical Society*, 5th series, 38 (1988), 63-84.

3 J. A. Chartres, 'Food Consumption and Internal Trade', in A.L. Beier and R. Finlay (eds), *London 1500-1700: the Making of the Metropolis* (London, 1986), pp. 442-54; L. Schwartz, 'London 1700-1840', in P. Clark (ed.), *The Cambridge Urban History of Britain*, II, *1540-1840* (Cambridge, 2000), pp. 668-9.

4 Lorna Weatherill, *Consumer Behaviour & Material Culture in Britain 1660-1760*, 2nd edition (London, 1996), pp. 43-69.

5 Jan de Vries, 'Between Purchasing Power and the World of Goods: Understanding the Household Economy in Early Modern Europe', in J. Brewer and R. Porter (eds), *Consumption and the World of Goods* (London, 1993), pp. 85-132.

I

Drinking in England has experienced three cyclical peaks, within a long-term fall in the significance of alcohol as energy source as diets diversified: in the late twentieth century; in the great Victorian boom (sustained at historically very high levels from the 1860s to the early 1900s); and in the second quarter of the eighteenth century.[6] Each reversed for a while this long term decline, and each, with the possible exception of that we currently experience, raised public concerns and policy responses. The most recent has been masked by preoccupations with other drugs, and the second saw a battle royal between the beerocracy and their allies and the temperance movement.[7] The cycle of central concern in this chapter also experienced intense public debate, repeated efforts to draft effective legislative controls, the application of orders from county benches to ginger up Justices' administration of the statutes, and a widespread network of common informers called to assist Excise and Customs officials and to bring cases into the Courts of King's Bench or Common Pleas.[8] The gradual success of controls, effectively changed the national drink market.

Before looking in regional detail at this first great historical cycle of drink and the struggle for control, it is important to establish the relative shares of the major drinks in the period. Consistent data survive for England and Wales for the years 1684-1785, and these can be used briefly to describe drinking patterns. Treating the Excise data on drink taxed as a full measure of the market, and converting these figures to the typical units of consumption in the period, small beer fell in market share pretty consistently, displaced perhaps by hot-water beverages; strong beer, symbolised by London porter from the 1720s, rose; wine and cider retained a fairly consistent but small place in the national 'bar'; but spirits rose from a level akin to wine in the 1680s to a peak in the mid-1740s approaching the level of small beer. This great hump in the curve of spirits was sustained into the early 1750s, before falling back, only recovering from the mid-1780s.[9]

These spirits were predominantly home-produced gin, and concern over excess centred upon London. Excise records do not identify the finally retailed product precisely, merely the origins of the proof spirit, but the first statement

---

6 Josephine A. Spring and David H. Buss, 'Three Centuries of Alcohol in the British Diet', *Nature*, 270 (15 December 1977), 567-72.

7 Burnett, *Liquid Pleasures*, pp. 179-84; G. B. Wilson, *Alcohol and the Nation: A Contribution to the Study of the Liquor Problem in the United Kingdom from 1800-1935* (London, 1940), pp. 307-10; D.W. Gutzke, *Protecting the Pub: Brewers and Publicans Against Temperance* (London, 1989), pp. 1-29.

8 Jessica Warner and Frank Ivis, '"Damn You, Your Informing Bitch." *Vox Populi* and the Unmaking of the Gin Act of 1736', *Journal of Social History*, 33 (1999), 299-330; there is recurrent evidence in Excise letterbooks of collusive activity between officers, who for long were not permitted to gain directly from the laying of informations, but who would gain a share of the spoils of confiscations, and 'informers', individuals, often those such as alehouse servants in an inferior power position, who formally laid the information.

9 J. A. Chartres, 'No English Calvados? English Distillers and the Cider Industry in the Seventeenth and Eighteenth Centuries', in J. A. Chartres and D. G. Hey (eds), *English Rural Society, 1500-1800: Essays in Honour of Joan Thirsk* (Cambridge, 1990), pp. 314-24.

holds for the boom years of the first half of the century: in the 1720s, 1730s, and 1740s, British spirits took about 80 per cent of the legitimate market, brandy around 10, and the residue comprised rum and the produce of Scotland and Ireland. Towards the end of the century, the position changed, with imported spirits taking a larger share of the total United Kingdom market. Although the later figures are far from perfect, between 1785 and 1805, rum took roughly a 25 per cent share of the UK market, and brandy 12-15 per cent; home-produced spirits retained a two-thirds share, half of this English.[10] As will be argued below, after the successful restriction of retailing in the early 1750s, the later eighteenth-century market for spirits developed a more discriminating character, and imported goods demonstrated these changing tastes.

Such evidence as exists for the distribution of the English distilling industry confirms a business concentrated upon London from early in the eighteenth century, and, by presumption, earlier. Unlike the data that survive for the brewing industry, direct statistics offering even a rough guide to the regional incidence of consumption are lacking for spirits. Thus the records of distillers that survive for 1713 provide the only quantitative guide to spatial distribution for the first half of the century. These display an industry heavily concentrated into London. More than half of the 334 distilleries were listed as lying in London or south-eastern England, 149 and 30 respectively, 44.6 and 9 per cent; the West Midlands, containing the three of the four distilling clusters ranked next to London, Bristol (40, 12 per cent), Gloucester (14, 4.2), and Worcester (12, 3.6), had 83 in all, 24.9 per cent of the total; the South-West, with Exeter at 13 (3.9 per cent), came next at 21 (6.3 per cent); and the North-West, with 14, held 4.3 per cent. Other regions returned small figures, and the North, with 4 distilleries, 2 in Durham and 1 in Northumberland ranked identically with Wales, and well behind Yorkshire (11, 3.3 per cent). Separately listed were 186 'compound distillers' undifferentiated geographically, who were rectifiers producing finished goods for sale.[11] If the presence of distilleries can be used as a proxy for spirit consumption in the absence of direct information, there was a heavy metropolitan concentration, and evidence of an apparent centre-periphery split in the adoption of this new taste.

Both 'strong waters' and 'spirits' were subjected to the first Excise, in 1654-5, for which returns disaggregated by county survive, and these suggest a rather different pattern.[12] All duties were farmed, and there were clearly political factors at work in some parts of the country that might have offset their value as indicators of relative consumption. Subject to this caveat, London accounted for 56 per cent of aggregate revenue, and with a trickle allocated to Surrey, the whole of 'strong waters', probably the home product. For spirits, almost certainly imports, and thus taxed at four times the rate, London ranked fifth with 6.5 per cent, behind Devon (40.6 per cent), Lincolnshire (30.1), Norfolk (10.4), and

[10] London, Custom House (hereafter PRO), Excise Revenue Accounts, 1662-1827, pp. 255-6.
[11] London, Public Record Office (hereafter PRO), Excise Letterbooks, CUST 48/11, p. 119.
[12] British Library (BL), Lansdowne Ms. 1215, 'Revenue Papers 1568-1758', f. 7, 'An Abstract of what hath beene Collected for Excise both in London & elsewhere in every Distinct County upon each perticular merchandize both inland and imported for one whole year ending the 25th of March 1655'.

Somerset (10.1). No returns under either head appeared for the counties of northern England, although their share of beer Excise, at just under 4 per cent for Yorkshire and 'Newcastle, Northumberland and Berwick' looked well behind that of the next available benchmark year, 1754-5, when strong beer in the comparable region took a 14 per cent share of the national total.[13] This suggests that these data may reflect the vagaries of the tax more than the realities of consumption and importation.

While this may represent the reality of regional standings in the league of spirit drinking, other evidence suggests that the taste diffused more quickly through England in the mid-seventeenth century, although exact quantification is not possible. Three probate inventories from the London Court of Orphans record by name and place debts owed to the estates of distillers of the City: Thomas Wills, 1672; Robert Maddox, 1698; and James Cart, 1706.[14] All three traded with the South-East and into East Anglia, but were clearly differentiated in their longer-distance traffic: Wills dealt mainly as far north as Newcastle under Lyme, and west to Wolverhampton, within a predominantly midland business; and on a larger scale, Cart focused upon the north and west, reaching limits at Edinburgh, Kendal, Ruthin, and Taunton.

Most interesting for present purposes was Maddox, who supplied the South-East and East Anglia from his London warehouse, but who had provincial warehouses at Exeter and York. In North-Eastern England he had two quite distinct distributive networks. One, presumably supplied direct coastwise, incorporated the great towns of the east coast region – running roughly north to south, Newcastle, Gateshead, South Shields, Sunderland, Durham, Stockton, Guisborough, Yarm, Whitby, Robin Hood's Bay, Scarborough, Seamer, Bridlington, Beverley, Hull, Gainsborough, Lincoln, Boston, King's Lynn, Norwich, Yarmouth, and Lowestoft. A second network was based upon the warehouse at York, though with some places probably supplied direct through Newcastle: North-West to Richmond and Barnard Castle; north to Northallerton; east to Pickering, Malton, and Pocklington; and west into Wensleydale, Wharfedale, and Airedale, as far as Askrigg, Threshfield, and Settle. Although but a single case, albeit a substantial one, Robert Maddox's trading links point to an earlier and more widespread diffusion of spirit drinking into North-Eastern England than other sources indicated.[15] By 1698, this new taste had spread widely though England, reaching the principal centres of the east coast but also the more remote market towns of the Dales.

---

[13] BL, Add. Ms. 38382 f. 5-6, Liverpool Papers, 'An account of the Number of Barrels of Strong Beer and Ale and of Barrels of Small Beer brewed in the several Collections of England…Midsummer 1754 to Midsummer 1761'. The North-East, constituted as above, took 14 per cent of strong beer, and 9.9 per cent of small beer, in 1754-5.

[14] Corporation of London Record Office (CLRO), Court of Orphans Inventories, 763, Thomas Wills, Citizen and Distiller (28 February 1672); 2301, Robert Maddox, Citizen and Distiller (10 June 1698); 2738, James Cart, Citizen and Distiller (July 1706).

[15] CLRO, Court of Orphans Inventories, 2301.

II

Evidence of the regional patterns of spirit manufacture and consumption is no better for the bulk of the eighteenth century. There is no direct evidence unifying figures for output, the distribution of distilleries regionally, and the range of retail outlets by location. Despite this, it is possible to infer the basic comparative position of North-East England within the industry and in the national profile of consumption.

The first half of the eighteenth century, the period of the great Georgian alcoholic binge discussed above, saw an expansion in the number of distilleries from the data of 1713, although consistent statistics are not available. Under the Act of 1748 that taxed each producing distillery in England and Wales at £5 per annum, numbers averaged just under 600, but this figure lay far above those for earlier and later years kept by the Excise: the latter provide some basis for the estimation of the split between the capital and the provinces. Ignoring for simplicity the divisions between malt and molasses distillers recorded for London, provincial distilleries held a 50 per cent share of the total in the decade 1751-60, with an annual average of 112; this fell to 40 per cent in 1771-80 (36.3 distilleries); and to 34 per cent in 1781-85 (14.3), when the series ceased.[16] These data are hardly certain evidence, but they suggest a pattern of rapid contraction in the third quarter of the century combined with intensified spatial concentration of the industry into London and away from the provinces.

Figures exist for the mid-1780s that allow the comparison of the numbers of distilleries with output. In all, the provincial corn distillers produced 42.7 per cent of the England and Wales total, with a 7 per cent share of the much smaller molasses distillation, all in Bristol. On average, those distilleries defined as outside London, were therefore larger, but this would clearly be a misleading impression. Well over a third of this 'provincial' output was concentrated into just two Excise collections, Hertford with 29.7 per cent, and Surrey with 6.8 per cent, leaving a mere 6.2 per cent shared between the other five districts. Significantly, for the present study, Northumberland was represented along with Bristol, Gloucester, Rochester, and Worcester. At 0.7 per cent of the national total revenue, Northumberland's £4900 was the equivalent of about 25,000 gallons of proof spirit.[17] The industry was therefore concentrated heavily into the metropolis and surrounding districts, and into a limited number of provincial centres, including the North-East.

A second set of figures allows a further but still imperfect assessment of the North-East's standing in the supply of spirits at the end of the century. In the 'Pitt Papers' returns were provided for the Excise year ending July 1796 for the taxation of British and Foreign spirits by Excise Collections, and for the same period revenues for retail spirit licences. Put together, the two sets of data confirm the North-East as a significant area for the consumption of spirits and as

[16] Custom House, 'Excise Revenue and Statistics, 1662-1785', p. 36.
[17] PRO, CUST 48/22, p. 293 (5 January 1786).

a region involved in their importation, but probably not one engaged in their home manufacture to any significant degree.

Unfortunately for the historian, the year of the Pitt survey was unrepresentative: it was a year of dearth, and for most of the year mashing of corn for distilling was suspended. British spirit manufacture was thus artificially low in the figures: revenue was only a little above £210,500, 89 per cent from the three leading districts of 1785, London, Hertford, and Surrey. Bristol, Worcester and Gloucester completed the returns, along with four new entrants compared with 1785, Liverpool, Dorset, Plymouth, and Preston; none was recorded for any of the North-Eastern collections.[18] While this did not point with certainty to rank orders for production in normal years, it strongly suggests the marginal position of the North-East in manufacture.

Spirits were by this stage regarded as necessary luxuries, and the consequence of the suspension of home distilling was the giving over of the home market to foreign supplies. Here the North-East was much more strongly represented, as was the north in general, although London still accounted for almost three-quarters of total revenues from foreign spirits. The position of the northern collections in this import trade is summarised below in Table 4.1.

Table 4.1 Foreign spirit revenues by excise collection (1796)

Excise Collection in Rank Order	*Revenue to nearest £*	*% of England & Wales*
Liverpool	110,941	12.5
Bristol	50,786	5.7
Hull	25,384	2.9
Durham	18,882	2.1
Lancaster	7,299	0.8
Cumberland	5,911	0.7
Cornwall	5,073	0.6
London	660,113	74.2

Source: Public Record Office, PRO 30/8/288, f. 56, Pitt Papers, 1796

With a share of around a fifth of provincial imports, these northern districts were significantly represented in the total. The same source indicated the contents of each 'collection', the base unit of the Excise which approximated to some counties but was in no sense conterminous with them. These, moreover, were evidently different by 1796 from those used earlier in the century, as new collections had been added, often by subdivision, and some by division and recombination. In the North-West, 'Liverpool' encompassed the town and surrounding districts; 'Lancaster' comprised parts of the county and part of Westmorland, the remainder being included with 'Cumberland'; and 'Preston', which returned £70 for foreign spirits, covered 'a considerable portion of the

[18] PRO, PRO 30/8/288, f. 56.

inland parts of Lancashire, with part of Yorkshire'. The position in North-East England was similar, with 'Durham' including the principal part of the county plus Newcastle upon Tyne and North Shields; Northumberland, returning £251 in revenue, covered the remainder of the county; and 'Hull' the town and 'a small part of the County of Yorkshire near to it'. Significantly, James Delamain, son of one of Cognac's leading brandy houses, traded from Hull from 1788, and busily petitioned the Excise Commisioners over problems with duty in 1804 and 1805.[19] Import trades direct to the ports marked at least part of the regional demand normally supplied by British spirits, and indicated further that the locus of manufacture was no measure of consumption.

This was confirmed by the distribution of licences for the retailing of spirits for the same year. Whereas manufacture of British spirits and the import of foreign geneva, rum, and brandy was concentrated into a limited number of Excise collections, by the end of the century retailing was ubiquitous. Returns for the collections for North-East England, with those for London as a comparison, appear below in Table 4.2. Unfortunately, these data were the outcome of licence duty graded by the rateable value of the premises being licensed, and ranged between a minimum of £4 14s for a property of under £15 in seven bands up to £7 12s for a property of £50 and over.[20] There is thus no wholly satisfactory way to turn revenue figures into an approximate number of licences in order to compare distribution with population figures. If, however, the mean value of a licence is treated as £5, then numbers can be compared with the 1801 population, following the methods adopted by the Muis in their study of shops. These estimates, for the grouped collections, appear in the final column of Table 4.2.

[19] L. M. Cullen, *The Brandy Trade Under the Ancien Régime: Regional Specialisation in the Charente* (Cambridge, 1998), pp. 228-9; idem, *The Irish Brandy Houses of Eighteenth-Century France* (Dublin, 2000), pp. 191-2; PRO, CUST 48/37, pp. 263-4 (7 September 1804); PRO, CUST 48/38, pp. 326-8 (12 September 1805).

[20] Parliamentary Papers, 1870, XX, 'Spirit Retailers' Licences', p. 60.

Table 4.2 Revenue from spirit retail licences, London and North-East England, 1796 and approximate population per £ licence revenue

Excise Collection	*Revenue to nearest £*	*% England and Wales*	*Population per Licence*
Durham	4899	3.1	
Northumberland	1893	1.2	
North-East England	6792	4.4	241
Leeds	3983	2.6	
York	2652	1.7	
Sheffield	2554	1.6	
Whitby	2352	1.5	
Hull	1931	1.2	
Preston (20 %)	853	0.5	
Yorkshire	14325	9.2	309
Manchester	4737	3.0	
Liverpool	2891	1.9	
Preston (80 %)	3410	2.2	
Lancaster	1526	1.0	
Cumberland	2856	1.8	
Chester	3491	2.2	
North-West England	18911	12.1	279
London	26251	16.8	161
England and Wales	155949	100.0	266

Source: As Table 4.1. Population, as used by the H-C and L. H. Mui, *Shops and Shopkeeping in Eighteenth-Century England* (Quebec and London, 1989), Appendix 4, pp. 301-5, but with a more modest reallocation of Preston revenues to Yorkshire (20%, rather than 33%).

They appear to confirm our earlier inference, that the North-East as a leading sector in the industrializing economy, growing rather earlier than many other regions on the basis of the east coast coal trades and other industries, may have had advanced tastes for the luxury good of spirits. The figures of Table 4.2 are no sure guide, but the London figures, at roughly 40 per cent higher than the capital's share of total population, accords with some other indicators of its relative standing in consumer-oriented goods. When an appropriate discount is made for relatively higher London rents, the figures certainly look plausible. If these rough-and-ready estimates can be taken as indicators, then, the North-East stood relatively higher than the as yet less advanced regions of Yorkshire and the North-West, and well above the average level for England and Wales as a whole. If, as suggested earlier, spirit drinking was a vice of prosperity not despair, these figures may mark the region's relatively high levels of material comfort.

III

Long term evidence on a national basis thus leads to the conclusion that the North-East as a region was probably a leading sector among the non-metropolitan regions in the taste for spirits. While it held a significant position in the import of foreign spirits, it was not a major area of manufacture. None of Northumberland, Durham, and Yorkshire was a major distilling district: all appear to have been supplied largely from London. These counties had advanced and efficient merchandising and wholesaling systems, and ready access to the coasting trade for primary supply to major centres of distribution. The model that applied in the later eighteenth century was that pioneered by Robert Maddox in York at the end of the seventeenth century. A similar role has recently been demonstrated for Leeds in the 1770s and 1780s, where the town acted a redistributive centre for spirits and other luxuries from the east coast primary route for the whole West Riding and much of the North-West.[21] Spirits, with high value for bulk and stable in transit thus stood transport costs with ease, unlike beers. Situated on Britain's best coasting route, relatively short of grain, but with plentiful cheap carriage available back from London, and easy access to supplies from across the North Sea, the North-East had no need to develop a significant indigenous manufacture.

Yet the directories recorded many 'distillers' and related trades for the towns of the area. The section that follows describes the distribution of these dealers and trades, as a prelude to linking the region to surviving business records from the production side of the industry. Together they indicate how the coastwise supply to primary centres of distribution operated, and cascaded or trickled down from towns like Newcastle and Durham to lesser centres, to the holders of the 1350 or so retailing licences in the region, and to those private consumers supplied direct from their wine and spirit merchants.

Although it is imperfect, the *Universal British Directory* of 1793-8 allows some assessment of the distribution of spirit merchants and related businesses. As suggested earlier, the North-East lacked any distillers of its own by the mid-1790s, and they were pretty sparse in northern England as a whole. There were only five in Yorkshire, two each in Leeds and Hull, and one in Sheffield; Lancashire had three in each of Liverpool, Manchester and Warrington; one possible, a 'bone distiller' in Chester; and three in Staffordshire, two in Walsall and one in Wolverhampton. The single regional distilling link was Robert Stoker in Durham, who described himself as 'victualler and distiller of herbs', perhaps suggesting a tradesman making plant essences for mixing with spirits in the making of cordial waters.[22] Understanding the supply of spirits in the North-East is thus a matter of analysing the mercantile system.

---

[21] J. A. Chartres, 'Leeds: Regional Distributive Centre of Luxuries in the Later Eighteenth Century', *Northern History*, XXXVII (2000); C. E. Challis, G. C. F. Forster and S. J. D. Green (eds), *Essays on Northern History in Honour of Maurice W. Beresford*, pp. 115-32.

[22] P. Barfoot and J. Wilkes, *Universal British Directory of Trade, Commerce and Manufacture*, 5 vols (London, 1793-8), facsimile reproduction (Castle Rising, 1993), 2, part II, p. 875.

Table 4.3 Merchants and dealers in spirits, North-East England and North Yorkshire (1793-8)

Location	*Number*
Newcastle upon Tyne	23
Durham	9
Alnwick	8
Sunderland	8
York	7
Gateshead	5
Ripon	5
Stockton	5
Berwick upon Tweed	4
Scarborough	3
Barnard Castle	3
Darlington	3
Hexham	3
Knaresborough	3
Bishop Wearmouth	2
Bridlington	2
Whitby	2
Bishop Auckland, Chester-le-Street, Easingwold, Hartlepool, Morpeth, Pickering	Each 1
Total	**101**

Source Barfoot and Wilkes, *The Universal British Directory,* 2, part I, pp. 20-21, 75, 256-7, 286-7, 362; 2; part II, pp. 548, 759, 871-6; 3; part I, pp. 30, 237, 258, 518; 3; part II, p. 932; 4, part I, pp. 31-42, 43, 228, 314-5, 384-7, 486, 513-14, 515; 4, part II, pp. 742-3, 973-8.

The directory evidence suggests a clear and rational urban hierarchy of distribution, and summarised above in Table 4.3. Newcastle was clearly the dominant and central element in the trading system, and should perhaps be regarded as followed by the other main port, Sunderland, if Bishop Wearmouth were to be incorporated with it, as the *Directory* considered: 'now little better than the suburbs of Sunderland'. Leading towns followed the two principal ports in the rank order, in Durham, Alnwick, and York, and ports occupied more than half of the next eleven positions. The distinctively advanced and maritime character of the North-East in the eighteenth century is very clear in this distribution.

If it is proper to infer some hierarchy in the spirits trade from Newcastle at the top to Morpeth and Pickering at the bottom, then there should be some visible differentiation in function declared in the pages of the directory. Towns at the head of the distribution might be expected to display a more mercantile/ wholesaling character, whereas those at the lower end would lie closer to the retailers. To explore this is perhaps to press the evidence a little too hard, but the exercise does provide some suggestion of this functional differentiation. Newcastle contained 1 applying the term 'spirit merchant', 1 'importer of foreign spirits', and 6 other 'spirit dealers' unassociated with other trades, but only 2 'victuallers and spirit dealers'. Hull, for comparison, with 22 in the trade, had 19 using the term 'merchant', and only two 'dealers' including the only woman, Martha Robinson, 'brandy dealer and lodging house'.[23] All of Sunderland's entries (including Bishop Wearmouth) used the term 'spirit dealer', two in association with wine, and one, Eleanor Hogg (one of two women trading) also as grocer;[24] while Durham had 3 dealers in foreign spirits, 2 wine and spirit merchants, a brandy merchant (who was also the agent for the Phoenix Insurance), and a dealer in spirits; it also had Thomas Rippon, flaxdresser and dealer in brandy, rum etc., and the victualler and 'distiller of herbs', Robert Stoker.[25] Alnwick and Gateshead emphasised the shift towards mixed trade of less obvious status: Alnwick had two 'spirit dealers' and a wine and spirit merchant, but four who dealt in spirits in association with grocery and tea, and one also a linen and woollen draper; and Gateshead two corn and spirit merchants, two grocers, tea and spirit dealers, and one spirit dealer, brewer and victualler, John Hall at the Royal Oak.[26]

This drift towards multiple occupational names and lower status descriptors was clear towards the lower end of the distribution, but most of the towns with single traders contained 'merchants' in some form. Barnard Castle had three 'dealers in spirituous liquors', one also the postmaster; Morpeth a grocer and dealer in spirits; and Pickering a brandy merchant and druggist. The ultimate in multiple occupations was George Hunter at Hartlepool, boat builder, fishmonger, and brandy merchant.[27] Though this linguistic analysis of occupational descriptors is not wholly consistent, and certainly could not be sustained for the *Directory* as a whole, it does offer some support for the inferred stratification of the trading system in spirits. Behind these 'merchants' and 'dealers' lay the 1500 or so retailers discussed earlier, some, as we have seen in exploring multiple occupational categories, shading upward into the mercantile and wholesaling trades.

Did these trading structures look the same from the supply side, the main London-based distillers who despatched their British spirits? Unfortunately, surviving business records of the principal London distillers are poor for their provincial trades, at least for the eighteenth century. Gordon's sales ledgers for the period 1797-1803 record London trade only, perhaps half their business at the time. Fragments of their 'country ledger' showed three North-Eastern customers: Andrew Bone of South Shields, with an average ledger transaction for £73 in 1812-13, placing him into the middle-ranked customers; Joseph Barker at Haltwhistle (two transactions only averaging £53); and John Bushby, Culgaith, Westmorland (£74), but indicated no others north of Leeds and Manchester. No customers north of Keighley and Manchester appeared in their still more fragmentary 1820s ledger

23 Ibid., 3, part I, p. 353.
24 Ibid., 4, part I, p. 513.
25 Ibid, 2, part II, pp. 871-6.
26 Ibid., 2, part I, pp. 20-21, 4; part I, p. 43.
27 Ibid., 3, part I, p. 237.

accounts.[28] The Gordon records, therefore, suggest some North-Eastern trade, but are too limited to permit full appraisal of its significance.

Thus, for the final quarter of the eighteenth century, the only business records dovetailing in any way with the inferences drawn earlier from the structure of the North-Eastern distributive system come from an unusual new entrant to the spirits trade, the Bishop family of Maidstone in Kent. From 1781 or earlier, George Bishop manufactured *Maidstone Geneva*, an import substitute for Dutch gins, and the produce of other European geneva makers aiming at the English market – the Dutch at Schiedam, plus plants under the permission of the Emperor at Nieuwpoort, Louis XVI at Dunkirk, and the King of Sweden at Göteborg.[29] Though a modest element in the import trade behind the premium good, brandy, and colonial rum, geneva was an imported luxury and esteemed as such: accordingly, Bishop pitched his *Maidstone Geneva* at a price between the imported Schiedam product, and the very different English gins. It was intended to cream off some of the import market, and to provide a disincentive to the smuggling trade.

Significantly, for present purposes, the North-East was one of the markets targeted for the promotion of this new product. Thomas Stockdale at Scarborough wrote anxiously to Samuel Bicknell, the Bishops' London factor, in May 1787 expressing doubts about sales prospects for 'your geneva' when foreign spirits were expected to fall in price, and blamed their commercial traveller, Mr Radcliffe, for persuading him to keep the last puncheon received.[30] Another Scarborough customer expressed similar doubts: 'for I have A Nother foll won be sids it that I got befor wich I moust with out dout be losers by' and sought to return the puncheon to the Maidstone Geneva Warehouse in Bishopsgate Street, London, or divert it to Shields or Newcastle, 'whear I think there will be mor call for that sort of gin there'.[31] Despite these doubts, the distillery was at full capacity by January 1788, reporting orders 'from Newcastle to Penzance', being promoted by 'two riders constantly out for orders'.[32] In addition, George Bishop himself travelled to win orders, as did his nephew, who was in Rutland in late August 1788,[33] and in Newcastle in February 1789. There orders were buoyant 'as the stocks of the Scotch gin are nearly exhausted', pointing to another source of North-Eastern supply.[34]

A final case from the 1820s confirms the significance of the North-Eastern market. Nicholson had entered the gin trade some time after 1800, and by

---

28 United Distillers & Vintners Archives, unnumbered, Gordon's Ledgers, 1797-1840s, Ledger C, Country Ledger (1810s), no pagination.

29 *The Case of George Bishop, of Maidstone, Manufacturer of Geneva* (1784), Leicestershire Record Office (hereafter LRO) Exton Ms., DE 3214/67/9. I am indebted for reference to this archive to Professor Peter Clark.

30 LRO Exton Ms., DE 3214/6/32/1, letter from Thomas Stockdale to Messrs. Bicknell & Son (1 May 1787).

31 Ibid., DE 3214/364/17.

32 Ibid., DE 3214/6/51, letter from Sir William Bishop, Maidstone, to G. N. Edwards Esq, MP, Chandos Street, Cavendish Square, London (3 January 1788).

33 Ibid., DE 3214/118/8/2, letter from Sir William Bishop, Maidstone, to G. N. Edwards Esq (30 August 1788).

34 Ibid., DE 3214/364/14, letter from Sir William Bishop, Maidstone, to G. N. Edwards Esq, Catmouse Lodge, Rutland (13 February 1789).

1822 stood seventh in the ranking of rectifiers by output, a list headed by Hodge, Booth, Gordon, and Burnett. They rose rapidly thereafter, and held first place by the 1840s.[35] In the 1820s, they clearly specialised to some degree in the North-Eastern trade, though it would be fanciful to see this as the sole secret of their subsequent success. Their sales ledger for 1826-8 records over 420 separate customer accounts, of which three-quarters (315) were from the six northern counties, the bulk from east of the Pennines. It has been possible to identify 280 (89 per cent) of these northern customers with reasonable certainty by comparing the ledger record with the four trade directories covering the region compiled by William Parson for Edward Baines and published between 1822 and 1829. Such remarkable linkage at once allows an insight into the nature of the spirit trade at the end of our period, and powerfully validates the quality of these Baines directories as historical source material.

Table 4.4 North-East customers of J. and W. Nicholson, gin distillers (1826-8), and number of wine and spirit merchants (WSMs) in total

Durham			*Northumberland*		
Town	*Total*	*WSMs*	*Town*	*Total*	*WSMs*
Sunderland	20	8	Newcastle	21	12
Darlington	9	8	North Shields	3	3
Stockton	9	7	Brampton	2	1
Durham	7	4	Monk Seaton	1	0
Barnard Castle	6	4			
South Shields	6	3			
Gateshead	3	3			
Yarm	3	1			
Bishop Auckland	2	2			
Staindrop	2	1			
Wolsingham and Woolviston	1 each	0			
Total	**69**	**41**	**Total**	**27**	**16**

Sources: J. & W. Nicholson Ms., 2/1/2, Sales Ledger, sample of years 1826-8, pp. 1-444 [now deposited in Hackney Borough Archives]; W. Parson and Edward Baines, *History, Directory & Gazetteer of the County of York*, 2 vols. (Leeds, 1822-3); idem, *History, Directory, and Gazetteer of the County Palatine of Lancaster*, 2 vols. (Liverpool, 1824-5); idem and William White, *History, Directory and Gazetteer of the Counties of Durham and Northumberland and Berwick-upon-Tweed*, 2 vols. (Newcastle, 1827-8); and idem, *History, Directory and Gazetteer of the Counties of Cumberland and Westmorland, and that part of the Lake District in Lancashire, forming the Lordships of Furness and Cartmel* (Leeds, 1829).

[35] J. & W. Nicholson Ms., 2/1/30, 'Malt Spirits worked by the Rectifiers in 1821'; and figures accompanying draft cartel agreement (22 March 1844), 'Proposed allocation of proportions of 6,060,000 gallons', of which Nicholson's were to have 12 per cent; Seager, 9; Smith, 8; Booth, 7.5; and Gordon and Burnett, 5.5 each.

This analysis shows a strong wholesaling sector in the trade, as in the 1790s strongly concentrated into the major towns, but displaying a relatively stronger position for the major towns, and significant shifts in the urban hierarchy, particularly in the standing of Sunderland, Stockton and Darlington to Newcastle and Durham. The outcome for the North-Eastern counties, 34 per cent of the identified Nicholson customers, is summarised in Table 4.4. For simplicity, the 8 customers out of 96 for whom certain identification was impossible have been left in the total figures. While Nicholson's customer base may not be fully representative of the whole, it shows how a rapidly expanding distillery related to its ultimate retail customers – through an extensive system of wholesalers concentrated into a limited set of distributive centres.

Reflecting the fundamental changes in the industry, towards intense corporate and spatial concentration, this pattern is not surprising, and Nicholsons clearly applied a system of agencies, formal and informal, to supply their rising customer base. The patterns of Table 4.4 also reflect the changing profile of the North-East's urban system. In Langton's recent analysis, the North-East had enjoyed a 'precocity' in Britain's urban system, wholly attributable to Newcastle's maritime and coal-based development in the seventeenth century, but lost out in comparison with faster-growing regions during the later eighteenth.[36] The single great urban centre, Newcastle, saw its relative dominance within the region invaded over the same period, notably by the emergence of Sunderland and the south Durham ports. Thus, by the end of the eighteenth century, continuing to the 1820s and beyond, the North-East showed a greater plurality in its urbanism, and the pattern of centres observed in the Nicholson records suggests rational usage of that more complex system.

The 'wine and spirit merchant' thus accounted for 60 per cent of the region's customers, and only in the principal towns were there numerous 'others'. Who were these other customers? In Newcastle, two were purely spirit merchants, four were retailers or dealers, three at inns, the Black Bull, Quayside, the Black House, Pilgrim Street, and the Old Custom House, Sandhill, one Chemist and Druggist, one wholesale grocer, and one unidentified. The pattern was replicated in Sunderland: five spirit merchants or retailers; one tavern, the Coal Trade, Silver Street; two chemists and druggists; and two from the shipping trade, one master mariner and Horns & Scott, coal fitters and shipowners. Darlington's 'other' was a brewer, Robert Colling; Stockton's a mariner and Robert Stephenson & Co; and Durham's one spirit merchant, the Free Mason's Arms, New Elvet, and one unidentified. Barnard Castle was the other significant inland centre, where Hannah Heslop, brewer, grocer and tea dealer and James Wilkinson at the Black Horse, Newgate Street, were the other customers.

With few exceptions, then, wholesale businesses, some combined with naturally contiguous trades, dominated spirits distribution. The North-East was a major and attractive market for producers, notably so for the rising London firm of Nicholson, and wholesalers in its principal urban centres distributed to the hundreds

---

[36] John Langton, 'Urban Growth and Economic Change: From the Late Seventeenth Century to 1841', in Clark, (ed), *Cambridge Urban History*, II, Table 14.4, pp. 473-4, and pp. 486-9.

of retailers and private consumers. Ports predominated in this maritime region, the urban system adjusting to incorporate those growing in Durham, and the two inland centres, Durham and Barnard Castle, displayed their redistributive functions for the region.

IV

There were holes in this regulated system attributable to three causes: smuggling; the Scots producers; and illicit stills. While the impact of these cannot be estimated with certainty, they require assessment to complete our picture of the trade in the North-East. The first would be expected to have a significant role, in that the region was predominantly maritime in its trade, with many small havens and landing places in addition to its numerous and developing ports, and it was served by the North Sea, offering easy access to the main source of bootleg spirits in the eastern Channel, Dunkirk. Unless the scrutiny of the Customs cutters was regionally defective, it would appear that smuggling in the North-East was attenuated by comparison with the major centres, places like Paglesham in Essex, Deal and Ramsgate in Kent, the creeks of Chichester harbour, and those of south Devon.

There was, of course, smuggling activity. Complaints occurred as early as April 1721, when the boldness of smugglers, defiant of the Excise officers and beating them, was reported especially in the counties of Surrey, Sussex and Northumberland: troops were requested as controls.[37] Illicit imports to Hull may have served the North-East: in 1744, Joseph Cockburne was released on bail for supplying 'the most notorious smugglers in the North with run goods', specifically 2410 gallons of foreign brandy.[38] Complaint occurred intermittently at other peaks in concern, in the 1740s, but no direct estimates appeared before the mid-1770s. In a document called 'Proposed Review of the Smuggling Laws' from Mr Pitt, undated but on internal evidence from 1776 or 1777, Excise surveys were applied to assess the extent of illicit trade and its impact upon revenue. The Excise collections for Durham, Richmond and York were among the 19 of 33 that appeared in the assessment, but not Northumberland. Durham was among the least problematic areas, with only two ships of 50 and 100 tons active, with crews of 40 and 60, and carrying 4 to 12 guns respectively, and no land smuggler gangs reported: around 700 gallons of brandy, arrack and geneva were illegally imported by this group, along with over 50,000 pounds of coffee and tea. York, by comparison, had seven ships between 40 and 200 tons, with 14-50 men, and guns, but with far lower illegal landings, but Richmond provided the North-East's worst case, with 6 ships, of 80-150 tons, 20 to 50 men, 10 to 20 guns, distributing the booty by gangs of 40 to 50.[39]

A successor survey of 1783 reported 88 smuggling vessels of up to 250

---

37 PRO, CUST 48/11, pp. 445-6, 446-7, memoranda on smuggling (29 April 1721).

38 PRO, CUST 48/13, pp. 471-2 (order of 7 September 1744).

39 A. L. Cross, *Eighteenth Century Documents Relating to the Royal Forests, the Sheriffs and Smuggling Selected from the Shelburne Manuscripts in the William L. Clements Library* (New York and London, 1928), XXX, 'Proposed Review of the Smuggling Laws from Mr. Pitt', pp. 237-41.

tons active in the Canterbury collection, between the ports of Dover, Deal, Ostend, Dunkirk, and Lydd, one skippered by a John Major, but provided information only on York in the north. There eight ships were held to be working the coast between Hull and Cloughton, the largest of 160 tons, and five of 30 or under: by inference, the problem was perceived as modest.[40] At the same time the Admiralty reported upon ships allocated to the prevention of smuggling: 17 covered the south coast from Sheerness to Land's End, but only 3 the east coast from Lowestoft to St Abb's Head, with a further 3 covering thence to Shetland for fishery protection 'during the season'.[41] Records of seizures are available thereafter to 1793, but without the same geographical specificity, but if we assume that the same three ships – the *Myrmidon*, the *Kite*, and the *Brazen* – remained on the same station throughout this period, they managed only 23 seizures in eleven years. One seizure by the *Myrmidon* – responsible for 17 of these 23 – of the lugger or barque *Endeavour* in October 1788 was made in the Thames, and the ship was described as in the regular trade from Maidstone to London, indicating that it had been reallocated, perhaps replaced by the *Lowestoffe*, active in the early 1790s.[42] None of the contemporary investigative evidence thus indicated smuggling as a major issue for the North-East, though it clearly contributed something to regional levels of the consumption of spirits, tea and tobacco.

More insistent as a problem, at least in the eyes of the London primary distillers, was the entry from the 1770s of new and substantial Scottish lowland distillers into the English trade, under what were held to be beneficial effective rates of taxation. This may have had some adverse impact on their business with the North-East, where illicit sales of Scottish spirits continued well into the nineteenth century, as Philipson argued, reflecting a regional taste as well as the fiscal motive.[43] English distillers succeeded in securing 'equalizing duty' to counter the unfair competition from the Scots, and short-run figures survive allowing us to observe the extent of this trade, 1786-7, summarised below in Table 4.5. Additions to this duty in 1788 led to complaint from the principal producers for the English market: James Stein at Kilbagie; John Stein, Kennetpans; Robert Stein of Kincaple; James Haig, Canonmills; and John Haig at Lochrin.[44] They secured no redress, but Scottish distillers enjoyed an advantage in duty averaging20-40 per cent well into the 1830s, creating a motive for evasion and for illicit cross-border land traffic.[45] Such 'smuggling' was effectively condoned, especially in the North-East, and even regarded as a meritorious trade.

---

[40] PRO, CUST 48/21, pp. 236-9 (26 November 1783).

[41] PRO, CUST 48/21, pp. 223-6 (1 November 1783).

[42] PRO, ADM 7/353, 'An Account of Smuggling Vessels, of uncustomed and prohibited Goods made by His Majesty's Ships and Vessels commencing the 22nd May 1783'.

[43] John Philipson, 'Whisky Smuggling on the Border in the Early Nineteenth Century', *Archaeologia Aeliana*, 4th series, XXXIX (1961), 151-63. I am indebted to Dr. R. B. Weir for this reference.

[44] PRO, CUST 48/23, pp. 322-4 (20 February, 26 February 1788).

[45] John Owens, *Plain Papers relating to the Excise Branch of the Inland Revenue Department from 1621 to 1878* (Linlithgow, 1879), pp. 464-5, 467; J. Scarisbrick, *Spirit Manual: Historical and Technical* (Burton-on-Trent, 1891), pp. 58-9.

Table 4.5 Scottish penetration of the English spirit market (1786-7), payments of Equalizing Duty

Location	*Equalizing Duty (£)*	*Share of Total (%)*
Bristol	4700	6.2
Hull	1807	2.4
Liverpool	214	0.3
Newcastle	1913	2.5
Stockton	57	0.1
London	66598	88.5
Total	**75289**	**100.0**

Source: PRO, CUST 48/23, p. 205, Excise Letterbooks (15 November 1787). Figures have been rounded to the nearest £.

The clustering of spirit dealers in the major towns on both sides of the border – there are rather more in Carlisle, Penrith, and Berwick than other trade considerations might suggest – certainly indicates its extent. Correspondence to the Excise Board in 1807 reported grave concern over smuggling into the Tweed, particularly by ships from Folkestone: 20,000 casks of spirits were being run there, with 100 seamen landing them, and another 100 lying ashore in ambush to distribute them, including many deserters from the Navy. The smugglers had agents in Berwick, with gangs in every town, and it was recommended to place a cutter at the mouth of the Tweed to cut off the traffic.[46] Two years later, Rice Atchison, a fisherman and well-known smuggler of Tweedmouth was arrested with an anker of geneva, clandestinely landed in Berwick Bay, and fined £100.[47] In 1824, illicit traffic across the border was put at 10,000 gallons a week, when Carlisle spirit merchants sought greater controls, and patrols in the Solway Firth.[48] However, the bulk, as is clear from the figures of Table 4.5, was raw malt spirit sent for rectification into gin or other compounds in London, and, contrary to the inferences drawn by Philipson,[49] little was probably sent for direct consumption as 'whisky'. The romantic cross-border traffic under cloak of darkness, was probably only a modest overall contributor to the regional market, though this thistle continued to provoke the Exciseman until the equalization of duties in 1856 and 1857.[50]

The same probably applied to our final source of leakage from legitimate trade, the work of the illicit distiller. While such figures provide good stories, they occur only infrequently in the Excise records. Certainly, the work of Philipson and Child has demonstrated the existence of half a dozen covert

---

[46] PRO, CUST 48/42, pp. 503-6 (1807). An anchor was a small cask, normally 10 wine gallons in capacity.

[47] PRO, CUST 48/48, pp. 239-41 (25 November 1809).

[48] PRO, CUST 48/112, pp. 247-9 (3 March, 24 June 1824).

[49] John Philipson and F. Austin Child, 'Remains of Illicit Distilleries in Upper Coquetdale', *Archaeologia Aeliana*, 4th series, XXXVIII (1960), 108.

[50] For comparative rates of duty, Owens, *Plain Papers*, pp. 464-5.

distilleries in Upper Coquetdale alone, and there must have been many others, but few appeared in the official record.[51] It was, no doubt, much more difficult to police stills in the wild and remote country of the borders than in lowland England, where the distinctive odour of distilling was almost impossible to mask, but the absence of extensive Excise evidence surely indicates the low level of such problems. The one case identified came from Richmondshire, in 1822, and was more comic than evidence of a serious threat to revenue control. Thomas Coates, a farmer at Bean Hill, Kirkby Ravensworth, between Richmond and Barnard Castle, was found to have an illicit still hidden in a farm cottage in June 1821. He had brought in James Johnson, 'a Scotchman', to set up the worm and still, and run the business to produce 'whiskey', which they were selling locally at 3 shillings a bottle. That the business ran for a maximum of a few months, had a still of only 15 gallons capacity, and that Coates did not appear to support his plea of 'not guilty' indicated that it was not a serious challenge to legitimate supply in the southernmost part of the region.[52]

V

North-East England seems never to have developed a significant distilling industry, even late in the eighteenth century when modest activity grew in other urban centres traditionally supplied from outside, such as Birmingham, Liverpool and Plymouth. Yet, on the evidence of this study, it was a very significant market for spirits, both home-produced and imported. Though the evidence is less plentiful than one would wish, Robert Maddox's distributive network at the end of the seventeenth century shows us a complex supply system attracted by precocious economic development to the North-Eastern market. Subsequent evidence from the distillery records shows a region continuing to be supplied largely from outside throughout our period, and revealing a complex and integrated structure of wholesalers supplying the retailer in inn or public house, and the private customer.

The use of business records with those of the Parsons/Baines' directories for the 1820s provides an extraordinary level of successful linkages, and shows something of the business activity behind the words 'wine & spirit merchant' and similar trades on the face of the directory. A wholesale trade largely invisible from Excise records and unclear from the directories is thus shown to have linked Geordies and their gin. The Scots and the 'owlers' undoubtedly helped. With easy access to shipping, London and then Leith may have squeezed prospects of successful distilling in the North-East, the latter being one of many sources for a modest but continuing illicit cross-border traffic that lasted to the 1850s. England's most advanced economic region of the later seventeenth century thus

---

[51] Philipson and Child, 'Illicit Distilleries', pp. 99-112.

[52] PRO, CUST 103/110, Excise Trials, pp. 455-64 (22 May 1822), Attorney-General and Coates, Court of Exchequer.

joined in the age of spirits, though more modestly than London, and provides an important and distinctive case-study of provincial trade and distribution.

Chapter 5

The Sociability of the Trade Guilds of Newcastle and Durham, 1660-1750: The Urban Renaissance Revisited[1]

REBECCA KING

The most influential model of early modern sociability argues that the post-Restoration period witnessed the development of a distinctively new leisure culture, in which towns became centres for the consumption of polite recreation. Borsay and Clark, amongst others, emphasise the lack of recreational facilities in pre-Restoration towns, contrasting the highly developed pleasure-seeking culture of the Georgian town with an earlier period when urban communities 'principally served as a site for trade and guild-based manufactures'.[2] In the later seventeenth century commercial expansion and industrial growth allowed urban centres to become arenas of sociability, hosting a growing number of public performances of music and a revived provincial theatre.[3] Inhabitants and visitors could display their gentility at assemblies, which were increasingly held in purpose-built rooms. Walks and gardens were constructed in many urban centres, which also permitted maximum opportunities for personal display. There was a growing appetite for sporting activities, which Borsay suggests were often held in or just outside towns, including horse-racing, bowling and cock-fighting.[4]

This theory that patterns of socialising were transformed in the later seventeenth century by an 'urban renaissance' has become the dominant narrative in accounts of early modern leisure and recreation. However, the current model is

---

[1] I would like to thank Joanne Bailey, Chris Brooks and Adrian Green for commenting on drafts of this chapter. For a more detailed exposition of the material presented here see R. F. King, 'Aspects of Sociability in the North East of England 1600-1750', University of Durham, unpublished Ph.D. dissertation (2001).

[2] P. Borsay, *The English Urban Renaissance: Culture and Society in The Provincial Town 1660-1770* (Oxford, 1989), *passim*; P. Clark, *British Clubs and Societies 1580-1800: The Origins of an Associational World* (Oxford, 2000), *passim*; R. Porter, 'Material Pleasures in the Consumer Society' in R. Porter and M. Mulvey Roberts (eds), *Pleasure in the Eighteenth Century* (London, 1996), p. 21.

[3] Borsay, *Urban Renaissance*, pp. 16-18, 28-37, 200-211, 224, 117-149; J. H. Plumb, 'The Commercialization of Leisure' in N. McKendrick, J. Brewer and J. H. Plumb (eds), *The Birth of a Consumer Society: The Commercialization of Eighteenth-century England* (first edition 1982, reprinted London, 1983), pp. 275-280.

[4] Borsay, *Urban Renaissance*, pp. 150-96. However, for a case-study of horse-racing in the north east, which argues that the majority of horse-races were held in rural communities see King, 'Sociability', pp. 129-87.

not without its weaknesses, including a tendency to overlook important continuities in the culture of sociability, such as the on-going significance of traditional institutional association.[5] This chapter exposes the important role which trade guilds played in the social lives of their members from the pre-Restoration period until the mid-eighteenth century. It is primarily based on the records of six trade guilds in the North-East; the Newcastle Hostmen, Barber Surgeons and Shipwrights, and the Durham Mercers, Barbers and Curriers. The first part of the chapter describes the regular conviviality of trade companies in the first three-quarters of the seventeenth century before exploring how this was challenged by changing attitudes to communal celebrations from the last decades of the century. As we will see, guild sociability was ultimately resilient and the guilds of Durham and Newcastle continued to enjoy many of their customary festivities. The second part of the chapter shows how guilds expanded their sphere of activity in this period by embracing newly popular modes of socialising. Companies not only incorporated rising leisure activities into their social calendars, but also acted as an important exemplar for the development of a new institution of sociability, the club.

Trade guilds were important economic institutions in early modern urban centres, and until the third decade of the eighteenth century companies regulated most of the trades practised in incorporated towns. Provincial guild control of trades began to decline gradually from the late seventeenth century, but enforcement only declined seriously from the mid-eighteenth century.[6] In 1600 there were sixteen guilds in the city of Durham, and thirty-six guilds in Newcastle, all of which were still active by the mid-eighteenth century.[7] Not only did all the guilds survive as operational institutions, but membership levels also remained viable until at least the early eighteenth century. In Newcastle, admissions to some guilds may have declined after 1700, but there was no crisis in admissions. In the Newcastle Joiners guild, for example, there were almost as many enrolments between 1725 and 1749 as there had been between 1650 and 1674.[8] The Newcastle Shipwrights, experiencing increased prosperity as the shipping trade expanded, saw their admissions peak as late as 1733. The three Durham guilds studied here also enjoyed healthy entry totals in the first half of the eighteenth century.[9]

---

[5] J. Barry, 'The press and the politics of culture in Bristol 1660-1775', in J. Black and J. Gregory (eds), *Culture, Politics and Society in Britain 1660-1800* (Manchester, 1991), pp. 49-50.

[6] M. J. Walker, 'The Extent of the Guild Control of Trades in England c.1660-1820; A Study Based on a Sample of Provincial Towns and London Companies', University of Cambridge, unpublished Ph.D. dissertation (1985), pp. 69, 94, 126, 164-165, 60, 391; F. W. Dendy (ed.), *Extracts From The Records Of The Merchant Adventurers Of Newcastle-Upon-Tyne*, Surtees Society, vol. I, 93 (1895), pp. xxxix-xlvii.

[7] C. E. Whiting, 'The Durham Trade Gilds - continued', *Transactions of the Architectural and Archaeological Society of Durham and Northumberland,* 9, 3 (1943), 347 and passim; C. E. Whiting, 'The Durham Trade Gilds, Part I', *Transactions of the Architectural and Archaeological Society of Durham and Northumberland,* 9, 2 (1941), passim; Walker, 'Guild Control', p. 123.

[8] D. Woodward, *Men at Work: Labourers and Building Craftsmen in the Towns of Northern England, 1450-1750* (Cambridge, 1995), p. 54.

[9] D. J. Rowe (ed.), *The Records Of The Company Of Shipwrights of Newcastle Upon Tyne 1622-1967*, vol. I (Surtees Society, 181, 1970), pp. 3-4; DUL, Bramwell Bequest, Mercers, Curriers and Barbers Bundles.

The companies were not only economic organisations, but also played a vital social role in early modern towns, where the pressures of constant immigration increased the potential for disharmony. Company celebrations provided regular opportunities for men competing within the same trade to develop and strengthen a sense of group identity that minimised conflict both within the guild and within the wider urban community.[10] Ritualised social interactions between guild members were expressions of the ideals of guild fraternity and civic pride, which were also articulated in company ordinances. The charters and orders of the Durham and Newcastle trade companies, like those of the London guilds, emphasised the importance of brotherly unity. In 1649, for example, the Newcastle Shipwrights passed an order explaining that their rules existed so that 'brotherly love and amity may be continued amongst the said society and every one of them'. This ideology of fraternal unity was enacted in charitable giving to members and their families who were suffering financial hardship, attendance at the marriages and funerals of guild members, and ritualised feasting at guild dinners.[11]

A large proportion of the middling sort of men took part in guild celebrations, either as apprentices, journeymen or master craftsmen. The gentry also participated in guild sociability, and those claiming the status of gentleman entered the most prestigious guilds in increasing numbers from the late sixteenth century onwards. These individuals were able to join guilds either as apprentices, or as honorary members. In Newcastle, the proportion of gentlemen's sons among apprenticeship enrolments increased from the late sixteenth century onwards. The growing desirability of apprenticeships drove up the premiums, resulting in a decline in the proportion of yeomen apprentices, particularly in élite companies such as the Newcastle Merchant Adventurers. At the same time there was also a sharp decline in the enrolment of apprentices whose fathers were husbandmen.[12] In the course of the seventeenth century some gentlemen also began to enter trade companies as honorary members.[13] Admission to guilds was in demand among those who did not intend to practise the relevant trade because membership of certain guilds conveyed political power and influence within the civic administration, and membership of any Newcastle or Durham trade company conferred the right to vote in parliamentary elections.[14]

---

[10] J. Ellis, 'A Dynamic Society. Social Relations in Newcastle-Upon-Tyne 1660-1760', in P. Clark (ed.), *The Transformation of English Provincial Towns* (London, 1984), pp. 190-227; Barry, 'Bourgeois Collectivism?', p. 89.

[11] TWA, GU/SH/4/1 (16 May 1649); C. W. Brooks, 'Apprenticeship, Social Mobility and the Middling Sort, 1550-1800', in Barry and Brooks (eds), *Middling Sort,* pp. 76-77; D. M. Palliser, 'The Trade Guilds of Tudor York', in P. Clark and P. Slack (eds), *Crisis and Order in English Towns 1500-1700* (London, 1972), pp. 109-11; Barry, 'Bourgeois Collectivism?', pp. 95-104.

[12] Dendy (ed.), *Merchant Adventurers*, vol. I, pp. 67-68; Whiting, 'Durham Trade Gilds, Part I', 236-7; TWA, GU/BS/2/1, fol. 63; Brooks, 'Apprenticeship, Social Mobility', pp. 54-62.

[13] M. C. Jacob, *Living the Enlightenment: Freemasonry and Politics in Eighteenth-Century Europe* (Oxford, 1991), p. 38; Whiting, 'Durham Trade Gilds - continued', 325-30.

[14] Woodward, *Men at Work*, p. 29; K. Wilson, *The Sense of the People: Politics, Culture and Imperialism in England, 1715-1785* (first edition 1995, reprinted Cambridge, 1998), pp. 297-9. Durham was not enfranchised until 1678; A. J. Heesom, *Durham City and its M.P.s 1678-1992* (Durham, 1992), p. 19, *passim*.

Women played a central role in company festivities throughout the seventeenth and early eighteenth century. Wives and widows not only attended company feasts, but were also expected to be present at other guild occasions, including funerals. The Durham Mercers charter of 1561, for example, stipulated that when a guild member died a sermon should be preached at St. Nicholas, where 'all brethren and sisters must be present'. The funerals of the wives of guild members were also regarded as guild occasions, and a Newcastle common council order on funeral regulation, passed in the 1670s, assumed that members of all the Newcastle guilds attended the funerals both of members of the company and of their spouses.[15] Several companies also welcomed the new wife of a guild brother by attending their wedding. The Newcastle Barber Surgeons guild required members to attend one-another's weddings, and in 1746 a newly-married member was fined for not making the customary present of gloves to the stewards, clerk and beadle.[16] It seems likely that wives also attended the celebrations that were held when new members joined the guild, as they did elsewhere in the north. Trade companies valued the presence of women at guild festivities, and provided the wives and widows of guild members with important opportunities for association.[17]

Having established the profile of participation in company social occasions we must now examine the range and significance of guild celebrations. In the early and mid-seventeenth century the members of the trade companies of Newcastle and Durham gathered for frequent and extensive guild celebrations. Each company marked the milestones in the lives of its members as well as celebrating important events in the calendar of the institution itself. The guilds were central to the funerals of the members of trade companies and their households, which involved socialising both before and after the burial.[18] Assembling to share food and alcohol provided an opportunity for fellow guild members and their families to pay their respects to the deceased, comfort one-another, and to reaffirm their bonds.[19] These funeral social gatherings were often prolonged, and the 'gathering together at the funeral house and serving the people there' frequently lasted more than three hours in Durham in the 1690s.[20] After a long period of communal eating and drinking, the bearers, usually chosen from among the members of the trade company, carried the body to the church. The Newcastle Shipwrights noted that 'when any brother or sister of the company died

---

[15] A. Clark, *Working Life of Women in the Seventeenth Century* (first edition 1919, reprinted London, 1982), pp. 171-2; F. Heal, *Hospitality in Early Modern England* (Oxford, 1990), pp. 336-7; Whiting, 'Durham Trade Gilds, Part I', 251, 236; Whiting, 'Durham Trade Gilds - continued', 283, 290; TWA, GU/CF/10.

[16] Dendy (ed.), *Merchant Adventurers*, vol. I, p. 67; TWA, GU/BS/2/2 (26 May 1746).

[17] Woodward, *Men at Work*, p. 73.

[18] R. Houlbrooke, 'Death, Church, and Family in England Between the Late Fifteenth and the Early Eighteenth Centuries', in R. Houlbrooke (ed.), *Death, Ritual, and Bereavement* (London, 1989), p. 33; D. Cressy, *Birth, Marriage, And Death: Ritual, Religion, and the Life-Cycle in Tudor and Stuart England* (first edition 1997, reprinted Oxford, 1999), pp. 435-455; R. Houlbrooke, *Death, Religion, and the Family in England, 1480-1750* (Oxford, 1998), pp. 255-294.

[19] Cressy, *Birth, Marriage, And Death*, pp. 427, 444-5.

[20] C. Gittings, *Death, Burial, and the Individual in Early Modern England* (Beckenham, 1984), pp. 105-11, 154, 114, 116, 120, 151; DUL, DCG, Mercers photocopies/4, undated transcript of Durham Common Council order on funerals, bound after 23 September 1696, and before 2 October 1691.

that his or her Corpse were carried to the church or other place appointed by free brethren of the company'. Members and their families could borrow funeral equipment from their guilds, including the pall or cloth for the corpse, mourning cloaks, and plate on which to serve the funeral fare.[21] Trade companies sometimes also gathered to celebrate weddings, and these too involved long celebrations. There was often eating and drinking before the couple left for the church, accompanied by a procession. After the marriage was solemnised the festivities began in earnest, and usually included drinking, feasting and dancing. Wedding meals, like funeral dinners, could be served on plate borrowed from the trade guild.[22]

The important days in the calendar of each individual guild were also marked by communal celebration. Company meetings were often celebrated by the sharing of food and drink, and some guilds spent company funds on festivities to mark the admission of new members.[23] In other guilds all new members, or sometimes only those master craftsmen who had migrated from another town, were required to provide a breakfast or dinner for the whole company as part of their conditions of admission.[24] The grandest festivities of the year celebrated the annual main meeting day, the most important day in the guild calendar. Companies usually held a feast in honour of their main annual meeting, which was often marked by elaborate celebrations. In 1682 the Durham Mercers began their festivities by assembling at St. Nicholas Church 'then and th[e]re to have a Sermon made to the glory of God and edifying of the people and Company'. After leaving church the guild held their meeting, followed by a dinner, at which fourteen bottles of wine '& 2 Bottles of Sacke' were drunk. The company paid for the Durham town musicians to play for them, so that members and their wives could either dance or listen to the music.[25]

Guild socialising had already undergone some change by the mid-seventeenth century. Some days of company celebration were lost as town governments ceased to fund festivities on the days of the ritual year in the course of the sixteenth century.[26] These changes in the patterns of corporation spending had an inevitable effect on the calendar of guild sociability, which also shifted its focus away from some of the days of the ritual year.[27] However, the later seventeenth century witnessed a more significant period of transition, in which some individuals became less committed to socialising with their guilds at funerals and dinners, while others remained protective of their customary celebrations.

---

[21] Rowe (ed.), *Shipwrights*, vol. I, pp. 18-19, 32; DUL, DCG, Mercers photocopies/3, 59A; TWA, GU/HO/1/2, pp. 451-2.

[22] Dendy (ed.), *Merchant Adventurers*, vol. I, pp. 67-8; TWA, GU/BS/2/2 (26 May 1746); Cressy, *Birth, Marriage, And Death*, pp. 350-76.

[23] Whiting, 'Durham Trade Gilds, Part I', 237; DUL, DCG, Curriers/1 (18 February 1670); TWA, GU/BS/2/1, fol. 45.

[24] DUL, DCG, Curriers/1 (5 July 1678); DUL, DCG, Barbers/1, 8th consent in 'a note of all the consents of the whole company as followeth 1617', fols. 19v-21v.

[25] TWA, GU/BS/2/1, fol. 45; DUL, DCG, Mercers photocopies/4, copy of 1632 ordinances; TWA, GU/HO/1/1, pp. 383-384; DUL, DCG, Mercers photocopies/3, 30.

[26] R. Hutton, *The Rise And Fall Of Merry England: The Ritual Year 1400-1700* (Oxford, 1994), pp. 38-40.

[27] J. J. Anderson (ed.), *Records of Early English Drama: Newcastle Upon Tyne* (Toronto, Manchester, 1982), pp. xv, 67.

In the course of the seventeenth century there was a general weakening of the older tradition of communal mourning, which resulted in changes to funeral practices. The level of donations to the poor at funerals declined, and invitations to funeral dinners were increasingly restricted to the intimate associates of the deceased.[28] At the same time the families of deceased guild members, and members of the company themselves, seem to have become less committed to choosing bearers from among the ranks of the trade company. In 1672, for example, the Newcastle Shipwrights complained that whereas guild members and their wives had once been carried to their burials by shipwrights, 'now of late the contrary is used and practised to the great wrong and prejudice of the said company and contrary to the useage and custome'.[29] Some guild members were also increasingly unwilling to be compelled to spend several hours at the funerals of every member of the company and their household. The Durham common council reported that the customary long funerals were inconvenient for 'persons of businesse' because they were 'thereby neglecting their owne necessary occasion and business'.[30] From the 1670s the corporations of Durham and Newcastle acted to regulate what many perceived as the time wasted in funeral attendance, restricting the pre-burial eating and drinking to no more than two hours 'after the time invited'.[31]

While some members of trade companies wished to curtail the time they spent at funerals, many others seem to have wished to continue the tradition of leisurely eating and drinking before burials. The Newcastle and Durham common councils clearly anticipated opposition to the provisions of the funeral orders and care was taken to limit evasion of the new rules, either by individual guild members or officers of the companies. In Newcastle householders were warned not to attempt to gain extra time by inviting their guests to arrive 'betwixt 2 hours'. If this stratagem was attempted, then the allotted time was calculated from the earlier of the two hours. The household where the funeral was held was fined for any infringement of the rules, and guild members who stayed at a funeral longer than two hours were fined twenty-one shillings each. Strong measures were also included to prevent trade guild officials from ignoring the new regulations. If any guild's stewards failed to comply with the notice, then the fine was to be doubled to forty-two shillings, and the eldest sons or apprentices of that company were to be debarred from gaining the freedom of the town.[32]

From the later seventeenth century, however, the guilds were slowly forced to alter their practice, allowing members to attend funerals for a shorter period of time, and recognising the new trend for bearers to be chosen from among

---

[28] K. Wrightson and D. Levine, 'Death in Whickham', in J. Walter and R. Schofield (eds), *Famine, Disease and the Social Order in Early Modern Society* (Cambridge, 1989), pp. 156-65; Cressy, *Birth, Marriage, And Death*, p. 443.

[29] Rowe (ed.), *Shipwrights*, vol. I, pp. 18-19.

[30] Ibid.; DUL, DCG, Butchers/2 (1 January 1697).

[31] Cressy, *Birth, Marriage, And Death*, p. 453; TWA, GU/CF/10; DUL, DCG, Butchers/2 (1 January 1697).

[32] TWA, Gu/CF/10; DUL, DCG, Butchers/2 (1 January 1697).

the close friends and relations of the deceased. Despite their obvious regret, the Newcastle Shipwrights Company was forced to recognise that the members of the guild were no longer unanimously committed to the obligation to attend the entire funeral of members. In 1672 the guild not only amended their rules to allow friends and relations from outside the company to carry the corpse, but if non-guild bearers were chosen, allowed their members to leave the funeral after the register had been called, rather than accompanying the corpse to the grave.[33] In 1734 the Newcastle Barber Surgeons also changed their rules to permit members to leave fifteen minutes after the register had been taken. These resolutions obliged members to appear at company funerals to pay their respects, but allowed them to leave early in the social proceedings of the funeral, which were also curtailed by the new corporation regulations.[34]

As many guild members became less committed to spending time at funerals, they also became less interested in attending celebrations to mark the initiation of new members. Such festivities had traditionally been valued as occasions to welcome new recruits and reaffirm the fraternal ties between all the existing members. From the early eighteenth century, however, members began to be expected to pay a sum of money into the guild coffers instead of organising a feast. In the Durham Barbers guild, for example, newly admitted freemen continued to fund free-making celebrations into the 1690s. In 1717, however, the guild decided that all future entrants should pay a financial penalty rather than provide food and drink, and that this money should 'goe forward for the use of the Trade & not be expended'.[35] Companies also appear to have become increasingly reluctant to spend money from guild funds on sharing food and drink to celebrate the admission of new members. Those trade companies that had previously required members to provide meals increasingly preferred to maximise their income by collecting the penalty fees, and other guilds chose not to spend their money on such festivities.[36]

Both the inclusivity and extent of guild sociability had been eroded by the mid-eighteenth century. In the earlier seventeenth century companies held frequent celebrations attended by all the members of the guild. However, by the mid-eighteenth century, the company calendar tended to be dominated by one large-scale annual celebration, while spending on other occasions had declined. The accounts of the Durham Mercers guild survive from 1664, for example, and expenditure on social occasions other than the day of the annual main meeting peaked in the late seventeenth and early eighteenth century, declining steadily from the second decade of the eighteenth century. Between 1732 and 1750, a mere two shillings was spent on food or drink on days other than the main meeting day. Although guild officials became less willing to spend money from the company stock on regular celebrations involving the whole company, they continued to spend money at meetings of guild officials, or small groups of members.[37] The

---

33 Ibid.; Rowe (ed.), *Shipwrights*, vol. I, pp. 18-19.

34 TWA, GU/BS/2/2, p. 384; TWA, GU/CF/10; DUL, DCG, Butchers/2 (1 January 1697).

35 DUL, DCG, Barbers/2, fol. 61; DUL, DCG, Barbers/3, fol. 20.

36 TWA, GU/BS/2/1, fol. 129; DUL, DCG, Barbers/2, fol. 61; DUL, DCG, Barbers/3, fol. 20.

37 DUL, DCG, Mercers photocopies/3, 56B.

growing tendency to recruit from the urban community itself, rather than the surrounding rural area, and the narrowing in the social origins of apprentices must also have affected the atmosphere of trade guilds, making eighteenth-century companies less open and more club-like than their sixteenth-century counterparts. The Newcastle Merchant Adventurers guild, for example, drew 41 per cent of its apprentices from Newcastle by the mid-1680s, and a little over a third of the company's intake were sons of members of the guild.[38]

From the later seventeenth century there were also attempts within some trade companies to severely limit expenditure on the main guild celebration. In 1690, for example, the warden of the Newcastle Hostmen banned 'festivalls and treats' 'in w[hi]ch the company expended vast sums of money'.[39] In 1702 the Newcastle Barber Surgeons decided that they would limit the expense of audit dinners to fifteen shillings per annum, and three years later the company decided that only forty shillings would be expended on each head-meeting day. In 1716 the Barber Surgeons took the more drastic step of announcing that no money whatsoever should be spent on an auditing feast. In both these guilds, however, the majority of members were sufficiently committed to the customary annual guild celebrations to ensure that these attempts to economise failed to curtail spending. The Newcastle Hostmen, for example, flouted their ban on guild feasting only a year after it was agreed. From 1691 to the 1720s the company continued to celebrate two annual occasions, the main meeting, and the auditing of the accounts. The Newcastle Barber Surgeons guild only obeyed their order against guild celebrations for three years, and in 1728 the guild's audit feast cost the princely sum of £2 2s.[40]

The annual feast of the Durham Mercers guild was also threatened by shifting spending priorities among some members, who were happier to spend money on other things, including maintaining funeral equipment and prizes for horse-races. In thirty of the years between 1666 and 1750 the company passed a resolution not to hold either a communal sermon or feast on the guild meeting day. In some years this decision was probably taken because the company was in financial difficulties, and needed to save money.[41] However, it seems that the irregularity of celebration in the Durham Mercers Company in the later seventeenth and early eighteenth century was not primarily due to financial difficulties. An examination of the company's accounts shows that in many of the years in which the guild cancelled the annual celebrations it could certainly have afforded to hold them. In at least half of these years the account was in credit at the end of the accounting year, so that the company could have afforded to provide a communal sermon and feast.[42]

---

[38] Brooks, 'Apprenticeship, Social Mobility', pp. 56-9, 63-5.

[39] F. W. Dendy (ed.), *Extracts From The Records Of The Company Of Hostmen Of Newcastle-Upon-Tyne,* Surtees Society, 105 (1901), pp. liii, 145.

[40] Ibid., pp. liii, 145; TWA, GU/BS/2/2, pp. 122, 128, 143-4, 205, 225, 317; TWA, GU/HO/1/2, pp. 401, 414, 451-2, 461-2, 709-10.

[41] DUL, DCG, Mercers photocopies/4 (16 October 1666); DUL, DCG, Mercers photocopies/3, 69, 71, 13.

[42] DUL, DCG, Mercers photocopies/4 (7 October 1703); DUL, DCG, Mercers photocopies/3, 25, 71, 69.

Although some guild members were urging restraint, they only succeeded in moderating expenditure on company festivities, because many members wished to continue to enjoy frequent association within their guild. In several years the Durham Mercers Company voted to hold a feast, and a later meeting of the company then reversed that decision. At their quarterly meeting in October 1684, for example, the guild agreed to gather for a meal and sermon, but the celebrations were cancelled at another meeting held twenty days later.[43] Even if those who wished to reduce spending on company celebrations succeeded in passing an order banning the festivities for that year, the resolution might be evaded. The accounts show that in at least five of the years when such a restraining order was passed a feast or a sermon was subsequently held. In the account for the year to January 1680, for example, various members were fined for absence at the company dinner, although the guild had previously voted not to assemble for either a dinner or a sermon in that year.[44]

Despite occasional attempts to reduce spending on entertainment, company celebrations remained an important mode of urban sociability until at least the mid-eighteenth century. Although the frequency of gatherings tended to decline from the later seventeenth century in both Newcastle and Durham, most of the trade companies continued to celebrate on occasions other than the annual dinner until at least the 1740s. Guild meetings were sometimes accompanied by eating or drinking, especially when fines were paid or when capital lent out to a guild member was repaid. The Newcastle Shipwrights were still enjoying celebrations on days other than their main annual celebration in the 1750s.[45] While celebrations on the days of the ritual year had declined, some festivities continued to be held on these days. The Durham guilds marked the beating of the boundaries, a ceremony descended from the Pre-Reformation Rogation Day processions, until at least 1730.[46]

Throughout the period, these occasional guild festivities were supplemented by regular company funerals. There was some reduction both in the prominence of guild members in the funerary rituals, and in the length of time that members were expected to stay.[47] However, many tradesmen continued to view the funerals of members and their households as company occasions. Most of the guilds did not alter their rules regarding participation in funerals, and companies continued to enforce attendance, by fining those who were late, or who did not appear. The guilds also continued to contribute money towards the funerals of guild members as a form of charitable giving.[48] Companies remained committed to investing in funeral equipment and were still hiring out burial cloths and cloaks in

---

43 DUL, DCG, Mercers photocopies/4 *(3 October 1684, 23 October 1684), copy of 1632 ordinances; DUL, DCG, Mercers photocopies/3, 24.

44 DUL, DCG, Mercers photocopies/3, 47B, 30, 31.

45 DUL, DCG, Barbers/3, fols. 218r, 232r; TWA, GU/SH/1/1, account for 1755; DUL, DCG, Mercers photocopies/3, 51A.

46 TWA, GU/SH/1/1, account for 1678; R. Hutton, *The Stations of the Sun: A History Of The Ritual Year In Britain* (Oxford, 1996), pp. 277-87.

47 TWA, GU/CF/10; DUL, DCG, Butchers/2 (1 January 1697); Rowe (ed.), *Shipwrights*, vol. I, pp. 18-19; TWA, GU/BS/2/2, p. 384.

48 TWA, GU/BS/2/1, account for 1681; TWA, GU/BS/2/2, pp. 165, 373.

the mid-eighteenth century. In the Newcastle Shipwrights Company, for example, demand for funeral equipment remained high, and the guild continued to lend out their funeral cloaks and handsome velvet pall until 1758, if not beyond.[49] Evidently, guild members were proud to belong to their trade company, and wanted to be able to conduct the funerals of their relatives using a pall that bore the arms of their guild, even though many of them could have chosen to borrow funeral equipment from their parish church instead. The parish of St Oswald's in Durham, for example, owned a coffin by the early seventeenth century.[50]

Not only did guilds continue to socialise at the funerals of members, but they also continued to gather for at least one annual celebration throughout the first half of the eighteenth century. Communal eating and drinking remained an important part of the self-image of the trade company as a fraternity of brothers, sisters and their households. The Durham Mercers Company, for example, held their main meeting day dinner of 'four dishes of Meat' in an inn in the town from 1735. In 1742 the guild decided that they would continue to hold an annual dinner in one of the Durham alehouses, sharing food costing up to £2 2s.[51] Not only did annual company social occasions survive beyond the mid-century, but these festivities could be impressive events, which included feasting, music, a sermon, and particularly in the Durham guilds, a procession. The sums spent on these celebrations were sometimes surprisingly large, as in 1737, when the Newcastle Barber Surgeons spent ten guineas on t/he dinner to celebrate their main meeting.[52]

The core festivities of the guild social calendar survived into the mid-eighteenth century and guild sociability was also reinvigorated from the later seventeenth century by involvement in the new political calendar of public celebration and in commercialised leisure. The trade companies of Durham participated in the city's regular civic processions from the last decade of the seventeenth century to beyond the mid-eighteenth century.[53] The guilds marched on various occasions, including the arrival of the Bishop in the city and the anniversary of the accession of the current monarch. Jacob Bee, a member of the Durham guild of Skinners and Glovers, witnessed the procession that welcomed Bishop Crewe and his wife into the city in August 1700. Bee recorded in his diary that the couple were 'mett with a very great company, both gents, tradesmen and others, besides every street in his way to the castle, the streets and windows were see [sic] clad with people 'twas almost innumerall: all the trads' banners was displayed: the mayor and aldermen was there'.[54] The city's guilds also held processions for Restoration Day, celebrated on the 29th of May, and for

---

[49] TWA, GU/HO/ 1/2, account for 1741; Rowe (ed.), *Shipwrights*, vol. I, p. 32; TWA, GU/SH/1/2, account for 1758.

[50] Gittings, *Death, Burial*, p. 116; Cressy, *Birth, Marriage, And Death*, pp. 432-5.

[51] DUL, DCG, Mercers/1 (6 October 1735, 30 September 1745).

[52] DUL, DCG, Mercers photocopies/3, 76; DUL, DCG, Mercers/1 (26 June 1710, 1 October 1722); Mackenzie, *Newcastle*, p. 88; TWA, GU/BS/2/2, p. 401.

[53] DUL, DCG, Mercers photocopies/3, fol. 34; DUL, DCG, Curriers/2, account for 1706; DUL, DCG, Barbers/3, fol. 5; Whiting, 'Durham Trade Gilds - continued', pp. 286, 333-4; Whiting, 'Durham Trade Gilds, Part I', p. 248.

[54] J. C. Hodgson (ed.), *Six North Country Diaries*, Surtees Society, 118 (1910), p. 60; DUL, DCG, Mercers photocopies/3, 52A.

Gunpowder Treason Day on November the 5th, and sometimes marked these days with eating and drinking before or after their procession.[55]

It seems likely that many individual guild members attached political significance to guild celebrations on political anniversaries, which reinforced the importance of company sociability. The festivities on such days were innately politicised, because certain days of celebration were closely associated with particular political loyalties. Restoration Day, the anniversary of Charles II's entry into London in 1660, was widely abandoned after 1688 because of its connection with the exiled Stuarts, for example. After the Hanoverian accession Restoration Day became a focus for the expression of Jacobite sympathies, and was also celebrated by the politically impotent Tories.[56] In Durham the anniversary seems to have been marked by annual guild processions from 1713 to 1749, which can probably initially be accounted for by the political leanings of Nathaniel Crewe, bishop of Durham from the 1670s to the 1720s. Crewe was a suspected Jacobite, and a contemporary noted that the city was dominated by 'Rory Toryism', for 'none but men of that kidney are in favour with our worthy good bishop.' However, the Durham trade companies continued to hold celebrations on Restoration Day in the years after Crewe's death in 1722, when the see of Durham was held by two Whig-leaning bishops in succession. Processions on Restoration Day continued until at least the mid-eighteenth century, probably because they were popular.[57]

Although the Durham trade companies did have an unusual attachment to a day that was strongly associated with Tory sympathies, many of the days celebrated by the town's guilds did not have the Tory associations of Restoration Day. The companies celebrated the anniversary of Gunpowder Treason, which was widely observed in Britain throughout the eighteenth century, and the Durham guilds also marked the anniversaries of the accessions of both George I and George II. The variety of days celebrated by the Durham trade companies defies any attempt to infer the ideological convictions of the majority of their members. However, the celebration of days that had both Whig and Tory associations meant that guild sociability gained an added significance for members of all political affiliations.[58] Newcastle was relatively unusual during this period in that the town's trade guilds do not appear to have taken part in the civic processions that marked political and religious landmarks after the Restoration. None of the three Newcastle companies studied here seems to have mounted independent processions in the later seventeenth and first half of the eighteenth century, although at least one of the town's other guilds is known to have organised its own processions. However, decline in company sociability on days of the ritual year was partly compensated

[55] DUL, DCG, Barbers/2, fol. 76; Whiting, 'Durham Trade Gilds - continued', p. 333; DUL, DCG, Mercers photocopies/3, 55.

[56] Hutton, *Stations of the Sun*, pp. 288-91; Hutton, *Merry England*, pp. 289-90, 257-8; D. Cressy, *Bonfires And Bells: National Memory and the Protestant Calendar in Elizabethan and Stuart England* (London, 1989), pp. 64-6.

[57] Heesom, *Durham City and its M.P.s*, pp. 19-21; DUL, DCG, Mercers photocopies/3, 79.

[58] Hutton, *Stations of the Sun*, pp. 396-7; DUL, DCG, Barbers/3, fols. 34, 40; DUL, DCG, Mercers photocopies/3, 59A.

for by the guild gatherings that occurred in the course of political treating. On election day in 1747, for example, the victorious candidates, provided a 'handsome Treat' for the freemen 'class'd into their respective Companies'.[59]

Not only was guild sociability revitalised after the Restoration by the new political celebrations, but trade companies also showed their flexibility by engaging in fashionable commercial leisure pursuits. From at least the later seventeenth century the trade guilds of Newcastle and Durham were financing horse-racing in the two towns, consistently contributing towards prize money. The Durham Mercers, for example, donated money to prizes for races from 1687 to 1739, often giving several guineas a year.[60] Attending horse-races was popular among both men and women from all social levels, so giving to the horse-races was guaranteed to please the households of both the trading and non-trading members of the company. At least one guild, the Durham Mercers, also participated in newly fashionable club life. From 1708 until 1718 the company socialised together at 'club nights', which could involve substantial outlay. In 1709 the sum of £2 10s 11d was spent on one such evening, probably on food and drink.[61] Trade companies were also occasionally choosing to socialise in the coffee houses of the two towns, as the Newcastle Barber Surgeons did in 1704 and 1705, spending small sums of money on food or drink. From the later seventeenth century trade companies were also more likely to celebrate in inns than in private houses, because alehouses had come to be perceived as the obvious location for much institutional sociability.[62]

Trade guilds were effective institutions of association throughout the pre-1750 period and were sufficiently influential to provide an important template for the development of the club, which became a highly significant institution in the course of the eighteenth century. Clubs and societies began to appear from the later sixteenth century and by 1750 the club was fairly well established as an arena of sociability both in London and in the provinces. At least thirty-five different societies had been founded in the north east by the mid-eighteenth century, ranging from a highly successful clerical charity to relatively informal clubs that seem to have been primarily devoted to drinking and conviviality.[63] A variety of institutions probably helped to create an appetite for more formalised modes of association, including the secular continental academies that appeared during the Renaissance period. However, in general, British clubs tended not to model themselves on either the Italian patron-led academies, or the state academies of France. England itself had an older tradition of voluntary association outside the trade guilds, in religious confraternities. These bodies were privately organised,

[59] Wilson, *Sense of the People*, pp. 294-7, 302-3; *Newcastle Journal* (4 July 1747); E. E. Mackenzie, *A Descriptive And Historical Account Of The Town And County Of Newcastle Upon Tyne, Including The Borough Of Gateshead* (Newcastle, 1827), p. 88.

[60] DUL, DCG, Mercers photocopies/3, 57; Whiting, 'Durham Trade Gilds, Part I', 206; Whiting, 'Durham Trade Gilds - continued', 346.

[61] R. W. Malcolmson, *Popular Recreations In English Society 1700-1850* (Cambridge, 1973) pp. 50-51; DUL, DCG, Mercers photocopies/3, 47B, 48B, 56B.

[62] TWA, GU/BS/2/2, pp. 136, 143; Clark, *Clubs*, pp. 39-40; DUL, DCG, Mercers/1, 6 October 1735 (30 September 1745).

[63] *Newcastle Courant* (20 August 1711); *Newcastle Courant* (7 August 1725); Clark, *Clubs*, pp. 60-93.

membership was voluntary, and sociability was an important part of their appeal. However, it seems likely that these organisations had relatively little direct impact on the formation of clubs and societies, because they were no longer active by the later sixteenth century. Confraternities were suppressed by legislation in 1547, and had been in decline since the 1530s.[64]

Enthusiasm for institutional sociability was probably most strongly fuelled by the vitality of association in trade companies. The individuals and groups that established clubs were able to draw on the flourishing and highly visible exemplar of guild sociability. Residents of incorporated towns regularly witnessed company members assembling at funerals, weddings and processions. Large numbers of middling sort men and their wives experienced guild sociability from the inside, attending company feasts, sermons and funerals. Non-members of the guild also occasionally attended guild dinners, either as guests, or as employees of the company.[65] As the seventeenth century wore on increasing numbers of the gentry experienced the culture of the guilds as members. Guild organisation was a national model, which was culturally available even to those in towns that did not have their own guilds, and to those living in rural areas.[66] Not only was guild sociability prominent, but contemporaries recognised it as a successful and important form of association.

The institutional practices of trade companies were ideally suited to the urban context in which they had developed, and clubs were predominately urban institutions, which made use of many of the traditions of the companies.[67] Early provincial clubs and societies sometimes modelled their rules on guild ordinances, and many societies copied the organisational procedures of the trade guilds, including the titles of officers, election arrangements, and the requirement that members swear oaths of secrecy about the organisation's affairs. The officials of clubs in the north east, for example, used various titles, including 'steward', 'warden' and 'assistant', which were all in use by trade companies in the region.[68] Not only did clubs draw on the organisational structure of the guilds, but they also performed many of the same functions as guilds, including providing for burial, and supporting penurious members. Like trade companies, many clubs and societies reinforced fraternal bonds among members by marking the life-cycle events of members, and by socialising at communal feasts and processions. In terms of membership, both trade companies and societies were supported by a solid core of middling sort members, whilst many of the gentry also participated. Gentry participation would have been more marked in élite clubs than in lower status trade guilds, but many societies, including benefit clubs, were also

64 Clark, *Clubs*, pp. 13-25.

65 Rowe (ed.), *Shipwrights*, vol. I, p. 95; *Newcastle Courant* (12 October 1728); DUL, DCG, Mercers photocopies/4 (6 October 1682); DUL, DCG, Barbers/3, fol. 191r; DUL, DCG, Mercers photocopies/3, 21, 41.

66 Brooks, 'Apprenticeship, Social Mobility', pp. 56-62.

67 Barry, 'Bourgeois Collectivism?', pp. 98-9.

68 *Newcastle Journal* (22 June 1745); *Newcastle Journal* (28 April 1744); *Newcastle Courant* (31 May 1735); D. J. Rowe (ed.), *The Records Of The Company Of Shipwrights of Newcastle Upon Tyne 1622-1967*, vol. II, Surtees Society, 184 (1971), p. 298; Dendy (ed), *Merchant Adventurers*, vol. I, pp. 284-5; Clark, *Clubs*, pp. 23-24, 223.

dominated by the middling sort.[69] Like the guilds, clubs were overwhelmingly masculine in their membership, though women were able to participate in both society and guild social events. The rhetoric used to justify the importance of clubs in the early modern town was also borrowed from the traditional discourse of the trade guilds.[70]

It has recently been suggested that the voluntary basis of club membership distinguished socialising within societies from guild association, and that sociability in clubs was a distinctly new form of leisure. Clark argues that whereas trade guilds were semi-official and connected with town government and economic regulation, clubs were operating outside official control, and individuals could choose whether or not to join.[71] It is certainly true that in urban communities membership of a guild was more or less essential in order to practise many trades successfully, whereas individuals were not bound to join any club. However, from the seventeenth century onwards, a significant minority of those who joined guilds entered as honorary members, with no intention of practising the company's trade. These men joined in order to gain the political advantages that membership conferred, but also to enjoy the good fellowship of guild social occasions.[72] Furthermore, many of those who joined provincial clubs were motivated by an expectation of both economic benefit and conviviality, in the same way that guild members joined companies in order to practise their trade, but also to enjoy guild sociability.[73] The association of both guilds and clubs was governed by a similar ethic of communal conformity, and although membership of societies was indeed voluntary, club life was often ritualised and ordered, with a plethora of rules controlling behaviour. Members might be fined for absence from club meetings or funerals, or for unacceptable behaviour such as excessive drinking, swearing and gambling.[74]

The change in patterns of social interaction in the post-Restoration period seems to have been less significant than the urban renaissance model would suggest. There was certainly an increase in the provision of commercialised leisure in towns after 1660, but the current master-narrative must be modified to take account of the resilience of older forms of socialising, such as guild celebrations. Company festivities were an important mode of socialising in towns in the mid-eighteenth century, just as they had been in the early seventeenth century. The guilds of Newcastle and Durham were successful in the long term because they were prepared to modify their institutional practices when it became necessary for them to do so. Companies had traditionally demanded that their members invest

---

69 Brooks, 'Apprenticeship, Social Mobility', pp. 54-62; Clark, *Clubs*, pp. 211-15.

70 B. Hill, *Women, Work and Sexual Politics in Eighteenth-Century England* (Oxford, 1989), pp. 89-90; Clark, *Clubs*, pp. 23-4, 178, 198-204, 228, 265-70; TWA, 1160/1; Rowe (ed.), *Shipwrights*, vol. I, pp. 129-31.

71 Clark, *Clubs*, pp. 21-2, 24.

72 Brooks, 'Apprenticeship, Social Mobility', p. 54; Jacob, *Enlightenment*, p. 38.

73 Clark, *Clubs*, pp. 84, 153, 328-9; Brooks, 'Apprenticeship, Social Mobility', pp. 54, 78; Walker, 'Guild Control', pp. 13, 17, 20, 22-3.

74 DUL, DCG, Curriers/2, p. 30; TWA, GU/BS/2/1, fol. 120; TWA, GU/BS/2/2, p. 257; DUL, DCG, Curriers/2, p. 30; TWA, GU/BS/2/1, fol. 120; TWA, GU/BS/2/2, p. 257; Clark, *Clubs*, pp. 250-51; *Articles of Pot's Box* (Newcastle, 1787), pp. 17-21; TWA, 1160/1, pp. 15, 44, 98, 64.

large amounts of time in guild association, despite the many other modes of recreation that individuals were able to enjoy.[75] From the later seventeenth century onwards, however, many members were unwilling to devote so much of their time and money to socialising within their trade company. While some guild members remained committed to gathering at frequent company funerals and at many occasions of socialising throughout the year, others seem to have begun to expect a more pluralistic sociable life. These individuals probably wished to be able to enjoy guild celebrations alongside many other kinds of recreation, including horse racing and the emerging provincial clubs, without damaging their livelihoods.[76]

Trade guilds responded by altering their rules, allowing members to stay at funerals for a shorter time, but ensuring that all members of the guild would continue to attend company funerals.[77] Companies also reduced the occasions of incidental socialising, concentrating on one principal social occasion per year, which acted as a focus for the celebration of guild unity. After the Restoration trade companies took part in the new political calendar of celebration, and absorbed into their activities many of the newly fashionable forms of sociability, such as frequenting coffee-houses.[78] Their celebrations continued to involve large numbers of middling sort men and women, and many of those higher up the social scale also participated. Company sociability endured because guild members and their households enjoyed the celebrations, and because the festivities continued to symbolise a set of civic values that had survived the test of time. The success of the trade companies encouraged emulation, and clubs were heavily indebted to the guilds, sharing many of their ideals and practices.

---

[75] R. Longrigg, *The History of Horse Racing* (London, 1972), pp. 20, 23-4; G. R. Scott, *The History of Cockfighting* (London, 1957), pp. 93-5, 99, 102.

[76] Longrigg, *Horse Racing*, pp. 46-7; Clark, *Clubs*, passim.

[77] TWA, GU/BS/2/2, p. 383; TWA, GU/CF/10; DUL, DCG, Butchers/2 (1 January 1697).

[78] DUL, DCG, Mercers photocopies/3, 81, 73.

Chapter 6

'A Clumsey Countrey Girl': The Material and Print Culture of Betty Bowes*

ADRIAN GREEN

Cultural historians of the eighteenth century have claimed an unprecedented importance for material and print culture in this period, when increased consumption of material goods was accompanied by an expanded role for printed texts in shaping attitudes towards consumption.[1] Yet the novelty of material consumption and its relationship to print can be exaggerated; the volume and range of material goods and their promotion in print had been increasing since the late fifteenth century.[2] Neither material abundance nor the prevalence of print in themselves determined the cultural significance of things and texts in the eighteenth century. It was their content and form and the altered meanings associated to them, that made print and the materiality of eighteenth-century life distinct from earlier centuries. As signifiers of 'taste' material goods and printed texts were self-consciously regarded as defining social identities. Such a role for texts and things was scarcely new to the century after 1660, but the prevalence of contemporary comment in print about material life, whether condemned as luxury or exonerated as taste, has led historians to regard this period as creating a peculiarly modern mode of cultural interaction, partly expressed through the individualised consumption of material and print culture.

From the late seventeenth century, élite status no longer relied upon gentility being associated to family and lineage, but was newly asserted through learnt codes of behaviour that defined polite taste and marked out a special role for material consumption.[3] It has been argued that this more modern mode of creating

---

* Rebecca King has provided invaluable assistance during the research for this paper; I am also grateful for the advice of Joanne Bailey, Chris Brooks, Harriet Guest and Matthew Johnson.

[1] J. Brewer and R. Porter (eds), *Consumption and the World of Goods* (London, 1993); J. Brewer, *The Pleasures of the Imagination: English Culture in the Eighteenth Century* (London, 1997).

[2] L. Jardine, *Worldly Goods: A New History of the Renaissance* (London, 1996); D. Gaimster and P. Stamper (eds), *The Age of Transition: the Archaeology of English Culture 1400-1600* (London, 1997); J. Thirsk, *Economic Policy and Projects: The Development of a Consumer Society in Early Modern England* (Oxford, 1978).

[3] F. Heal and C. Holmes, *The Gentry in England and Wales 1500-1700* (London, 1994), pp. 46-7 and *passim*; P. Corfield, 'The Rivals: Landed and Other Gentlemen', in N. Harte and R. Quinault (eds), *Land and Society in Britain, 1700-1914* (Manchester, 1996), pp. 1-33.

social identities fostered the growth of individualism at the expense of the family. Reading is similarly supposed to have promoted a more rational sense of self in the eighteenth century. In relation to women, it has been argued that individual reading encouraged not only a heightened sense of self but actively dissuaded women from engaging in a family through marriage.[4] The documented material and print culture of Betty Bowes provides an opportunity to test these assumptions about the role of material and print culture in eighteenth-century life, and to examine the relationship of one individual in North-East England to wider cultural practices.

Following her death, an inventory was taken of the estate of 'Mrs Elizabeth Bowes of Elvet, Durham'.[5] Betty was unmarried, and the courtesy term 'Mrs' was applied in the patriarchal context of family accounts. This was not a formal probate inventory, but a family document drawn up as part of the private bureaucracy that created and sustained the wealth of the Bowes family.[6] Compiled a week after her death, the inventory itemises plate, furnishings and household utensils by room, and unusually lists over eighty books by title. Few book lists exist in print for early to mid-eighteenth-century women, and the publication (see Appendix) and discussion of the Bowes book list here is intended as a contribution to the study of the consumption of print culture.[7] Betty's provincial position as well as her unmarried status make her a particularly significant case. For she was less integrated with metropolitan print culture than the subject of John Brewer's study of reading through Anna Larpent's diary. Anna was the wife of a government censor of literature in London.[8] Betty was an unmarried gentlewoman with her own income, in Durham.

In many respects Betty's books, furnishings and mode of living, fit well with recent research into reading, gender and gentility. For those who prospered most from North-East England's coal trade participated in the élite culture of eighteenth-century England as a whole. The context of Betty's life also indicates the continued importance of family in framing material and print consumption. Betty's library and furnishings as well as her unmarried status, appear to have been the product of family concerns rather than an example of the 'enlightened domesticity' that contemporary commentators and historians have argued put women off men.

---

[4] I. Q. Brown, 'Domesticity, Feminism and Friendship: Female Aristocratic Culture and Marriage in England 1660-1760', *Journal of Family* History, 7 (1982), pp. 406-24.

[5] Strathmore Papers, Durham Record Office D/St/E8/4-14.

[6] See D. McCollum-Oldroyd, 'Accounting and Estate Management in North-East England c.1700-1770, with particular reference to the Bowes estates', University of Durham, unpublished M. Phil. dissertation (1998).

[7] I. Rivers (ed.), *Books and Their Readers in Eighteenth-Century England* (Leicester, 1982); J. Raven, H. Small and N. Tadmor (eds), *The Practice and Representation of Reading in England* (Cambridge, 1996).

[8] J. Brewer, 'Reconstructing the Reader: Prescriptions, Texts and Strategies in Anna Larpent's Reading', in Raven *et al* (eds.), *Practice and Representation,* pp. 226-45, and idem, *Pleasures of the Imagination,* pp. 56-7 and *passim.*

Context

The Bowes were one of Durham's principal county gentry families. Their estates at Streatlam in Teesdale and Gibside near the Tyne were amassed through opportune marriage from the fourteenth century, and fierce Protestantism and coal wealth underpinned the further rise of the family from the late sixteenth century. By the eighteenth century, the Bowes' were wealthy coal owners and Whig gentry.[9] Born in 1699, Elizabeth Bowes was the third of eight surviving children of Sir William Bowes of Streatlam and Elizabeth Blakiston of Gibside. After her father's death in 1707, Betty was resident either at Gibside or more regularly at Bowes House in Durham, situated on the South Bailey. South Bailey was the most prestigious address in Durham, next to the Cathedral close and at the furthest end of the peninsula that housed the county and professional gentry. Bowes House was built by Sir William Bowes in the fifteenth century, split into tenements in the sixteenth century and redeveloped into a large town house in 1689 by Cuthbert Bowes. Part of a wider pattern of the gentry returning to residence in town during the seventeenth century, the Bowes' decision to reform a house on this site represents an assertion of gentry lineage and their long-standing place in Durham society.[10] Despite the association of Bowes House with the family as a whole, it was mainly occupied by the unmarried and widowed women of the family. The unmarried Bowes daughters lived there with their widowed mother, and Betty and Jane held the lease after Lady Elizabeth's death.[11] Other gentry houses in Durham were also most often occupied by the women of the family, and not infrequently by unmarried women sharing a house together.[12] Urban residence offered benefits of sociability and amenities for well-off eighteenth-century women in the North-East as elsewhere.[13]

Whereas Jane remained resident in the Bailey house, Betty made preparations to move to her own house in Elvet in the year after their mother's death in 1736.[14] She took a lease from the Cathedral's Dean and Chapter estate, and her brother arranged a mortgage in her name with the City Corporation to build a new architect-designed house. A Mr Nesham was paid £1 19s 3d for 'planning the House'; a fraction of its total cost of £225 15s 1½d.[15] Situated close to the race-course, Elvet had developed in the early eighteenth century as a second gentry quarter outside the Baileys on the peninsula. Newspaper advertisements reveal that several houses were occupied by unmarried or widowed genteel women, mainly living on rentier incomes that they usually controlled.[16] Betty's finances, however,

---

9 M. Wills, *Gibside and the Bowes Family* (Newcastle upon Tyne, 1995).

10 Now 4 South Bailey; A. Green, 'Houses and Households in County Durham and Newcastle upon Tyne, c. 1570-1730', University of Durham, unpublished Ph.D. dissertation (2000).

11 Durham University Archive, Hudlestone Papers; Durham Cathedral Archive, Dean and Chapter Rental Books; D/St/E8/4.

12 Green, 'Houses and Households', pp. 270-74.

13 A. Vickery, *The Gentleman's Daughter: Women's Lives in Georgian England* (London, 1998), p. 9 and *passim*.

14 D/St/D13/5/25-7.

15 D/St/E8/7/1-5; D/St/E8/9-13; now part of Royal County Hotel, remodelled in the 1770s.

16 Green, 'Houses and Households', p. 233.

were under the control of her brother. Sir George administered the incomes of his sisters, using their capital to finance the expansion of the Gibside estate.[17] Betty's involvement in the estate was limited to funding the schoolmaster's salary at Tanfield, though she expressed an interest in the family trade in correspondence with her brother: informing him *c.*1727 that 'we have had very Rainey weather which I am feared will Prejudice the Cole trade'.[18] She had to report her expenditure accounts to Sir George, to such a degree that her account book includes entries as detailed as those that regulated estate revenue. For instance, in April 1734, 'Elizabeth Bowes bought of Alison Maydwelli: 45 wine glasses, 6 beer glasses, 12 flowered wine glasses, 12 water glasses; and plates flowered; 2 quart decanters, and a Box to put them in for £4, 6 shillings and tuppence.'[19] The yearly balance in the ledger for Betty's account shows £200 in 1723 when it begins on her maturity, rising with interest to £2000 in 1742, after moving to her own house, and over four and a half thousand pounds in 1758. Her income was disposed of mostly in cash withdrawals, but also included occasional coaches out of Durham, lace livery for her boy, and payments to tradesmen – including booksellers.[20]

Despite establishing an independent household, family remained of central importance in Betty's life. Her Elvet house was the location for some of Sir George Bowes' political activities, and in 1739 Betty was hosting social events to gather votes for his re-election as MP for the county.[21] This family-orientated political activity parallels the recent recognition by historians that élite women participated in politics; the books in Betty's house included 'A book of old sets of Parliament'.[22] The portraits on her walls provide further evidence for her familial obligations. The family portraits in 1759 were in the drawing room and best parlour, except for 'Miss Bowes's picture' (Jane's portrait) which was relegated to the 'Best Bed Chamber', a guest room upstairs, a location that may reflect poor relations between the sisters. This might also be inferred from Jane's reputation as 'a celebrated beauty and extremely vain', and may partly explain Betty's move to her own house, leaving Jane resident on the Bailey.[23] The other family portraits were all downstairs. In the best parlour were 'George Bowes Esqr' and 'Doctor Bowes the Solicitor'; in the drawing room, 'Mrs Liddell' her sister Peggy, and her brother 'Mr Thomas Bowes' as well as her late sister in law 'Miss Verney'.[24] This

---

[17] Wills, *Gibside,* p. 15; D/St/D13/4/15; D/St/D/13/5/28 & 35.

[18] D/St/E15/5/86; Elizabeth to Sir George Bowes 26 May *c.*1727. Glamis Castle Archive, Bowes Letter Books.

[19] D/St/C1/3/71-73.

[20] D/St/C1/3/67-70 & D/St/C1/2/22.

[21] Durham Cathedral, Dean and Chapter Library, Sharp Mss. 125.

[22] See E. Chalus, 'Women and Electoral Politics in the Late Eighteenth Century', in E. Chalus and H. Barker (eds), *Gender in Eighteenth-Century England: Roles, Representations and Responsibilities* (London, 1997); idem, 'Élite Women, Social Politics and the Political World of Late Eighteenth-Century England', *Historical Journal*, 43, 3 (2000), pp. 669-97.

[23] Wills, *Gibside*, pp. 15, 65; Jane also spent more time in London than Betty, for example chaperoning their niece Mary Eleanor during the 1750s.

[24] D/St/E8/4-14.

woman had died tragically young, at the age of fifteen, within months of her marriage to Sir George in 1724.[25]

The association of Eleanor Verney's death with her marriage may well have discouraged Betty from seeking marriage for herself. A pair of poems by Mary Astell and Lady Mary Wortley Montagu were written as complimentary responses to Eleanor Bowes' death, and both turn on the fateful fortunes of marriage.[26] Astell, the daughter of a Newcastle coal merchant, was famously unmarried and in her writings advised women not to marry unless they could find a man into whose hands they could entrust their moral life. Astell was personally committed to celibacy intellectually and physically, and thought of sexuality as destructive; her poem 'On Mrs Bowes' Death' suggests the marriage was fatal. Lady Mary Wortley Montagu gave a more ironical treatment of the brief marriage than Astell. She held ambivalent feelings about marriage both before and after her union with Edward Wortley Montagu, Sir George Bowes' principal partner in the coal trade. In her youth Lady Mary discussed potential suitors in terms of providing a route into 'heaven', 'hell' or 'limbo'. In her poem 'On the Death of Mrs Bowes', Lady Mary considered Eleanor to have achieved heaven and avoided limbo.[27] The death of Eleanor presumably held commensurate responses for the young sister-in-law Betty, who almost certainly knew these poems.[28] Eleanor Verney's mother was a neighbour of Lady Mary at Twickenham, and her antagonism towards Lady Mary's independence has been attributed to the poem that implied her daughter had been killed by Bowes' sexual vigour.[29]

In 1727 Betty wrote to her brother in London, where he was preoccupied with lobbying for the coal trade, while Mrs Verney chaperoned their sister Peggy around town. The purpose of Betty's letter was to encourage Sir George to make a second marriage match:

> I am sorry to have your Assurance that you have no thoughts of making your addresses to Miss Skidens if she is amicable to you and your hopes of Sucksess, which I think you need not fear if you be but harty in the affair. Sure no business can be an excuse, nor will it if you begin rightly to set about matremony, if as you have often told me that you and Peggy are to be the supporters of our family.[30]

While George and Peggy were to marry to the advantage of the family, the prospect of Betty marrying was evidently regarded as a lower priority that might risk diluting the family's wealth. Peggy later married Thomas Liddell, who

---

[25] Eleanor, daughter and heiress of Thomas Verney, married Sir George 1 October 1724, died 4 December 1724, Wills, *Gibside*, pp. 11-12.

[26] Poems printed in R. Perry, *The Celebrated Mary Astell: An Early English Feminist* (Chicago, 1986) pp. 489-90; I. Grundy, *Lady Mary Wortley Montagu: Comet of the Enlightenment* (Oxford, 1999), pp. 239-41 and 296-97.

[27] Grundy, *Lady Mary*, pp. 239-41, 368; a redrafted version of the poem is in *The Letters and Works of Lady Mary Wortley Montagu* (London, 1893), vol. II, p. 485.

[28] No surviving correspondence links Betty to Lady Mary, though Grundy notes that many of her acquaintances are unknown, Grundy, *Lady Mary*, pp. 193, 240-41, 298-300 and *passim*.

[29] Grundy, *Lady Mary*, pp. 298-300.

[30] Glamis Castle Archive, Bowes Letter Books (1 February 1727).

represented a key ally for Bowes in the north-east coal trade as the younger son of the Ravensworth estate neighbouring Gibside. Bowes himself was reportedly so affected by the death of his first wife that he did not remarry till twenty years later (and gave his only daughter Mary Eleanor, both his wives' names). In her letter, Betty identifies herself unfavourably with George's marital fortunes, though she may not yet have been entirely reconciled to a life without men:

> it's time you were begun for you like me have little time to loose, there' is not great difference in our age, you indeed have many advantages I have not, as being a fine Gentleman and of great Estate, which are two undeniable things with the Ladies, I can Pretend to nothing who am but a clumsey Countrey Girl with a Small fortune - Just enough to maintain me at Durham.

This self-characterisation as a 'clumsey Countrey Girl', is not so personal as might first appear and has close parallels in other gentry correspondence between the North-East and London. Rebecca King's research into élite sociability has shown that 'correspondents writing from the North-East often assumed a stylised position of faux-ignorance towards friends or kinfolk experiencing the delights of London'.[31] Katherine Carr wrote to her brother Ralph in the 1730s, styling herself 'a Poor auQuard Country Girll' in a manner almost identical to Betty.[32] Yet, the demure expression of inferiority as an unmarried sister in the country did not preclude familiarity with London and actually supported notions of virtue associated to being unsullied by city living. Betty herself visited London, and a portion of family plate was inventoried there as part of her estate at her death.[33] She also went to Scarborough and Bath for health reasons in the early 1730s, but spent the majority of her time in the provincial context of Durham.[34]

Betty's public identity was inevitably closely associated to her brother, as in the notice of her death that appeared in the *Newcastle Courant* on 24 November 1759:

> Monday Night died at Durham, Miss Betty Bowes, Sister of George Bowes, Esq; of Gibside, Member of Parliament for the County of Durham; a Lady whose friendly and benevolent Disposition gained her great Esteem, and whose charity to the Poor will make her Loss severely felt by them, as it is justly regretted by her Friends and Acquaintances.[35]

Thomas Gyll recorded in his diary that Mrs Betty Bowes had died 'of the gout in her stomach'.[36] Betty's coffin and skeleton have recently been excavated, and it is

[31] R. King, 'Aspects of Sociability in the North-East of England, 1600-1750', University of Durham unpublished Ph.D. dissertation (2001), p. 260.
[32] King, 'Aspects of Sociability', p. 260.
[33] D/St/E15/2/2.
[34] Elizabeth to Sir George Bowes, 19 June *c.*1730, Glamis Castle Archive, Bowes Letter Books; D/St/C1/2/123, Francis O'Neal, London to Mrs. Elizabeth Bowes, Bath (20 December 1733).
[35] J. Styles (ed.), *Eighteenth-Century Provincial Newspapers* (Reading, microfilm unit 6, series 4); *Newcastle Courant* (Newcastle Papers, Reel 12, 1759-1763).
[36] 'The Diary of Thomas Gyll', *Six North Country Diaries II*, Surtees Society (1910), vol. 118, p. 207.

likely that she suffered from a peptic ulcer since her early thirties, when a cure in Bath proved unable to remedy her condition. Betty's burial with her mother in a vault beneath the choir of the small parish church of St. Mary the Less, opposite Bowes House on South Bailey, underscores the family's prominence among Durham's protestant élite and the particular importance of urban residence and burial for the unmarried and widowed women of the family.[37]

Texts

The importance of family in Betty's life extended to her library. The list of books in the 1759 inventory includes many titles that were first published in the late seventeenth or very early eighteenth century, though most went through numerous later reprints.[38] It is thus difficult to know the exact date of the books in the list, and whether they were acquired by Betty. It is probable that the early books formed part of a family collection given to her by her mother. The fact that the books were inventoried as a separate category, and by title, also implies that they were part of a family library, with the books holding similar status to the family plate in Durham and London. However, Betty had many books published after her mother's death and payments to booksellers in her financial accounts. Her library was not simply an heirloom though it was founded on family taste.

The inventory largely identifies volumes by an abbreviated version of title, with authors only given for *Works*. The identification of authors with their entire corpus rather than individual texts, implies an emphasis on the content of the text rather than the personality of the author.[39] 'John Earl of Rochester' is the only name to appear without connection to title, genre or collected works, and does so twice; reflecting familiarity with his notoriety. Betty very probably had John Wilmot's death-bed oration repenting his rakish London life and celebrating his provincial domesticity, rather than his libertine works. Given the limited presence of other plays and poems in the list, the duplicate reference to the earl of Rochester probably relates to one of the many publications produced in the debate following Burnet's publication of *The Libertine Overthrown* in 1680.[40] The moralistic concerns of the collection are also reflected in *The Case of Impotency*; George Abbot's account of the earl of Castlehaven's rape and sodomy trial, among other

---

[37] A ledger slab records that the three coffins in the Bowes vault contain 'DAME ELIZABETH BOWES / MDCCXXXVI / AND HER DAUGHTER / ELIZABETH BOWES / MDCCLIX / JANE BOWES MDCCLXX', N. Emery, 'Excavations at the Church of St. Mary the Less Durham City' (unpublished), vol. I, pp. 11 and 137; D/St/C1/2/123. I am very grateful to Norman Emery for showing me his report.

[38] E.g. William Beveridge's *Private thoughts upon religion, digested into twelve articles, with practical relations form'd thereupon* (1709), went through five editions by 1748.

[39] M. Foucault, 'What is an Author?' in J. Harari (ed.), *Textual Strategies: Perspectives in Post-Structuralist Criticism* (London, 1979), pp. 141-60.

[40] J. Redwood, *Reason, Ridicule and Religion: the Age of Enlightenment in England 1660-1750* (London, 1996), pp. 44 and 176-9.

élite infidelity trials. Alternatively, these scandalous texts could be read as erotica.[41]

Although we cannot account for the specific presence of each text, the book list does present a coherent collection. The majority of the list is recognisably standard fare for an eighteenth-century gentry library. In addition to the Bible and Shakespeare, there was an English Dictionary and works of political history. The presence of Titus Oates' *A Display of Tyranny*, justifying the Glorious Revolution of 1688, along with Clarendon's *History of the Rebellion* among other works, suggests a need to explain the convulsions of the seventeenth century. The Tory 'patriot' Bolingbroke is also present among these books, though the interest may have lain more in his religious views. With Bolingbroke, Locke and several divines in the list, the texts are commentaries and not originals. Betty seems to have lacked the seminal texts of key debates, but the range of secondary accounts disseminating key eighteenth-century concepts, seems to imply sincere interest rather than canonical display.

Inventories cannot be relied upon as a complete record of possessions, and Betty's book list may not record all the books she read or even possessed, especially if she gave away books before she died. Yet the lacunae in the list as a 'standard' gentry library, makes it the more interesting and distinctive. Sermons are largely absent, and there is surprisingly little about health or gardening, and almost no imaginative literature. Fielding, Richardson and Defoe's fiction are absent. The predominant category is religious works; commentaries on debates as well as manuals to devotion. These commentaries shade into 'moral philosophy' debates, starting with Locke and Filmer and following through eighteenth-century topics as well as a number of later seventeenth-century writings (many of which remained in print throughout the eighteenth century). These texts are related to the prescriptive literature, and both genres involve issues relating to gender relations. Finally, a few poems and plays are included, with a couple of the classics in translation. Questions of religion are paramount in the list; even though this was the 'Age of Enlightenment', the vast majority of books printed were religious.[42] Many of the most earnest religious books here were intended for personal and private devotion. For instance, John Humphrey's *A Private Psalter, or Manual of devotion* (1683), or John Kettleworth's *Practical Believer* (1688), subtitled *The articles of the Apostles Creed drawn out to form a true Christian's heart and practice in two parts.* The religiosity of the list suggests that Betty was to some degree a pious woman.

That Betty read her books is convincing given the intellectual context of her family, noted for their earnest attitude to female education.[43] Betty's niece, Mary Eleanor, was encouraged in precocious intellectual pursuits; interested in botany, she also published a poetical drama *The Siege of Jerusalem* in 1769. Mary

[41] P. Wagner, 'Trial Reports as a Genre of Eighteenth-Century Erotica', *Journal of Eighteenth-Century Studies*, 5 (1982), pp. 117-21; see also C. Herrup, *A House in Gross Disorder: Sex, Law and the 2nd Earl of Castlehaven* (Oxford, 1999); D/St/E8/4-14.

[42] R. Porter, *English Society in the Eighteenth Century* (London, 1990), pp. 279-82.

[43] Wills, *Gibside*, pp. 63-5; R. Arnold, *The Unhappy Countess* (London, 1957), pp. 17-18.

Eleanor was more famous for her two failed marriages, both blamed on intellectually inferior husbands attracted to her massive inheritance. Her unhappy marriage to the ninth earl of Strathmore was ascribed to her education by Jesse Foot, who thought the late earl of Strathmore 'was not calculated to make even a good learned woman a pleasing husband'.[44] This would seem to fit Pollock's suggestion that well-educated upper-class women found it difficult to find happiness in marriage.[45]

Given the prominence of marriage in contemporary associations with the Bowes family, it seems appropriate to dwell on the theme of female marriage fortunes contained among the texts in the list. Indeed, gender relations appear to have been a prominent theme in these books. Molière explored a wide range of human relationships and their tensions in different works, but neatly Betty only had *The School for Husbands* on marital relationships and gender relations. Among the prescriptive literature, Betty had Richard Allestree's popular *The Ladies Calling*, which reasserted the confining cage of femininity. The optimistic orthodoxy over gender relations was further represented in George Savile's *The Lady's New Year Gift or Advice to a Daughter*, written in 1688. Savile claimed that the compensating qualities of the female sex should 'cure' men, though young women were seldom permitted to make their own choice of marriage partner.[46] Whatever the choices made by Betty, she was provided for and supported by her brother, although such a reciprocal relationship was not necessarily analogous to the hierarchical manner in which a wife was expected to behave towards a husband.[47]

In marked contrast to the conservative prescriptive literature, Betty had the more radical tracts of Mary Astell: *A Serious Proposal to the Ladies* and more unusually her *Essay in Defence of the Female Sex*. Family patronage through associations with Astell in Newcastle may explain their presence in the list. Yet the message in these texts remains significant; Astell considered women's intellectual incapacity to be acquired not natural, and urged women to engage in intellectual pursuits for religious ends.[48] Family patronage also supported the publication of Elizabeth Carter's translation of Epictetus, completed in 1756 and published in 1758. The subscription list includes Samuel Bowes, Esq. and Rumsey Bowes, Esq. of Binfield [Berkshire], George Bowes of Gibside, Co. Durham, Esq. and Mrs Eliz. Bowes, of Durham.[49] Given that Carter wrote in Newcastle Betty may well have known her, or Elizabeth Montagu (a Robinson of York) who promoted Carter's publication. Montagu flattered Mrs Carter that 'one would think [her poems] had been composed on the banks of Hyssus, rather than on those of the Tyne' and Mrs Carter wrote back describing the frivolity and cultural suffocation of the

---

[44] Wills, *Gibside*, p. 75; Arnold, *Unhappy Countess*, *passim*.

[45] L. Pollock, '"Teach Her to Live Under Obedience": the Making of Women in the Upper Ranks of Early Modern England', *Continuity & Change*, 4, 2 (1989), pp. 231-58.

[46] A. Fletcher, *Gender, Sex and Subordination in England 1500-1800* (London, 1995), pp. 387-9.

[47] L. Pollock, 'Rethinking Patriachy and the Family in Seventeenth-Century England', *Journal of Family History*, 23, 1 (1998), pp. 3-27.

[48] Perry, *Celebrated*, pp. 56-97; Fletcher, *Gender, Sex & Subordination*, p. 365.

[49] I am grateful to Harriet Guest for this information.

North-East.[50] Yet this correspondence shows that characterisations of the North-East as provincial could be combined with literary production (partly via correspondence with London) as well as consumption. Richardson thought Mrs Carter 'an example that women may be trusted with Latin and even Greek and yet not think themselves above their domestic duties' and Dr Johnson echoed this view: 'My old friend, Mrs Carter, could make a pudding as well as translate Epictetus'.[51] Epictetus placed virtue above health, pleasure or possessions and regarded marriage as a universal duty necessary among other tasks to make a person a member of a community and ultimately part of the human race. Epictetus' Stoicism appealed to Lady Mary Wortley Montagu, but how did a spinster such as Betty regard the essential requirement of marriage?[52]

The book list contains other writing by women. Mrs Catherine Cockburn, for example, wrote five stage works and later developed an interest in philosophy and published works in explication and defence of Locke. It might fit Betty's collection better if she had Cockburn's defence of Samuel Clarke (1675-1729), a metaphysician and moralist whose most significant work was a sophisticated defence of natural religion. Betty also had *Against Natural and Reveal'd Religion*. Female literary activity may also be present among the unpublished manuscripts in the list. More women wrote for themselves and friends than published in this period, and mention of 'an old written book' in the list may indicate Betty's own writing: potentially including copies, annotations and reworkings of poems and prose as well as 'original' writing. Many women's writings were only found in the drawers of their closet desks after death, and if pious, celebrated in funeral sermons. As Anthony Fletcher has argued, the experience of spirituality and examination of religion among élite women provided a meaningful channel of relief from subordination, at the same time as encouraging an internalisation of gender roles.[53] There was also of course the issue of class, and Roy Porter has observed that the endorsement of 'philosophical religion' in line with moderate behaviour that was opposed to 'enthusiasm', was one mode by which the educated and propertied élite justified their own manner of living against the 'vulgar'.[54]

Material culture

Betty's manner of living was certainly genteel. Her furniture was entirely of mahogany and walnut, with even the garrets containing 'A Mahogony Cistern with Brass keeps, a tea tray Mahogany, an old Tea Board and old Tray Mahogony', while downstairs there was 'a mahogony close stool', as well as mahogany tables, settees, beds and chests of drawers. As Vickery has remarked, 'mahogany objects

---

[50] *Letters from Mrs Carter, to Mrs Montagu, between the Years 1755 and 1800*, vol. I (1817), p. 14, letter iv, Deal (1 November 1758).

[51] Quoted in R. Lonsdale, *Eighteenth-Century Women Poets* (Oxford, 1990), pp. xxx-xxxii and 165-71.

[52] Grundy, *Lady Mary*, pp. 36-7.

[53] Fletcher, *Gender, Sex and Subordination*, pp. 347-63.

[54] Porter, *English Society*, p. 281.

embodied the social distinctions of provincial gentility'.[55] Betty probably spent a great deal of her time in the Old Elvet house and health problems may have enforced her domesticity, though she shared her house with companions who presumably afforded female sociability that included reading. The inventory refers to 'Old Mrs Thorps Room', furnished less elaborately than Mrs Bowes' room on the same floor. Downstairs was 'Mrs Thorps Little Room' containing a 'Mahogany round table, six chairs with green check'd covers' and 'a green window curtain', indicating her own space within the house and containing furniture that marked out her status as genteel. An undated letter concerning the seeking of a boarding room for a friend's daughter, who was to go to school in Durham, mentions that they 'w[e]nt to advise with Nanny Grey at Miss Betty Bowes'.[56] It would also seem feasible that the other unmarried or widowed women with houses on Elvet engaged in a sociability of reading, along with those married women in Durham whose husbands were regularly elsewhere. Although such practices are seldom documented, the bookshops in Durham that advertised in the newspapers indicate a considerable market for print.

The Elvet house was a substantial establishment, with thirteen rooms plus garrets, kitchen and laundry, with forty-four sash windows repainted in 1762.[57] Despite the specialisation of room use, there was no 'Library' or reading room as such. The inventory lists 'Books' separately at the end of the document, so their location in the house is uncertain though it might be inferred from the list that they were all together. The three line breaks may suggest units of shelving, though the storage of books need not dictate where they were read. Both men and women are presumed to have read in their personal closet and Betty had Edward Wettenhall's *Enter into thy closet, or, A method and order for private devotion*.[58] The importance of the closet as a mental space meant that it could be idealised as the monastery in miniature. Astell, conversely, advocated a 'protestant monastery' where women's worship could be formally recognised and encouraged outside the secrecy of closets.[59] The devotional aspect of Betty's book collection suggests she may have read in such a personalised space.

The most likely location for Betty to read in was 'Mrs Bowes Room' and its adjacent Dressing Room, on the first floor. The 'Yellow bed', referring to the painted frame which held the 'Feather Bed', was matched by '2 Yellow Window Curtains'. The '8 mahogony chairs with work'd Bottoms', sat in by favoured visitors, probably displayed Betty's own needlework.[60] The presence of a bed in the room conferred a degree of intimacy that entailed unspoken degrees of rank and access. The 'pound walnut tree Table' may have acted as a desk. The presence of '10 China Figures and Basons' also presumably held associations for Betty.

[55] Vickery, *Gentleman's Daughter*, p. 161.
[56] D/St/C2/3/100/17.
[57] D/St/E8/4-14.
[58] M. Girouard, *Life in the English Country House* (London, 1978), pp. 164-80.
[59] Perry, *Celebrated,* pp. 99-119.
[60] See S. Frye, 'Sewing Connections: Elizabeth Tudor, Mary Stuart, Elizabeth Talbot, and Seventeenth-Century Anonymous Needleworkers', in Frye and K. Robertson, *Maids, Mistresses, Cousins and Queens: Women's Alliances in Early Modern England* (Oxford, 1999), pp. 165-82.

Their likely presence alongside books is suggested by Joseph Addison's description of *A Lady's Library* of 1711.[61]

'Mr Addison's Works' heads the list of Betty's books, and Addison's status as the 'the model of the middle style' would seem almost emblematic of this library. His *Lady's Library* essay underscores the ways in which material and print co-existed in élite female culture, and the satire turns on books as artefacts being treated by women as ornaments. Sir Roger de Coverley found that 'The very sound of a lady's library gave me a great curiosity to see it'. Sir Roger was impressed by the 'very beautiful order' in which Leonora's great many books were ranged:

> At the end of the folios (which were finely bound and gilt) were great jars of china placed one above another in a very noble piece of architecture. The quartos were separated from the octavos by a pile of smaller vessels, which rose in a delightful pyramid. The octavos were bounded by tea dishes of all shapes, colours, and sizes... That part of the library which was designed for the reception of plays and pamphlets, and other loose papers, was enclosed in a kind of square, consisting of one of the prettiest grotesque works that ever I saw, and made up of scaramouches, lions, monkeys, mandarines, trees, shells, and a thousand other odd figures in china ware.[62]

While Betty had no room set aside as a 'library' her books were presumably stored by size and probably placed in juxtaposition with china ornaments. In the 'Little Dressing Room' off 'Mrs Bowes' Room', there were '6 Walnut Tree Chairs; Window Curtains the same', 'fire tools', 'a carpet' and '11 little China things upon the Chimney piece'. In the 'Best Parlour' on the ground floor, an alternative location for Betty to have displayed her books, was a marble table, '2 glass Lampes and Bracketts; 2 China Branches and bracketts; 3 China Jarrs, and a Dish' as well as '8 Yellow Damaske Bottome Chairs', 'Mahogany settees' and 'a Mahogony Card Table'.

Leonora, like Betty, was a woman living without men; widowed with no children, Sir Roger managed her estate 'an hundred miles distant from London', and she was determined not to venture on a second unfortunate marriage. As a result 'Leonora has turned all the passions of her sex into a love of books and retirement. She converses chiefly with men [...] but it is only in their writings'. Leonora's sensibilities in reading carry over into her material culture: 'As her reading has lain very much among romances, it has given her a very particular turn of thinking, and discovers itself in her house, her gardens and her furniture'. The narrator continues, 'What improvements would a woman have made, who is so susceptible of impressions from what she reads, had she been guided to such books as have a tendency to enlighten the understanding and rectify the passions, as well as to those which are of little more use than to divert the imagination?'[63]

---

[61] *The Spectator*, no. 37 (12 April 1711) in J. G. Fraser (ed.), *Essays of Joseph Addison*, vol. I (London, 1915), pp. 217-22.

[62] Ibid.

[63] *Spectator*, no. 37, pp. 217-22.

The Spectator is probably accorded too much influence as the first 'lifestyle magazine', but fifty years later Betty Bowes would seem to bear a significant resemblance to Addison's admonishment, in her furnishings and books, if not in her mind. The cursory catalogue of books in *A Lady's Library* bears some relation to the Bowes inventory. Betty had commentaries on Locke; Leonora had 'Locke of human Understanding; with a paper of patches in it'. Philosophical religion is alluded to in 'Father Malbranche's Search after Truth, translated into English'; while devotion is sniffed at, in 'A Prayer-book; with a bottle of Hungary water by the side of it.' Those archetypal feminine texts, Culpepper's *Midwifery* and *The Ladies Calling* are present among both Leonora's and Betty's books; although part of the satire here may relate to the reality that men read them as well.[64] The widowed Leonora had *The fifteen Comforts of Matrimony* but Betty perhaps unsurprisingly did not. Sir Roger also noted '*Clelia*: which opened of itself in the place that describes two lovers in a bower', and found 'A Dictionary for the explanation of hard words' and 'All the Classic Authors in wood; A set of Elzevirs, by the same hand.' Addison's book list is instructive in exploding pretension, but fails to dissuade the view that Betty was sincere in her reading. The similarities between a satire of 1711 and a library of 1759 suggests considerable continuity in the arrangement of élite women's material and print culture.

A more real comparison is with Lady Mary Wortley Montagu's book lists. When Lady Mary left for Italy in 1739 she drew up a list of over 500 entries; novels, plays, classics, and history, in French, Latin, Italian and English. French literature outnumbered English and there were several local histories describing the north of England. Betty had Abel's *Compleat French Master* but no books in French. Among her histories, were *The History of ye Church and State of Scotland* and a *Compleat History of Europe* but the collection contains no regional history. By her death in 1762, Lady Mary's library contained some seven hundred titles amounting to fifteen hundred volumes.[65] This was a vast number of books, but the real contrast is in the far more literary character of the collection in comparison to the Bowes list.

Conclusion

Betty's unmarried status may be thought to place her in a small subset of society, the 'women without men' neglected by historians before Hufton.[66] The increase in the number of unmarried women during the eighteenth century has been partly attributed by Brown to a 'rational domesticity', centrally created through reading, which put women off men; 'one of the chief characteristics of Enlightenment domesticity was a willingness to delay marriage or remarriage or even to refuse marriage altogether.'[67] This might seem to fit Betty, unmarried and with lots of

[64] See T. Hitchcock, *English Sexualities 1700-1800* (Basingstoke, 1997), p. 50.
[65] Munby (ed.), *Sale Catalogues*, pp. 51-79; Grundy, *Lady Mary*.
[66] O. Hufton, 'Women Without Men: Widows and Spinsters in Britain and France in the Eighteenth Century', *Journal of Family History*, 9, 4 (1984), pp. 355-76.
[67] Brown, 'Domesticity', p. 410.

books, and it certainly accords with Addison's satire. Yet the overt message of the texts in the list, with the exception of Astell, was that they frequently endorsed marriage as a prerequisite of a virtuous life. Moreover, Betty appears to have lived firmly in the context of her wealthy and influential family. Her books, houses, furnishings and unmarried status were all to some degree the product of family encouragement and constraints, that must have cut across any individualised, rational sense of self, which Ariès and Chartier would have us believe was promoted by eighteenth-century reading habits.[68]

Chartier has emphasised that 'if it is to exist the history of reading must be radically distinguished from a history of what is read'.[69] Yet we know enough about Betty to place her within what Stanley Fish termed an 'interpretative community', where people make sense of texts in ways characteristic of a particular group.[70] As Tadmor has demonstrated, there was a sociability of reading among élite women, and our impression of private individual reading has been exaggerated by excessive attention to contemporary critics of idle women.[71] Betty's library does not fit the old stereotype of 'idle' eighteenth-century women avidly consuming 'middle-class' novels. Instead, it is predominated by religious and philosophical texts; more in keeping with an older tradition of individual devotion and contemplation. Betty also presumably read and discussed her reading with other women in Durham. The context of her life suggests that her material and print consumption was framed by family concerns and female sociability that were inextricably linked to the more individualised meanings of her material and print culture.

North-East England provided the locational context to Betty's life; predominantly resident in Durham and at Gibside, with occasional visits to York and Scarborough, Betty only participated to a minimal degree in the national social scene, at London and Bath. Contemporaries primarily associated North-East England with coal, and the Bowes were celebrated beneficiaries of the trade. Their business relied upon industrial workers, and Gibside's elaborate landscape park, created during Betty's lifetime, was overlooked by adjacent mining settlements whose 'sooty faces' were able to see into its 'Elysian fields'.[72] Durham was an equally distinctive place, dominated by its ecclesiastical associations, but as a gentry centre possessing many of the characteristics typical of county towns, with female sociability paramount among them. While North-East England was distinctive, contemporary correspondence characterised it as provincial. Sociability and literary activity in the country was presented as peripheral to the cultural epicentre of London. Yet, our 'clumsey country girl' was able to participate in

---

[68] P. Ariès and R. Chartier, *A History of Private Life Volume III: Passions of the Renaissance* (Cambridge, Mass., 1989), pp. 1-19.

[69] R. Chartier, *The Order of Books* (Cambridge, 1994), pp. 5 and 23-7.

[70] S. Fish, *Is there a Text in this Class? The Authority of Interpretative Communities* (Cambridge, Mass., 1980).

[71] N. Tadmor, '"In the Even My Wife Read to Me": Women, Reading and Household Life in the Eighteenth Century', in Raven *et al* (eds), *Practice and Representation*, pp. 162-74.

[72] See D. Levine and K. Wrightson, *The Making of an Industrial Society: Whickham 1560-1765* (Oxford, 1991), pp. 274-5.

forms of consumption that are more easily characterised as national rather than regional. As so often, the study of material culture demonstrates that the seemingly straightforward reflection of cultural activity in documentary accounts does not tell the whole story.

This individual case study into the consumption of print and its material context, points to a number of conclusions. Betty's pretty china figures, mahogany furniture and books, demonstrate that the processes by which female élite culture was created and consumed in eighteenth-century North-East England were common to eighteenth-century England as a whole. Family influence and the seventeenth-century character of the book collection also indicate considerable continuities in the factors framing the consumption of material and print culture up to *c.*1760. Family appears to have been more significant for Betty than regionality; the absence of regional histories among her books suggests a lack of engagement with the north of England as a geographical frame of identity. The regional context was significant in other ways: Betty's likely associations with Mary Astell, Mary Wortley Montagu, Elizabeth Montagu and Elizabeth Carter, in person and in print, reveal that female literary culture of national standing was created and consumed in North-East England between 1660 and 1760.

Appendix: Elizabeth Bowes' Book List[73]

'Books' in the 'Inventory of Plate, Household Goods etc., in the House of the late Mrs Elizabeth Bowes in Elvet Durham taken 26th and 27th November 1759'.

Mr Addison's works, 3 volumes,[i] Jos. Taylor d.d.[ii]
The Iliad of Homer, 4 vols Genuine Ecclesiastical History[iii]
The Works of Shakespeare in volumes[iv]
The Book of Psalms,[v] The Works of Mrs Catherine Cockburn, 2 vols[vi]
A paraphrase & Comment of ye Epistles and Gospels[vii]
A poem occasioned by ye much lamen'd Death of Mrs Hester Buckw'th[viii]
Primitive Christianity in 3 parts[ix]
A Book of Sermons,[x] Cause of the decay of Christian Piety[xi]
History of the Rebellion[xii]
The Ladys Library II Vols[xiii]
Compleat History of Europe II Vols[xiv]
The Ladys Calling II Vols[xv]
The Cooks and Confectioners Dictionary[xvi]
Plays written by the late Mary Baker[xvii]
Pious Breathings,[xviii] Letters from ye Dead to ye Living[xix]
John Earl of Rochester,[xx] A Serious Proposal to the Ladys,[xxi]
A Discourse Concerning the Sacrament[xxii]

[73] D/St/E8/4-14. Notes cite probable authors with dates of known editions; identified from *Dictionary of National Biography*; M. Drabble, *Oxford Companion to English Literature* (Oxford, 1993); *WorldCat* (Computerised catalogue of historic published material) and *Eighteenth-Century Short Title Catalogue*.

A help to devotion,[xxiii] The Case of Impotency[xxiv]
The Case of Conscience[xxv]
An Essay in Defence of the Female Sexe,[xxvi] Youngs works[xxvii]
Compleat French Master[xxviii]
Memoirs of Manners,[xxix] On the most memorable events of the old and new testamt [xxx]
Bakers Chronical[xxxi]
Burkett on the new Testament[xxxii]
The Committee of Comedye[xxxiii]
A large Bible[xxxiv]
The works of Mr Pope 1 Volm[xxxv]
The Truth of Christian Religion[xxxvi]
The Protestant Evidence[xxxvii]
1 large Common Prayer Book[xxxviii]
Poems on Several Occasions[xxxix]
7 Massi[v]e Books,[xl] Lencias morals 4 vols[xli]
Help to worthy Communicantcy[xlii]
The School for Husbands[xliii]
The Essays of Councils Civile Morals[xliv]
A Vindication of King Charles[xlv]
The history of ye Church and State of Scotland[xlvi]
History of the Life and Death of the holy Jesus[xlvii]
A book of old sets of Parliament[xlviii]
An old written Book[xlix]
Practical discourse concerning Future Judgement[l]
The Ladys New Year Gift[li]
Comment upon the Epistles and Gospels[lii]
Method for private devotion[liii]
Works of Edmd Young LLD[liv]
The Whole Duty of Man[lv]
Moral Reflections[lvi]
A display of Tyranny[lvii]
The Chritian defence agst the fear of Death[lviii]
Discourses upon several Divine subjects[lix]
Private thoughts upon Religion[lx]
The Old Religion demonstrated[lxi]
The Poor of the Tabernacle[lxii]
The Government of the Tongue[lxiii]
Necessity & advantage of Publick Prayers[lxiv]
The Protestant monastery[lxv]
John Earl of Rochester,[lxvi] The Life and Death of Thomas Wolsey[lxvii]
The spiritual worship exalted[lxviii]
Private Psalter,[lxix] Psalms and Hymns[lxx]
Shakespeares works[lxxi]
The Travels of Cirus[lxxii]

The Practical Believer[lxxiii]
A Brief history of the Times[lxxiv]
An English dictionary[lxxv]
Great Importance of prinicipal Duties[lxxvi]
Against natural & reveal'd Religion[lxxvii]
Thos Browns Works[lxxviii]
The Sufferrings of John Coustos[lxxix]
Monsieur Scarren,[lxxx] Christian Blessedness[lxxxi]
The common lights of Subjects[lxxxii]
Plurality of worlds,[lxxxiii] A Comedy[lxxxiv]
3 written books[lxxxv]
The works of Epictetus[lxxxvi]
A Bible[lxxxvii]
History of ye Old & New Testament & an Explanation with Cutts[lxxxviii]

Notes to Appendix

---

[i] *The Spectator.*
[ii] John Taylor? (b.1694-d.1761) dissenting divine.
[iii] *A New History of Ecclesiastical Writers*, Louis E. Du Pin (edns. 1692-1724).
[iv] Several editions.
[v] Generic title.
[vi] Catherine Cockburn (b.1679-d.1749).
[vii] George Stanhope (edns. 1705-1751).
[viii] Charles Gildon (b.1665-d.1724), (1708).
[ix] William Cave (edns. 1673-1728).
[x] Generic title.
[xi] Richard Allestree (b.1619-d.1681), (1695).
[xii] Edward Clarendon, *The History of the Rebellion and Civil War* (1702-4).
[xiii] Attributed to Mary Wray, compiled writings of Jeremy Taylor, William Fleetwood etc. (edns. 1714-1739).
[xiv] D. Jones (b.1676-d.1720), civil and military history, 1600-1714 (1701-2 edn).
[xv] Richard Allestree (1673, reprints up to 1720).
[xvi] John Nott (1723 and later edns).
[xvii] Mary Baker; unidentified, manuscript?
[xviii] Saint Augustine (edns. 1701-1750).
[xix] Thomas Brown (edns. 1701-1750 and on).
[xx] John Wilmot (b.1647-d.1680); Gilbert Burnet's death-bed account, *Some Passages in the Life and Death of John Wilmot Earl of Rochester* (1680) or responses to it.
[xxi] Mary Astell (1694-97 and later edns).
[xxii] Edward Pelling (1685) explains the 'mystery' of the Catholic faith, viz. the Sacrament.
[xxiii] Prayers 'collected by a gentlewoman' (1710) or Samuel Bold's *An Help to Devotion* (1736).

[xxiv] George Abbot (3rd edn., 1719); élite infidelity trials.
[xxv] Sir Samuel Morland (b.1625-d.1695), (1695).
[xxvi] Mary Astell (1696 and later edns.)
[xxvii] Edward Young (b.1683-d.1765), cf. n. liv.
[xxviii] Abel Boyer (1694 and later edns.)
[xxix] Mrs Mary de la Rivière Manley (b.1663-d.1724), *Secret Memoirs and Manners* (edns. 1709-1736)
[xxx] Jacques Sauvin (b.1677-d.1730) 1723.
[xxxi] Sir Richard Baker (b.1568-d.1645). Succession of kings of England abridged and continued by Thomas Blount (1684).
[xxxii] Gilbert (b.1643-d.1715) or Thomas (b.?1635-d.1715) Burnet, both religious authors.
[xxxiii] Robert Howard (1665 and later edns.)
[xxxiv] Family bible.
[xxxv] Alexander Pope (b.1688-d.1744).
[xxxvi] Hugo Grotius, many seventeenth- and eighteenth-century edns.
[xxxvii] Probably one of many books *c.*1680 concerning The Popish Plot of 1678.
[xxxviii] *The Book of Common Prayer,* Thomas Cranmer (b.1489-d.1556), text finalised 1662.
[xxxix] Mary Barber (b.*c.*1690-d.1757) 1734-6; or Elizabeth Singer Rowe (edns. 1700-1799); John Tree's 'critical account of' English poetry (2nd edn., 1757); William Hutchinson, Durham antiquary (Ms., 1757).
[xl] Possibly manuscript collections.
[xli] Lencias unidentified, presumably Plutarch's *Moralia* trans. by Philip Holland (1603); 1684 or 1694 edn. (5 vols).
[xlii] John Kettleworth (b.1653-d.1695), (1683 and later edns. to 1737).
[xliii] Molière (b.1622-d.1673), *L'Ecole des Maris* (1661; London, transl. 1755).
[xliv] Francis Bacon (b.1561-d.1626), (1632 and later edns.).
[xlv] Thomas Wagstaffe (1693, 3rd edn. 1711).
[xlvi] Andrew Stevenson (1743) '...from accession of Charles I to restoration of Charles II', or John Spottiswood (d. 1639), A.D. 203 to end James VI (4th edn. 1677).
[xlvii] Jeremy Taylor (1649, 10th edn. 1742).
[xlviii] Parliamentary history.
[xlix] Manuscript collection.
[l] Sherlock Williams (1693, 12th edn. 1760).
[li] George Savile, marquess of Halifax (b.1633-d.1695), (1688, much reprinted).
[lii] George Stanhope (1705) duplicate copy or different edition of n. vii.
[liii] Edward Wettenhall (b.1636-d.1713) 'Enter into thy Closet' (3rd edn., 1670).
[liv] Edward Young (b.1683-d.1765).
[lv] Richard Allestree, attrib. (1658-1667; part 3 of *The Ladies Calling*, 1682).
[lvi] Pasquier Quesnal *Moral Reflections upon the Gospel of St. Matthew: To Make the Reading of it more profitable* (1706); William Darrell, *Moral Reflections on the Epistles and Gospels of Every Sunday* (1711); Viscount

Henry Bolingbrooke *Reflections Concerning Private Moral-Principles* (1752); also a regular title for funeral sermons.

[lvii] Titus Oates (1689).

[lviii] Charles Drelincourt (b.1595-d.1669), (1675 and later edns. by Daniel Defoe to 1747).

[lix] Gregory Thomas (1696) or John Norris, *Practical Discourses upon Several Divine Subjects* (edns. 1691-1728).

[lx] William Beveridge (b.1637-d.1708), (edns. 1709-1748).

[lxi] John Goodman (edns. 1684-1698).

[lxii] Published sermon; e.g. George Conway, *The blessedness of giving above that of receiving: a sermon preach'd at the tabernacle at Blandford* (1732).

[lxiii] Richard Allestree attrib. (edns. 1667-1721).

[lxiv] William Beveridge (b.1637-d.1708), (5th edn., 1714).

[lxv] Daniel Defoe (b.1669?-d.1731), (1726); or Sir George Wheler (b.1650-d.1723), (1698).

[lxvi] See n. xx.

[lxvii] George Cavendish (b.1500-d.1561), (1641); Wolsey (b.1475?-d.1530), Bishop of Durham 1524-1529.

[lxviii] George Myers (b.1653-d.1714) Quaker, (1721).

[lxix] John Humfrey (b.1621-d.1719), (1683).

[lxx] Generic title, perhaps Tom Sternold or John Wesley.

[lxxi] Second Shakespeare works, in one volume.

[lxxii] Chevalier Ramsay (b.1686-d.1743), (1727 and later edns. to 1753).

[lxxiii] John Kettleworth (b.1653-d.1695), (edns. 1688-1713).

[lxxiv] Sir Roger L'Estrange (b.1616-d.1704), (1687-88).

[lxxv] Bailey (1721); less likely Samuel Johnson (1755).

[lxxvi] George Bull (1714).

[lxxvii] Robert Jenkin (1702); less likely John Leland (1755) on Hume.

[lxxviii] Thomas Brown (b.1663-d.1704), Tory satirist and pamphleteer; *Works* (1707).

[lxxix] John Coustos, freemason released from Roman Catholic Inquisition at Lisbon by intervention of George II; Louis Pierre Boitard, William Strahan and Eberard Digby Pepys (1746).

[lxxx] Paul Scarren (b.1610-d.1660) French poet, dramatist and writer of prose fiction.

[lxxxi] John Norris (b.1657-d.1711), (1690, 1716).

[lxxxii] Benjamin Hoadly (b.1676-d.1761), (1719) debate over Corporation and Test Acts.

[lxxxiii] M. de Fontenelle (Bernard de Burier) (b.1657-d.1757), (1688 & 18th c. edns.).

[lxxxiv] Unidentifiable play.

[lxxxv] Manuscript collections.

[lxxxvi] Elizabeth Carter (b.1717-d.1806), celebrated 'blue-stocking' translation (1758).

[lxxxvii] Second bible.

[lxxxviii] Biblical introduction, perhaps Benrand Lamy (b.1640-d.1715) *Apparatus Biblicus* (1723).

1 Bowes House and St. Mary the Less Church, South Bailey, from the south

2 House on Old Elvet, Durham, occupied by Betty Bowes from c.1737-59, from the street

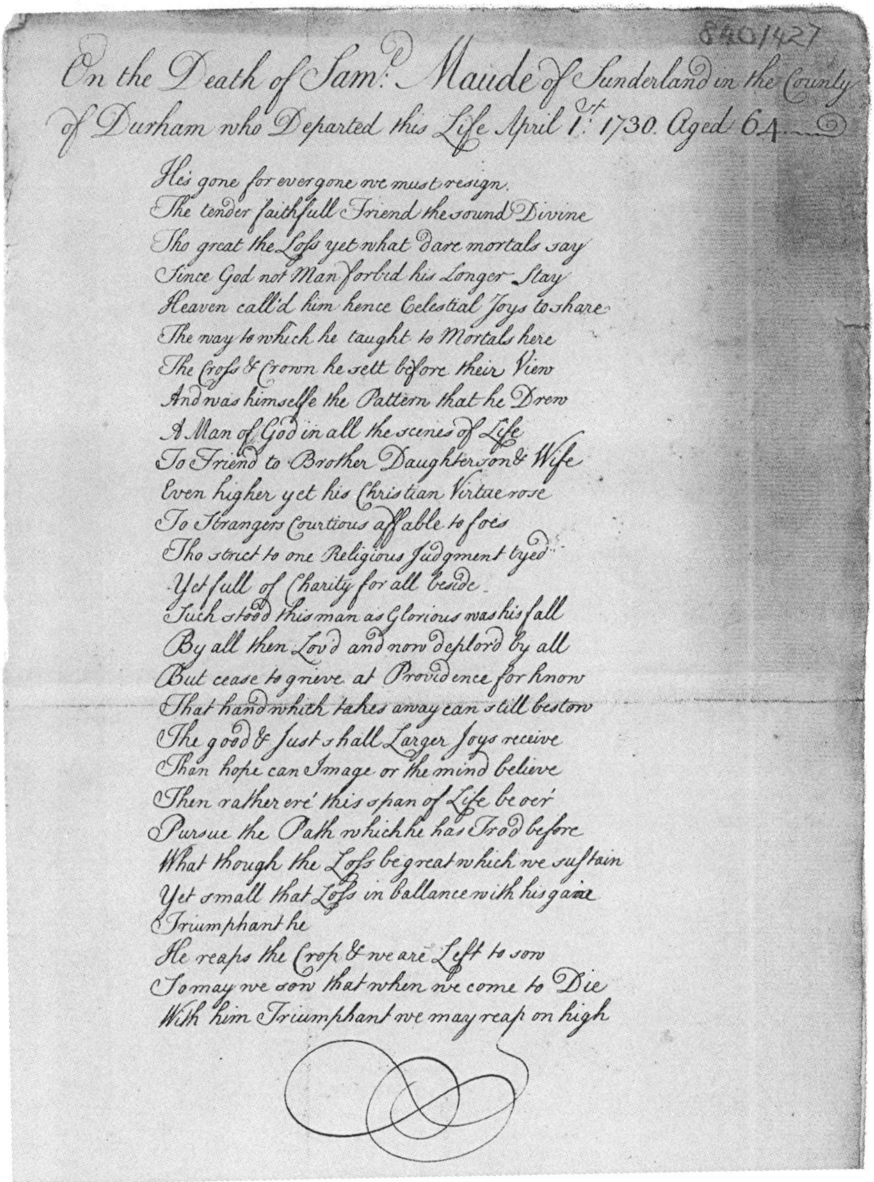

840/427

On the Death of Sam.ˡ Maude of Sunderland in the County of Durham who Departed this Life April 1.ˢᵗ 1730. Aged 64

He's gone for ever gone we must resign,
The tender faithfull Friend the sound Divine
Tho great the Loss yet what dare mortals say
Since God not Man forbid his Longer Stay
Heaven call'd him hence Celestial Joys to share
The way to which he taught to Mortals here
The Cross & Crown he sett before their View
And was himselfe the Pattern that he Drew
A Man of God in all the scenes of Life
To Friend to Brother Daughter son & Wife
Even higher yet his Christian Virtue rose
To Strangers Courtious affable to foes
Tho strict to one Religious Judgment tyed
Yet full of Charity for all beside
Such stood this man as Glorious was his fall
By all then Lov'd and now deplor'd by all
But cease to grieve at Providence for know
That hand which takes away can still bestow
The good & Just shall Larger Joys receive
Than hope can Image or the mind believe
Then rather ere' this span of Life be oer'
Pursue the Path which he has Trod before
What though the Loss be great which we sustain
Yet small that Loss in ballance with his gain
Triumphant he
He reaps the Crop & we are Left to sow
So may we sow that when we come to Die
With him Triumphant we may reap on high

3 Poem, 'On the Death of Samuel Maude of Sunderland' (1730)

4 'The Newcastle Assembly Rooms', from an engraving by Ralph Beilby

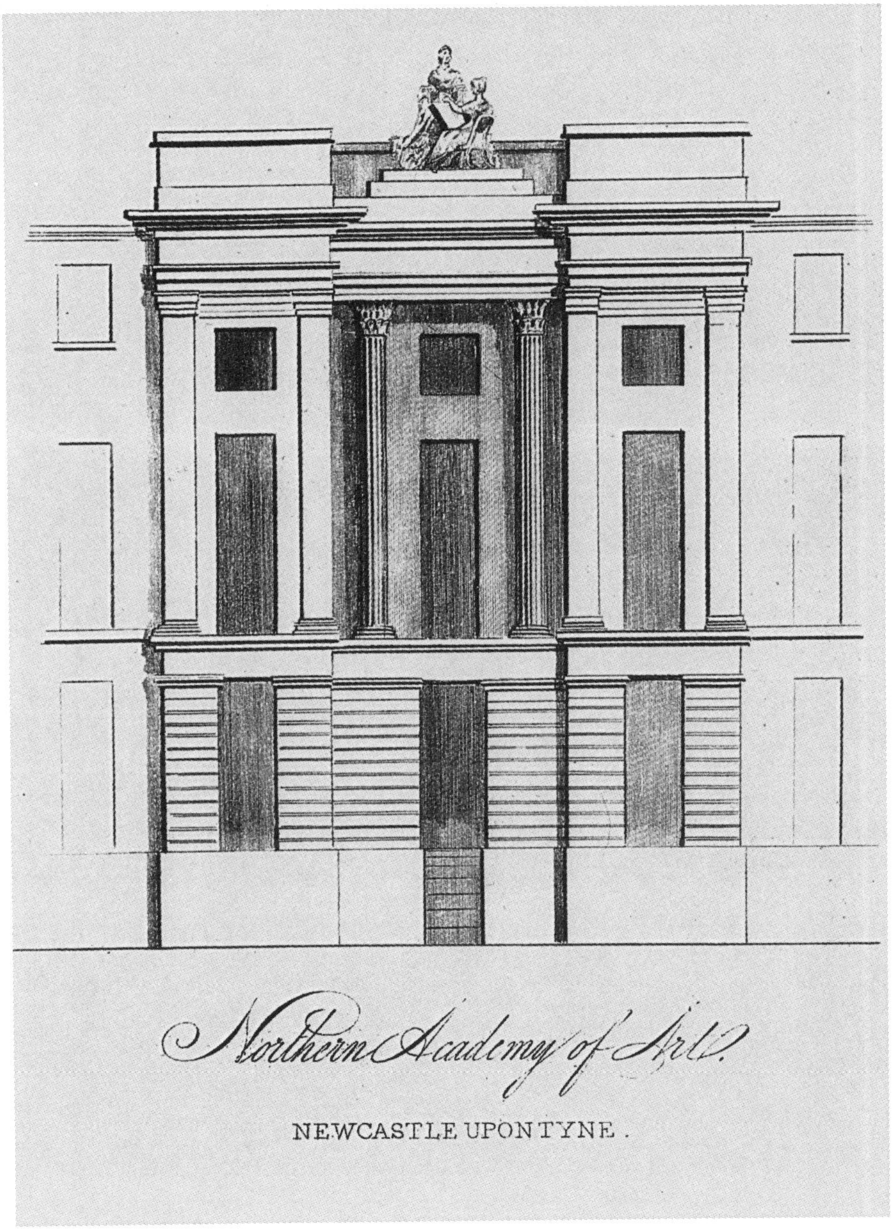

5 The Northern Academy of Art, Newcastle upon Tyne

6 James Ramsay, 'The Lost Child', exhibited, 1823

7 Statue of James Losh, Literary and Philosophical Society of Newcastle upon Tyne

Chapter 7

An Alternative Community in North-East England: Quakers, Morals and Popular Culture in the Long Eighteenth Century

RICHARD C. ALLEN

On Sunday, 30 January 1763, John Wesley addressed the Society for the Reformation of Manners in Seven-Dials, London, and quoting Psalm 94:16 asked 'Who will rise up with me against the wicked?'[1] Clearly, he was not alone in thinking that eighteenth-century British society was depraved and in need of reform. Abhorrence of ungodly behaviour in places of public diversion, such as inns or cockfighting arenas, led many to challenge some established and cherished social activities.[2] As elsewhere, in 1700 a society was established in Sandgate, Newcastle, for the reformation of manners, comprising twenty keelmen, who agreed to 'exert themselves in preventing tippling upon the Lord's day, and keeping Sandgate free of inmates'.[3] At the forefront of opposition to unreformed behaviour stood The Religious Society of Friends (Quakers). As early as 1701, Friends in Wales decided to translate and circulate John Kelsall's, *Testimony against Gaming, Musick, Dancing, Singing, Swearing and People calling upon God to Damn them. As also against drinking to excess, Whoring, Lying and Cheating...* (1682), to strengthen their resolve against such diversions.[4] This

[1] John Wesley, *A Sermon preached before the Society for Reformation of Manners: On Sunday January 30, 1763, at the chapel in West-Street, Seven Dials,* (London, 1763), and extracted from *The Works of... John Wesley* (14 vols., London, 1872), Sermon 52 (1872 edn). For further details, see R. B. Shoemaker, 'Reforming the City: the Reformation of Manners Campaign in London, 1690-1738', in L. Davison, T. Hitchcock, T. Kearn and R. B. Shoemaker (eds), *Stilling the Grumbling Hive: the Response to Social and Economic Problems in England, 1689-1750* (Stroud, 1992).

[2] Examples of social diversions in the early modern period are given in P. Burke, *Popular Culture in Early Modern Europe* (rev. edn, Cambridge, 1994); J. Barry and C. Brooks (eds.), *The Middling Sort. Culture, Society and Politics in England, 1550-1800* (Basingstoke, 1994); J. Brewer, *The Pleasures of the Imagination: English Culture in the Eighteenth Century* (London, 1997).

[3] John Sykes, *Local Records or Historical Records of Northumberland and Durham, Newcastle-upon-Tyne, and Berwick-upon-Tweed* (2 vols., Stockton-on- Tees: facsimile of the 1866 edition, 1973), I, p. 127.

[4] R. C. Allen, 'The Society of Friends in Wales 1653-1839: The Case of Monmouthshire', unpublished University of Wales Ph.D. dissertation (1999), ch. 6.

determination to counter undesirable developments in eighteenth-century life was shared by members in other areas of Britain and Ireland.

The regional particularity of North-East England has long been recognised by academics.[5] Its precocious modernity, typified by proto-industrialisation and a remarkably buoyant consumer culture is discussed elsewhere in this volume. This study of the North-East Quaker community and their response to the rise of consumerism offers a new perspective upon the existence and workings of a counter culture. Barry Reay has observed that as the 'middling sorts' accepted the principles of the 'reformation of manners', many nonconformists were admonished or expelled for indulging in popular and traditional pastimes. For Quakers and Methodists in particular 'culture was a serious culture, with no time for the frivolity and self-indulgence of drama, painting, sculpture, music and dance, or even less serious forms of popular leisure'.[6] Yet, as Reay has argued, such a reformation was never fully realised as these religious communities constantly had to exhort their congregations to be vigilant, especially in their relations with the 'world's people'.[7] The divergence between popular culture and reformed behaviour, and the problems associated with calls for plainness and a simple, godly life led many people to challenge the tenets of their meetings. Consequently, this call to austerity, especially by the Quakers, led to an inexorable decline in their membership as many found themselves unable to conform.

Quakerism appeared in Britain in the mid-seventeenth century, and from the Restoration of Charles II in 1660 the Friends sought to regulate their standards of personal morality and avoid the harmful effects of popular pastimes, which they considered immoral, frivolous or ungodly. Quakers have had a strong presence in the North-East from 1654 to the present day, with meetings throughout Northumberland and Durham.[8] During the first four decades, they suffered for their religious beliefs, were regarded as 'killjoys', 'cuckolds', and 'king-killers', and they were continuously persecuted by the authorities.[9] On 20 December 1688, the

---

[5] D. J. Rowe, 'The North-East', in F. M. L. Thompson (ed.), *The Cambridge Social History of Britain 1750-1950* (3 vols, Cambridge, 1990), vol. I, ch. 6.

[6] B. Reay, *The Quakers in the English Revolution* (London, 1985), p. 118.

[7] Ibid., p. 120.

[8] For example, meetings at Newcastle, Gateshead, South Shields, Berwick, Hexham, Alnwick, and Allendale in Northumberland; and at Darlington, Durham, Sunderland, Bishop Auckland, Stockton, and Raby and Staindrop in County Durham. For details, see John W. Steel, *A Historical Sketch of the Society of Friends "in Scorn Called Quakers" in Newcastle and Gateshead, 1653-1898* (London, 1899); Henry J. Cadbury, 'Early Quakerism at Newcastle upon Tyne: William Cotesworth', *The Journal of the Friends Historical Society* (hereafter *J.F.H.S.*), 50, 3 (1963), 91-6; Roger Howell, 'Early Quakerism in Newcastle upon Tyne: Thomas Ledgard's Discourses Concerning the Quakers', *J.F.H.S.*, 50, 4 (1964), 211-16; Ruth Sansbury, *Beyond the Blew Stone. 300 years of Quakers in Newcastle* (Newcastle: Newcastle upon Tyne Preparative Meeting, 1998); Marjorie Trotter, 'Of Sailing Ships, and Sealing Wax, and Ancient Quaker Meetings. The Religious Society of Friends in Sunderland 1653-1705', unpublished University of Sunderland M. Phil. dissertation (1999); Elizabeth O'Donnell, 'Woman's Rights and Woman's Duties: Quaker Women in the Nineteenth Century, with Special Reference to Newcastle Monthly Meeting of Women Friends', unpublished University of Sunderland Ph.D. dissertation (1999).

[9] Joseph Besse, *A Collection of the Sufferings of the People Called Quakers, 1650-1689*, 2 vols. (London, 1753), I, p. 189.

meeting-house at Sunderland was attacked by 'masters and mariners... a rabble of boys and the baser sort of people'. A contemporary observer commented that they 'broke open the house... pulled up and burnt the floors, doors, and windows, seats and roof of the house, totally demolishing it... [and] broke the windows of several houses of the people called quakers, as they passed the streets.'[10] Even though the Act of Toleration (1689) permitted Friends to worship freely, they remained the target of petty acts of intolerance. All too frequently they were imprisoned or fined for their refusal to pay church tithes and their reluctance to support or supply replacements for the local militia. In 1709, the Newcastle Company of felt-makers, curriers and armourers, insisted that 'no Quaker should be taken apprentice on pain of forfeiting £100'.[11] Despite the fact that Friends occupied a prominent place in North-East society as merchants, craftsmen and bankers,[12] this embargo had been imposed from at least March 1700 when Friends complained that they were 'inconvenienced' by the opposition of Newcastle merchants towards taking Quaker children as apprentices.[13]

Ultimately, Friends set themselves apart by preaching and practising a moral code which ran counter to the eighteenth-century social mores. The intention here is to explore the divergence between popular culture and Quaker beliefs in the North-East of England in the long eighteenth century, and consider whether the disciplinary code was indeed justified. In doing so, consideration will be given to the imposition of discipline and order, the reformation of manners and tastes, and the retreat from popular culture and society.[14]

Methods of discipline and order

Friends were determined to make sure that no member of their community infringed their code of behaviour. In conjunction with other meetings in England and Wales, they ensured that all aspects of life from birth to death were regulated. By their strict code of conduct, they distinguished themselves as a 'Peculiar

---

10 Sykes, *Local Records*, p. 123.

11 M. A. Richardson, *The Local Historian's Table Book, of Remarkable Occurrences, Historical Facts, Traditions, Legendary and Descriptive Ballads, &c., Connected with the Counties of Newcastle-upon-Tyne, Northumberland and Durham*, 8 vols. (Newcastle, 1846); Tyne and Wear Archive Service (hereafter T.W.A.S.) Ms. 3744/4 (Mf. 167). Monthly Meeting Minute Book no. 4 (1707-1759), 9 November 1709, no pagination.

12 Sansbury, *Beyond the Blew Stone*, pp. 38-9, 60ff. The change from radicalism to respectability is discussed in N. Morgan, *Lancashire Quakers and the Establishment 1660-1730* (Halifax, 1993); David Scott, *Quakerism in York, 1650-1720* (York, 1991); Allen, 'The Society of Friends in Wales', chs. 5, 6 and 9; T. J. Nossiter, *Influence, Opinion and Political Idiom in Reformed England. Case studies from the North-East, 1832-74* (London, 1975), pp. 131-2.

13 Durham County Record Office (hereafter D.C.R.O.) SF/Du/QM/2/1. Rough Quarterly meeting minutes (1672-1727), p. 152. As late as June 1733, Newcastle Friends were complaining that the Newcastle Company of Merchants were 'making By Laws that no merchant or member of that company shall take to be apprentice any person called a Quaker'. T.W.A.S., Ms. 3744/4 (11 April 1733).

14 T.W.A.S., Ms. 840/10. 'A copy of the State of the monthly meeting in Durham County as Drawn up by the after mention'd Friends when on that memorable visit in 1761'.

People'.[15] The testimonies of Friends upholding the disciplined life and warning against 'worldly' hazards were copied or published for the benefit of members. For example, in 1767, Joseph Phipps, a Quaker of York, warned Friends against 'a proneness to gratification of self, and the sensual part; an eager inclination at times to forbidden pleasure, an aversion to piety and holy walking'. For

> such is their frailty, it is an easy thing for them to fall in with temptation; but hard, if not impossible, effectually to resist it... This demonstrates the corruption of their nature... The corruption in the heart corrupts the actions, manners and language. Hence all the irregularities in conduct, and the profane and untrue speeches, all the common complemental falsehoods, to gratify the pride and folly of vain minds.[16]

Adherence to a prescriptive mode of behaviour helped the Society to regulate itself, and enabled members to conduct their affairs appropriately.[17] Various procedures, including the appointment of overseers, were employed by the monthly meetings to ensure the good behaviour of Friends and to pronounce judgements on those who brought the Society into disrepute. For example, on 13 July 1707 Robert Westgarth, a dyer, and Thomas Hodgson, a mariner, were asked by the Newcastle Preparative Meeting to 'take upon themselves the oversight of truth's affairs' while Joshua Middleton, a merchant, and Jeremiah Hunter, a dyer, regulated the affairs of the North Shields meeting.[18] Their appointment as overseers reflected their ability to uphold Quaker values. They counselled erring members and gave them an opportunity to explain their behaviour.

The level of control was such that, periodically, Friends were warned to be diligent at meetings of worship and avoid drowsiness. The Benfieldside Meeting were reminded of the counsel George Fox gave in 1688 that Friends should avoid 'sleeping in meetings and sottishness and dullness for its an unsavoury thing to see one sit nodding in a meeting and so to lose the sense of the Lord'.[19] At the Women's Quarterly Meeting in July 1709 members were told to be 'circumspect' and 'keep from drowsiness and sleep' in order to be 'truly concern'd to keep in that spiritual exercise of mind'.[20] In January 1747, when Raby Friends reportedly fell into the 'unseemly practice of sleeping' the Quarterly meeting were obliged to

---

[15] Issued in manuscript form in 1738, this code of conduct was eventually incorporated into *Christian and Brotherly Advices and Extracts from the Minutes and Advices of the Yearly Meeting of Friends held in London,* and from 1782 more commonly referred to as *The Book of Extracts.* See D. J. Hall, 'The Discipline of the Society of Friends', unpublished University of Durham M.A. dissertation (1972), ch. 2.

[16] Joseph Phipps, *The Original and Present State of Man, Briefly Considered* (London, 1767), and extracted from *The Friends' Library*, x (Philadelphia, 1846), p. 380.

[17] Cf. other nonconformist congregations who demanded equally good behaviour and high moral standards. See Robert Colls, *The Pitmen of the Northern Coalfield: Work, Culture, and Protest, 1790-1850* (Manchester, 1987), ch. 11.

[18] Sansbury, *Beyond the Blew Stone*, 39. For details on overseers, see R.T. Vann, *The Social Development of English Quakerism, 1655-1755* (Cambridge, Mass., 1969), pp. 128-43.

[19] T.W.A.S., Ms. 3744/38 (Mf. 174). Benfieldside Preparative Meeting Book (1768-1789) no pagination; a copy of George Fox's address on 'sleeping in meetings c.1668'.

[20] D.C.R.O., SF/Du/QM/3/1. Women's Quarterly meeting book (1679-1751 no pagination), 28-5-1709.

consider ways that the 'shameful practice' could be stopped.[21] Yet, the problem was still exercising them in 1761 when the Durham Quarterly Meeting condemned the deficiencies of members and their 'highly unbecoming behaviour in a place of solemn worship'.[22]

Throughout the period, Friends were constantly reproved for neglecting meetings. In August 1783, Hannah Ogden of Sunderland reflected in her notebook that the Shotton meeting which was once 'a considerable body' had so severely declined that it was 'hardly kept up. Many of those who frequent it being not in unity... The people seeming in general little acquainted with the Life of True Religion.'[23] Of course, it may well be that non-attendance at meetings stemmed from other causes, such as fraternisation with non-members or infidelity. The refusal to condemn or at least to acknowledge their failings would lead to the expulsion of the 'unworthy' member. In such cases, a paper of disownment was presented and the Friend barred from membership unless he/she repented to the meeting's satisfaction.[24] For example, on 12 May 1723 Shields Friends recorded that Laurence Coulby had expressed his desire to 'be one of the Church of England or a Roman of the ancient Religion'. They testified against him on 10 June, but hoped that in time he would recant and apply to be readmitted into fellowship.[25] Disownment was not a measure that Friends took lightly; rather it was only invoked if the recalcitrant member failed to repent. According to Richard Vann, however, the purpose of this disciplinary procedure was not primarily to reform the erring member, but rather to protect the reputation of the Society from the unwelcome attention of the wider community.[26]

Friends imposed these regulations from the cradle to the grave. By rejecting many of the traditional customs associated with rites of passage they set themselves apart from the wider community. At the South Shields monthly meeting in January 1702, members declared that they hoped to keep their meetings free from the 'spirit of the world', for only by being vigilant would Friends 'come to see the secret vertue and life of truth... wch is the blessing of all our assemblies'.[27] It has been observed that the relationship between Friends and non-Quaker family members and neighbours was subject to particular constraints. Notably, Quaker midwives were employed rather than experienced practitioners to avoid any interference by the 'the world's people', and to circumvent any attempt

[21] D.C.R.O., SF/Du/QM/2/2 (no pagination). Rough Quarterly meeting book (1727-1747), 6 November 1746.

[22] T.W.A.S., Ms. 840/10.

[23] T.W.A.S., Ms. 840/2. Memorandum Book of Hannah Ogden (3 August 1783), no pagination.

[24] For the consequences of disownment, see T.A. Davies, *The Quakers in English Society*, 1655-1725 (Oxford, 2000), ch. 8; M. Mullett, 'From Sect to Denomination: Social Development in 18th century English Quakerism', *Journal of Religious History*, 13, 2 (1984), 178-9.

[25] T.W.A.S., Ms. 3744/145 (Mf.179). North Shields Preparative Meeting (1720-1845 no pagination), 12-3-1723; T.W.A.S., Ms. 3744/233 (Mf.188). Newcastle Monthly Meeting Testimonies and Certificates (1706-1787), fol.14.

[26] Vann, *Social Development*, 138-9.

[27] T.W.A.S., Ms. 3744/3 (Mf. 167). Monthly Meeting minute book no. 3 (1674-1707), 12 November 1701/2, no pagination.

to baptise newborn babies who were unlikely to survive.[28] Childbirth was not an occasion for excessive festivity or undue sentimentality. Thus in 1709, Durham women Friends called upon members to be careful during childbirth not to invite too many women to attend them and 'to avoid making unnecessary provision of meat and drink'.[29] The Society had no formal baptismal ceremony, and the recording of the birth of a child was conducted in the same way as a business contract.[30] Quaker mothers also refused to be 'churched' as this was regarded by Friends as a superstitious tradition that had no scriptural justification.[31]

The Society of Friends placed great value on a good education,[32] endeavouring to secure every advantage for their offspring, and to protect them from contaminating influences.[33] Parents were required to bring up their children in a temperate way, which would ultimately lead to their 'convincement' when they were old enough to receive the personal message of 'Truth'. Mothers assumed primary responsibility for the instillation of 'good' behaviour. A testimonial to Elizabeth Holmes of Newcastle in April 1730 recorded that her life had been conducted with 'much prudence and propriety, being a faithful and loving wife, a tender and affectionate mother, a good mistress, an example of moderation, humility, charity and Christian practice to all'.[34] Co-religionists were also called upon to be careful in the 'virtuous education of our children' by offering 'honest and lawfull imployments that idleness and the evils ariseing... may be avoided', as well as an appreciation of 'plainness and simplicity... in habit, language and deportment'.[35] Fathers were required to institute a daily programme, which included Quaker ideology, prayers, and discipline.[36] The Coates family papers illuminate the way this worked. George Coates, a yeoman and blacksmith of Woodland in Lynesack, was considered to be:

[28] See Davies, *Quakers*, pp. 37-9; C. Trevett, *Women and Quakerism in the Seventeenth Century* (York, 1991), p. 60.

[29] D.C.R.O., SF/Du/Qm/3/1 (28 May 1709).

[30] *Extracts*, pp. 223-4.

[31] For 'churching' in the early modern period, see W. Coster, 'Purity, Profanity and Puritanism: the Churching of Women 1500-1700', in W. Sheils and D. Woods (eds), *Studies in Church History*, 27 (1990), 377-88.

[32] For studies of Quaker education, see D. G. B. Hubbard, 'Early Quaker Education, 1650-1780', unpublished University of London M.A. dissertation (1940); L. J. Stroud, 'The History of Quaker Education in England, 1647-1903', unpublished University of Leeds M.Ed. dissertation (1944); R. S. Mortimer, 'Quaker Education', *J.F.H.S.*, 39 (1947), 66-70; R. Randles, '"Faithful Friends and Well Qualified": The Early Years of the Friends' School at Lancaster', in M. Mullett (ed.), *Early Lancaster Friends,* University of Lancaster occasional paper no. 5 (Lancaster, 1978), pp. 33-42; G. Mason, 'Quaker Women and Education 1642-1840', unpublished University of Lancaster M.A. dissertation (1987).

[33] From *c.*1691, the Society began to establish their own schools based on a practical curriculum. See Hubbard, 'Early Quaker Education', chs. 6-7; Stroud, 'The History of Quaker Education in England', ch. 8.

[34] T.W.A.S., Ms. 840/8. A Testimony concerning Elizabeth Holmes from the Newcastle monthly meeting, 24 April 1738.

[35] D.C.R.O., SF/Du/QM/3/1 (28 May 1709).

[36] *Extracts*, pp. 48, 219.

> an affectionate and tender father, and great was his care for us his children that we might be kept in the fear of the Lord, often repeating unto us the advice that Christ gave his followers, first to seek the Kingdom of God and the righteousness thereof... and indeed what he advised others unto he practised himself, and the Lord blessed (him) both inwardly and outwardly... I sincerely desire that we his children may put in practice the many good advices he gave unto us.[37]

The constituent monthly meetings were encouraged to support the instruction of fellow members and to increase their levels of literacy. In April 1702, Friends at South Shields expressed concern about the education of William Rogers' youngest daughter who had left home and was 'like to have her education not amongst Friends'. They were anxious to ensure that she avoided the vanities, as they saw it, of the world.[38] Further references in the minutes between July and October 1708 indicate that while Newcastle Friends had both schoolmasters and mistresses, members at Shields were in need of a Quaker teacher who could provide an education for 'the safety of their children'.[39] These statements demonstrate the extent to which Friends sought to distance themselves from the corruption of the local community.[40]

In spite of the desire to lead a life separate from the corrupting influences of the outside world, in the early 1730s John Glen successfully ran a 'Meeting School' at Durham for the benefit of both members' and non-members', children. It may be that this was a way of making his school financially viable. Naturally, Quaker education was dominated by the need to inculcate spiritual and moral values, to focus upon heavenly concerns, and not those which led to vanity and worldly advantage.[41] Friends' children were taught:

> habits of regularity, of decency, and respectful subordination to their superiors, of forbearance, affection, and kindness towards each other; and of religious reverence towards their maker.[42]

Nevertheless, apart from Quaker studies, scholars at Durham were taught English, Latin, and possibly Greek.[43] Another school was established in 1737 at Hawthorne, County Durham, by Robert Forster who purchased the land and endowed the school.[44] In 1768, Edward Walton of Sunderland bequeathed a much larger endowment to Durham, Newcastle, and Raby Friends. In his will, he left sufficient funds for the establishment of several schools each providing for twelve poor

---

[37] Library of the Society of Friends, London (hereafter L.S.F.) Ms. vol. S179. J. J. Green, 'History of the Family of Cotes, Coats or Coates' (1906), typescript.

[38] T.W.A.S., MS.3744/3 (13 February 1702).

[39] T.W.A.S., Ms. 3744/4 (12 May, 13 July and 11 August 1708).

[40] A Quarterly Meeting minute in June 1711 enquired whether care was taken in the 'instruction of youth, and see how they [the constituent meetings] are provided with friends yt are schoolmasters'. By 1718, a minute from the monthly meeting clearly shows that by this date provision had been made for the education of Friends' children at both the Newcastle and the Shields meetings. See D.C.R.O., SF/Du/QM/2/1 (26 April 1711); T.W.A.S., Ms. 3744/3 (8 July 1718).

[41] *Extracts*, pp. 15, 126, 178, 190, 225.

[42] J. C. Lettersom, *Memoirs of John Fothergill M.D.*, 4th edn. (London, 1786), p. 137.

[43] Sansbury, *Beyond the Blew Stone*, p. 111.

[44] D.C.R.O., SF/Du/QM/2/2 (2 November 1738).

children (members and non-members); the employment of a school master, and any residual funds to be used for buying books and placing boys and girls into apprenticeships. Thereafter schools were founded at Sunderland, Shotton, Shildon and Bishop Auckland.[45] The interest generated from the bequest also meant that in June 1791 Friends were able to increase their expenditure on education at these four centres. They nevertheless believed that the annual salary was too small to encourage a schoolmaster of quality and thereby sought to increase the number of children to a maximum of twenty to offset the salary increase. Friends believed that the additional money would be better spent educating more poor children as it would be 'serviceable to the community [to have] a greater number of its members... obtain a more comfortable livelihood'.[46] From the mid-eighteenth century, therefore, there was an opportunity for at least a small number of Friends' children to be educated locally. Others who had more affluent parents or received support from the local meeting were sent away to the Quaker boarding schools at Ackworth in Yorkshire,[47] Wigton in Cumbria,[48] or Sidcot in Somersetshire.[49] For example, in 1780 eight children from the Newcastle meeting attended Ackworth,[50] while on 11 February 1799, Newcastle Friends paid the admission fees of £6.6s for John Watson's children to attend Ackworth as he could not afford pay for their education himself.[51]

As the eighteenth century progressed, most Quaker children benefited from a standard basic education.[52] In their wills Friends made special provision for their offspring and the children of poorer members. For example, in 1741 Jeremiah Hunter, a hostman, bequeathed his property at Newcastle and South Shields to his granddaughter, Sarah Tyzacke, but stipulated that his executors were to endeavour to place his granddaughter 'where she may have the benefit of such education as

---

[45] Sansbury, *Beyond the Blew Stone*, pp. 98-9.

[46] T.W.A.S., Ms. 3744/2 (Mf.167), Newcastle Monthly Meeting book no. 2 (1791-1809), pp. 82-4.

[47] See E. Vipont Foulds, *Ackworth School, From its Foundation in 1779 to the Introduction of Co-education in 1946* (London, 1959); Hubbard, 'Early Quaker Education', ch. 10; Stroud, 'History of the Quakers in England', pp. 98-102.

[48] D.C.R.O., SF/Su/116/1/2. Report and accounts of Wigton School, 1822.

[49] V. Leimdorfer, *Quakers at Sidcot 1690-1990* (Sidcot, 1990). These institutions were usually supported by subscriptions from the various meetings in the North-East or from individual donations. For example, the North Shields preparative meeting provided a list of members in September 1781 who annually paid a subscription to Ackworth. They were John Walker of the 'Square' (£1.1s); Joseph King (5s.), John Walker from Shields (2s.6d), Robinson Wakefield (£1.1s.), Joseph Flounders (5s.), Jane Champion (£1.1s), George Brown (10s.6d), Henry Taylor (£5.5s), Edward Appleby (10s.6d), and Robert Chapman (10s.6d). See T.W.A.S., Ms. 3744/145, 30-9-1781.

[50] Sansbury, *Beyond the Blew Stone*, p. 113. In some cases, Friends also paid for the education of non-members at Ackworth School. On 12 May 1795, Friends at the Shields meeting agreed to pay for the education of John Wright's nephew. The boy's mother had previously been disowned by the Society for marrying a non-member, but the meeting decided that in this circumstance they would consider the child to be a member 'until he is of an age to judge for himself in matters of religion'. This action was repeated in April 1796 and again in September 1799 for the nephews of George Wright and George Wakefield. See T.W.A.S., Ms. 3744/2, pp. 121, 139, 197.

[51] T.W.A.S., Ms.3744/2, p. 191.

[52] For example, see George Richardson, *Journal of the gospel labours of George Richardson : a minister in the Society of Friends, with a biographical sketch of his life and character* (London, 1864), xivff.

will be agreeable to my mind'.[53] Not everyone was so fortunate as Daniel Oliver recognised. The lack of a good Quaker education had exposed him to 'much evil communication' and a familiarity with 'hurtful amusements and... unprofitable books'. A consciousness of his limited education led him to contribute to the Royal Jubilee School at Newcastle in 1828.[54]

The emphasis that Friends placed on reading the Bible and the many books and articles they produced,[55] coupled with the growth of literacy within the movement cannot be overstated. Since the Society placed such emphasis on education, it undoubtedly helped to increase the numbers of those able to read, if not to write. Certainly, marriage registers indicate that members were sufficiently well educated to be able to record their own names. However, this is not a precise indicator for measuring literacy. The couple intending to marry may not have signed their own names but rather another, possibly the clerk, may have entered them into the registers. In the eighteenth and nineteenth centuries, Friends at Newcastle and Sunderland had access to well-stocked libraries at their meeting-houses.[56] A general survey of the Society does indicate that literacy was not merely the preserve of the 'better-off', for members who were artisans and labourers could also read and/or write.

Prominent Quaker journalists, such as Issac Thompson and Robert Doubleday, were fully committed to the spread of literacy in the region. In his *Newcastle Journal*, Thompson advertised the sale of *The Family Library or Instructor in Useful Knowledge* along with a commentary that 'the human mind... is like marble... which shows none of its inherent beauty till the skill of the polisher fetches out the colours and makes the surface shine'.[57] Robert Doubleday became the chairman of the Royal Jubilee Schools and, along with Revd. William Turner, helped promote the work of the Newcastle Literary and Philosophical Society in the late eighteenth century.[58] In 1823, the Newcastle Literary and Philosophical Society Annual Report stated that his 'deep knowledge on all subjects connected with literature and science, enabled him to fill the Chair [of the Literary and Philosophical Society] to the credit of the Institution and the delight of its Members'.[59]

A protestant work ethic lay at the heart of the Quaker way of life and its absolute rejection of worldly self-indulgence. As they believed that work was an end in itself, which should satisfy individual creative needs and exploit God-given talents, they sought to provide appropriate education and training. Apprenticeships

---

53 Durham Palace Green Archives (Special Collections) (hereafter D.P.G.A.) DPRI/1/1741/H9/1. The will of Jeremiah Hunter of Newcastle (11 July 1741).

54 Sansbury, *Beyond the Blew Stone*, pp. 116-17.

55 L. Wright, *The Literary Life of the Early Friends, 1650-1725* (New York, 1932); Cf. M. Spufford, 'First Steps in Literacy: the Reading and Writing Experiences of the Humblest Seventeenth-Century Spiritual Autobiographers', *Social History*, 4 (1979), 407-35.

56 T.W.A.S., Mf. 211-212. For details of the Sunderland Quaker library, see D.C.R.O., SF/Su/2, Sunderland Preparative Meeting (1706-1737), (11 December 1710, 10 November 1724), no pagination.

57 *Newcastle Journal* (18 July 1752).

58 For biographical details of Robert Doubleday (1753-1823), see Richard Welford, *Men of Mark 'Twixt Tyne and Tweed,* 3 vols. (London, 1895), II, pp. 120-21.

59 *Newcastle Literary and Philosophical Society Annual Report* (Newcastle, 1823), p. 3.

for the young were regarded as the optimum means of equipping members for a life of hard work and financial stability. In South-East Wales, for instance, Richard Clarke of Monmouthshire left a £30 legacy in 1697 for the 'placing forth of six poor boys apprentice to some handy craft trades', while in 1709 George Harris, a Quaker doctor, bequeathed £10 to his nephew 'to put him to apprentice to learn the art or mystery of physick or chyrurgery'.[60] In the North-East a similar pattern emerges. Members offered apprenticeships in businesses established by Quaker entrepreneurs, such as the Huntley family of Sunderland, the Middletons of Newcastle, or to local Quaker tradesmen.[61] For example, in September 1761 George Raw of Durham was bound as an apprentice to John Clark, a ship and tallow chandler, and baker of Sunderland.[62] The advantages were self-evident. Towards the end of the century, Bernard Ogden of Sunderland was apprenticed to Abel Huntley, a druggist in the town, and later became a well-known chemist who developed a copperas and pyroligneous works in the Deptford area of Sunderland.[63] The more prosperous members of the Society also took young women Friends into service as maids.

Occasionally, however, monthly meetings had to remonstrate with members about failing to secure positions for their children. In June 1751, James and Sarah Mason refused to obtain an apprenticeship for their son, and subsequently had their poor relief payments curtailed.[64] Three years later the erring couple offered a paper to the meeting regretting their earlier behaviour stating that:

> notwithstanding the labours that was bestowed on us, it was a sealed book unto us, but so soon as it appear'd clear to our understanding there was no more spirit of opposition left in us, being perswaded that unity and concord is the means by which the body is maintained... therefore [we] can freely condemn our proceedings and desires.[65]

Friends who were apprenticed to other members of the Society were strictly supervised in order to ensure that they did not associate too freely with the wider community. Sansbury has noted that no young men apprenticed in Newcastle were allowed to indulge in the popular pastimes of the period. They were denied the opportunity to fence, attend musical festivals, dances, playhouses, or have anything to do with cock-fighting.[66] In his indenture of apprenticeship in 1756, George Raw agreed to avoid taverns, inn and alehouses and 'any unlawful games'.[67] There is

---

[60] Public Record Office, PROB 11/446; National Library of Wales, LL/1707/33.

[61] See C. Brooks, 'Apprenticeship, Social Mobility and the Middling Sort, 1550-1800', in Barry and Brooks, *Middling Sort of People*, ch. 3, particularly 73ff.

[62] T.W.A.S., Ms. 3744/4, 13-9-1756. The indenture was provided the following month, but George's father would not agree to the placement of his younger son at the workhouse in London. Ibid. (11 October 1756; 8 November 1756).

[63] For further details of Ogden, see O'Donnell, 'Woman's Rights', pp. 52, 55.

[64] T.W.A.S., Ms. 3744/1 (Mf.215), Durham Monthly Meeting book (1675-1756), p. 151.

[65] Ibid., p. 166.

[66] Sansbury, *Beyond the Blew Stone*, p. 44. See also John Brand, *The history and antiquities of the town and county of the town of Newcastle upon Tyne*, (2 vols., B. White & Son, and T. & I. Egerton, London, 1789) I, p. 237.

[67] T.W.A.S., Ms. 3744/4 (11 October 1756).

evidence nevertheless of employers not fulfilling their obligations and Quaker apprentices behaving in a 'disorderly' way. In March 1761, Isaac Thompson intervened on behalf of the Newcastle meeting to examine the lodging of William and Sanders Gooding. He discovered that the premises were unsuitable and they were taken to board at Jane Greggs.[68] David Binns who was indentured as an apprentice draper to his uncle at Sunderland felt that he had been harshly treated. He subsequently wrote in his diary that his uncle had behaved 'very shabbily'. The salary he received was insufficient, and had not recompensed him for 'wear and tear, besides having all the necessaries to find, to equip myself for the journeys'. Nonetheless he admitted that he was at least partially to blame for not questioning it at the time, and recognised that his uncle may have felt that securing him further employment was sufficient recompense.[69]

Popular culture and Quaker moral reform

For Quakers who acquired wealth the pressure to emulate the conspicuous consumption of fashionable society was all too often overpowering. Michael Mullett claims that a gulf existed between the middling sorts and the better-educated and wealthy members who consequently abandoned their association with the Quaker faith.[70] In the North-East Quaker meetings attempted to counter local customs and pastimes, such as theatrical performances, musical festivals, dance, and sporting events, which they judged to be vain, gratuitous or simply pointless. Barry Reay has argued that as many members could not accept such an austere lifestyle there was a clash between the ideologies of popular culture and the Quaker 'godly subculture'.[71] The remorse of George Richardson of Newcastle (c.1780s), after visiting the countryside with friends on a first day afternoon instead of attending a meeting for worship, demonstrates the increasing divisions between Friends and the rest of society. As his 'conscience was awakened' he realised that he had 'forsaken the path of duty, and had been treading the broad way which leadeth to destruction'.[72] Such an unhealthy level of guilt made Quakers appear anti-social. Unable to share the simple pleasures of community life, they were forced to remain separate, and this in turn bred fear that their neighbours were still full of animosity and spitefulness towards them.[73]

The Foxian vision of an alternative community of believers, who rejected the paraphernalia of the parish church and society, was rooted in the importance of

---

[68] T.W.A.S., Ms. 3744/9 (Mf. 167). Monthly Meeting Rough book no. 9 (1758-1762), (8 March 1761), no pagination.

[69] T.W.A.S., Ms. 1203/1. Copy of the diary of David Binns, 1817-1824 (entry dated 20 November 1822).

[70] See M. Mullett, *Radical Religious Movements in Early Modern Europe* (London, 1980), p. 44.

[71] Reay, *The Quakers and the English Revolution*, p. 118.

[72] Sansbury, *Beyond the Blew Stone*, p. 101.

[73] Mullett, *Radical Religious Movements,* p. 90; Davies, *Quakers*, chs. 5-9, 14.

simplicity and plainness.[74] In keeping with this, women Friends in Durham denounced extravagance and the excesses of the world. They sought to keep their clothes plain 'as becomes women professing Truth' and reprimanded those who dressed immoderately.[75] Women Friends consistently sought to enforce the dress code. For example, on 28 July 1709 members were reminded that they should:

> keep out of all needless and superfluous Fashions, as that of cutting and powdering the hair and having too much compass in the browes of quoifes or setting our hoods over high and making mantoes with over wide sleeves, short lapps, and too much to pin upp behind and making them soe farr distant on the Breast and wearing great handkerchief to be puffed out.[76]

In October 1716, women Friends were advised to avoid imitating the 'foolish and indecent fashion of wearing hoppt pettycoats'.[77] Instead, the meeting urged members to wear 'modest apparel with the ornament of a meek and quiet spirit'.[78] Friends hoped that younger members would emulate their distinguished Quaker ancestors not only in their manner of attire but also by their actions. Children who attended Quaker schools, such as Ackworth in Yorkshire or Sidcot in Somerset, had to observe stringent rules on attire and behaviour.[79] In addition, in the eighteenth century all Newcastle apprentices were forced to keep their hair cut short and dress in plain clothing until they had completed their training.[80]

In 1720, leading Durham women Friends sensed that there was a spirit of 'uneasiness and dissatisfaction' in the monthly meetings as some young members were baring their necks, while others were 'wearing partly coloured clogs, and scarlet stockings wrought with points of silke of a different colour'.[81] A statement by women Friends later in the century highlights the increasing availability of fashionable goods and the levels of temptation, which led to:

> some Deviation in most of the meetings from that plainness of simplicity of Speech & Dress which Truth led our faithful ancestors & would still lead their

---

74 Braithwaite, *Beginnings,* passim; E.K.L. Quine, 'The Quakers in Leicestershire', unpublished University of Nottingham Ph.D. dissertation (1968), pp. 276-317; B. Reay, 'Quakerism and Society', in J. F. McGregor and B. Reay (eds), *Radical Religion in the English Revolution* (Oxford, 1984), ch. 6.

75 D.C.R.O., SF/Du/QM/3/1, 26-1-1700. Studies on Quakers and plainness include A. M. Gummere, *The Quaker. A Study in Costume*, (Philadelphia, 1901); J. Kendall, 'The Development of a Distinctive Form of Quaker Dress', *Costume,* 19 (1985), 58-74; D. J. Hall, 'Plainness of Speech, Behaviour and Apparel in Eighteenth-Century English Quakerism', in W. J. Sheils (ed.), *Studies in Church History,* 22 (1985), 307-18.

76 D.C.R.O., SF/Du/QM/3/1 (28 May 1709).

77 Ibid. (2 August 1716).

78 Ibid. (28 May 1709).

79 For details of the dress code for Sidcot school, see Richard Allen, 'Dress and Deportment of Monmouthshire Friends', *J.F.H.S.*, 57, 1 (1994), 52-53; details of attire in other Quaker schools are provided in Kendall, 'Development', 69-71.

80 Sansbury, *Beyond the Blew Stone*, p. 44.

81 D.C.R.O., SF/Du/QM/3/1 (4 August 1720).

> Descendants into which was cause of pain and if continued it may be a means to scatter the youth and lay wast the Testimony of Truth.[82]

Women were called upon to behave in a dignified manner and avoid gossiping. In July 1709, the Durham Friends cautioned against the 'sowing of discord or talebearing… whispering or causeing contention one against the other',[83] and this counsel was constantly reaffirmed.

Rules on plainness also applied to men who were expected to wear traditional Quaker clothing – knee breeches, white bibs and unmistakeable wide brimmed hats – and this clearly distinguished them from the rest of North-East society.[84] Although many Friends conformed, there were those who did not strictly observe the Quaker regulations.[85] In 1711, William Curry advertised a wide range of fine clothes and accessories in the *Newcastle Courant*, including silks, ribbons, and necklaces. Evidence indicates that this was the same William Currey of South Shields, who in 1714 experienced marital difficulties.[86] Occasionally, in the eighteenth century there were members who managed to uphold the dress code while at the same time succeeded in expressing their own individuality. Welford cites the example of Michael Doubleday who frequently wore 'a bright red cap, the top of which hung down behind his head' and was to be seen striding through the town holding a 'silver-headed pole as high as himself'. He was, Welford remarked, 'an object of wonder and admiration to the juvenile population'.[87] As a prominent Quaker, the example he set, albeit unwittingly, may well have been a contributing factor in the gradual relaxation of the rules on dress.

Plainness also applied to household furnishings. Friends' houses contained little embellishment and there was a marked absence of pictures or portraits. In 1709, Durham Women Friends were warned to furnish their homes plainly and not 'furbiloe [sic] their bed valance and window curtains or use any such foolish and unnecessary custome'.[88] As before, however, an examination of Friends' wills suggests that some members could not resist acquiring luxury goods. Clocks, watches, gold and jewellery were all listed as part of the estate as well as valuable items of clothing. In 1708 the will of William Maude, a wealthy woollen draper of Sunderland, bequeathed to his relatives several broad pieces of gold, a gold sceptre, along with a chair and cushion 'sent me from London'.[89] Similarly in

---

[82] T.W.A.S., Ms. 840/10. Letter to the Durham Quarterly Meeting concerning negligence, vanity and corruption in the Society of Friends (8 September 1761).

[83] D.C.R.O., SF/Du/QM/3/1 (28 May 1709). A wider study on 'gossip-mongers' or 'scolds' is in J. Addy, *Sin and Society in the Seventeenth Century* (London, 1989), ch. 8; D. Underdown, 'The Taming of the Scold: The Enforcement of Patriarchal Authority in Early Modern England', in A. Fletcher and J. Stevenson (eds), *Order and Disorder in Early Modern England* (Cambridge, 1985), pp. 116-36.

[84] *Extracts*, pp. 185-6.

[85] Kendall has pointed out that in terms of dress sense there were at least three categories of Quakers: 'gay Friends', 'plain Friends' and 'wet Friends'. See Kendall, 'Development', 58-9.

[86] *Newcastle Courant* (29 August-1 September 1771); Sansbury, *Beyond the Blew Stone*, p. 44.

[87] Welford, *Men of Mark*, II, p. 109.

[88] D.C.R.O., SF/SU/QM/3/1, 28-5-1709.

[89] D.P.G.A., DPRI/1/1708/M1/1-2. The will of William Maude of Sunderland (10 December 1706, proved in 1708).

1716, the inventory of Joshua Middleton of Newcastle revealed the extent of his fortune which, after the payments of his debts, was worth £3397 11s 1½d. Among many other valuable items, he left £5 in 'purse and apparel', several looking glasses and side tables, twelve rushia leather chairs, a clock worth £5, a copper coffee pot and tea pot, a coffee mill and seat of coasters, and brass kettles.[90]

The capacity to accept slight adjustments in their habits and clothing meant that the Society was able to stave off fundamental change and maintain its overall unity. This is illustrated by the regular revision of the questions asked of local meetings, and their incorporation into the *Book of Extracts*.[91] One interesting aspect of this, which has engaged the attention of Quaker historians, is the attitude towards the wearing of wigs.[92] Although this fashion was ubiquitous in the seventeenth and eighteenth centuries, there is little evidence to suggest that this unduly exercised Friends in the North-East. The few references available would seem to indicate that there was a grudging acceptance of such accessories. In 1701, Durham Friends called upon members who wore wigs to declare them, and to ensure that they were the 'same calibre and shape [as] resemble their former hair'.[93] Similarly, Friends at Newcastle and Shields were warned not to wear them as 'voluptuous' adornments.[94] In October 1721, members of the Newcastle and Shields meetings were reminded that they should avoid all 'superfluity', particularly the 'undecent cocking up of hats, undecent wigs, and unnecessary capes'.[95]

Friends' proclamations on plainness were calculated to deter members from slavishly following fashion, and protect them from the corrupting influences of the 'world's vanities'. Changes were inevitable, particularly as Friends were increasingly accepted or at least tolerated by their local communities. Eventually, the preference for broad brims and sober clothing became anachronistic. The inability to keep to the rule on plainness may also have been a precursor to a wider disaffection with the 'conservatism' of the Society or a reaction to the pressures by the local community to conform. This may certainly have been true of children who, having been teased by non-Quakers, would have been more inclined to question the Society's insistence on wearing plain clothes.

All forms of prose, plays and poetry, which ran counter to Quaker principles, were deemed unsuitable for the younger generation. In 1720, the London Yearly Meeting Epistle advised that they should not 'suffer romances,

---

[90] D.P.G.A., DPRI/1/1716/M8/1-2. The inventory was dated 21 October 1717, and the household goods were worth £125-6-8.

[91] See n. 15.

[92] One tract that has survived is John Mulliner, *A Testimony Against Perriwigs and Perriwig Making* (1677). Modern studies on the attitude of Friends to wigs are provided in Gummere, *The Quaker. A Study in Costume*, ch. 3; Marcia Pointon, *Hanging the Head* (New Haven, 1992), pp. 116-17; idem, 'Quakerism and Visual Culture 1650-1800', *Art History*, 20, 3 (1997), 411; E. Bell, ' "Vain Unsettled Fashions": the Early Durham Friends and Popular Culture, c. 1660-1725', *Quaker Studies*, 8, 1 (2003), 31-2.

[93] D.C.R.O., SF/Du/QM/2/1 (1 February 1701).

[94] T.W.A.S., Ms. 3744/3 (12 November 1701-2).

[95] T.W.A.S., Ms. 3744/4 (9 August 1721). This point was reiterated at a monthly meeting held at Durham in June 1726. T.W.A.S., Ms. 3744/1, p. 74.

play-books, or other vain and idle pamphlets, in their houses or families, which tend to corrupt the minds of youth, but, instead thereof that they excite them to the reading of the Holy Scriptures and religious books'.[96] Friends had made good use of the printing press to spread their message and educate their members, and this practice continued throughout the eighteenth and nineteenth centuries. Tracts written in newspapers and the writings of leading members helped Friends to consolidate their views, spread their message in the wider community, and counter the spread of anti-Quakerism.[97] In this respect, Friends in the North-East were no different. In response to a series of attacks in the *Newcastle Courant* in April and August 1739, particularly the vehement criticism of 'Domingo', Friends called for their critics to either argue their case more convincingly or else 'hereafter silent be!'[98]

Friends in the North-East opposed popular culture and sought to deal quickly with those who behaved badly in order to secure their 'reformation and amendment'.[99] The culture of the labouring orders, as the early eighteenth century poem by Edward Chicken, *The Collier's Wedding* suggests, was raucous, self-indulgent and intemperate:

> In former days when trade was good;
> And men got money, clothes and food...
> Then COLLIER LADS got money fast:
> had merry days while it did last,
> They lov'd to feast, drink, play and game,
> And swore without a sense of shame;
> They went to church but very rare,
> But miss'd not when a bride was there;
> Yet rested on the Sabbath day
> From ev'ry thing, but drink and play...
> And thus the Colliers and their wives,
> Liv'd drunken, honest, working lives...[100]

---

[96] *Epistles [from the Yearly Meeting of Friends... from 1681 to 1857]* (2 vols., London, 1858), I, pp. 157-8, and cited in D. Hall, *Plainness of Speech*, p. 314

[97] Cf. R. C. Allen, ' "Mocked, Scoffed, Persecuted, and Made a Gazeing Stock": The Resistance of the Religious Society of Friends (Quakers) to the Religious and Civil Authorities in Post-Toleration South-East Wales c.1689-1836', in Gilbert Bonifas (ed.), *Resistances, Publications de la Faculté des Lettres de Nice* (Nice, 2003).

[98] The first attack concerned Friends attitude towards baptism, while the second and third articles posed mathematical problems ending with an equation and the following rhyme: 'All round the moon I move & cut a whole Caper,/Frisking here & there like a Swaggering Quaker,/Here's pretty Tom-Titty by Timothy Tater,/Giving the following Answers & bubbles a Quaker.' *Newcastle Courant* (14 April 1739, 25 August 1739, 22 September 1739), and cited in Sansbury, *Beyond the Blew Stone*, pp. 52-3. The private ownership of books does not seem to have been particularly high. For example, in the inventory of Joshua Middleton in 1716 his books and 'severall small things' were appraised at £2. See D.P.G.A., DPRI/1/1716/M8/1-2. Friends were encouraged to borrow publications from the meeting and from one another. For a discussion on the development of Quaker literature in the eighteenth century, see R.G. Burtt, 'Quaker books in the eighteenth century', *J.F.H.S.*, 38 (1946), 7-18.

[99] T.W.A.S., MS.3744/3, 14-12-1703.

[100] Edward Chicken, *The Collier's Wedding* (written about 1710 and published 1741). This edition (Newcastle, 1829), pp. 1-2. See also R. W. Malcolmson, *Popular Recreations in English Society, 1750-1850* (London, 1973); B. Reay (ed.), *Popular Culture in Seventeenth Century England,* particularly

In contrast, Quakers advocated a well-ordered life, and held up as examples the reformed behaviour of new members. The conversion of Cuthbert Wigham of Cornwood is typical. Brought up as an Anglican, Wigham spent a large percentage of his time in 'loose and unprofitable company, delighting in vain sports'. In 1734, aged thirty, he had a 'road to Damascus' experience where, by his own account, he was 'awakened to a sense of his sinful and dangerous condition'. Briefly blinded, after receiving a visitation from God, he became aware of his wasted life and converted to Quakerism. He nevertheless found it difficult to relinquish his attachment to worldly pleasures, and had to be reminded that he should practise self-denial and avoid any association with his 'former wicked companions'. From this period onwards he 'laboured faithfully' for the Friends in Northumberland and often recalled his deliverance from 'the horrible pit of everlasting darkness', and was 'earnestly engaged to persuade and warn others to take heed to their ways, lest they should bring themselves into such distress as he had experienced.'[101]

Along with other nonconformists, Friends were convinced of the baneful influence of immoderate drinking.[102] George Fox advised inn-keepers that they should not let people have 'more drink than would do them good' and testified against 'wakes or feasts, their May-games, sports, plays, and shows, which trained up people to vanity and looseness'.[103] Clearly, such advice had little impact, as alcohol abuse in the eighteenth century was a serious problem.[104] In his visit to Newcastle in 1742, John Wesley wrote that he was amazed to witness 'so much drunkenness, cursing and swearing, even from the mouths of little children'.[105] Friends had counselled members from as early as 1701 to be more temperate and avoid 'undue liberty... in keeping and frequenting ale houses'.[106] A decade later they were concerned that some were still 'addicted to frequenting alehouses and drinking to excess',[107] and in 1712 the meeting called on Darlington Friends to exercise restraint and suppress the 'evil of alehouse haunting, and the disorders ariseing there from'.[108] This failed to have the desired effect, and in March 1713, the Quarterly meeting called upon them to name their 'disorderly' members.[109]

chs.1 and 3; H. Cunningham, *Leisure and Culture* in Thompson (ed.), *The Cambridge Social History of Britain,* vol. II; P. Burke, *Popular Culture in Early Modern Europe* (rev. ed., Aldershot, 1994); T. Harris, *Popular Culture in England, c.1500-1800* (London, 1995).

101 Steel, *A Historical Sketch*, pp. 1-4.

102 See comments in Robert Barclay, *An Apology* (8th ed., 1692), 512; Mullett, 'From Sect to Denomination?', 171-4; Reay, *The Quakers and the English Revolution*, pp. 118-20; Scott, *Quakerism in York*, pp. 14-15, 21-2.

103 J. Nickalls (ed.), *The Journal of George Fox* (Cambridge, 1952), p. 37.

104 For a detailed study of alehouse culture and efforts to curb excessive alcoholism, see P. Clark, 'The Alehouse and the Alternative Society', in D. Pennington and K. Thomas (eds), *Puritans and Revolutionaries* (Oxford, 1978), pp. 47-72; L. Davison, 'Experiments in the Social Regulation of Industry: Gin Legislation, 1729-1751', in Davison et al. (eds.), *Stilling the Grumbling Hive*, ch. 2. See also the chapter by John Chartres in this collection.

105 John Wesley, *The Works of... John Wesley*, I, p. 373.

106 D.C.R.O., SF/Du/QM/2/1, p. 159.

107 Ibid., p. 192.

108 Ibid., pp. 195-6.

109 Darlington Friends refused to comply, but by January 1715, although the minutes do not explain the circumstances, the matter had been internally resolved. Ibid., pp. 196, 200-201, 204-5.

It would be wrong to assume that Friends were simply concerned to restrict alcohol abuse or to preserve their reputation in the local community. By attacking excess, the Society was also trying to limit the consequences of such behaviour, namely the dangers posed to family relationships and business probity. Parents were quick to warn their children about the dangers of 'frequenting places of public diversion', and were vigilant in ensuring that their own behaviour would not encourage younger members to be 'exposed to the allurements of this world's pleasures which leads into the broad way and ends in destruction'.[110] Sunderland Friends had to deal with a crisis in John and Miriam Younger's marriage, caused by John's excessive drinking. Their constant quarrelling and John's drunkenness were judged to be a bad example to their children and servants as well as affording an opportunity for non-members to ridicule the movement. Younger consistently ignored their counsel to modify his behaviour and was testified against in February 1713.[111] In June 1714, he wrote to Sunderland Friends and explained that his business was suffering. Instead of repenting, he complained that his neighbours took advantage of him when he was drunk and attempted to defraud him of his rightful payments.[112] In February 1721, Robert Swanton of Shields was found guilty of 'shamefully abusing his wife and beating her' while intoxicated,[113] and in May 1733, Barlow Sheap of Sunderland was said to have not only 'brought shame and dishonour upon himself, as a man and a Christian', but had placed his family in 'imminent danger'.[114] Some members such as John Chipchase were prepared to admit that their drinking was the cause of their financial difficulties and sought help from the Sunderland meeting.[115] George Raw's immoderate drinking and the collapse of his finances in 1757 prompted the Society to intervene and act in *loco parentis* for his two sons.[116]

In most cases, Quaker employers instituted strict controls over alcohol consumption in their businesses,[117] although on rare occasions some apprentices or employees were able to hide their immoderate drinking. In his journal, David Binns secretly confessed to his enjoyment of alcohol and revelry. On 30 July 1818, when his friend John Feltman left his employment at Sunderland, they had a 'very

---

110 T.W.A.S., Ms. 840/11. Letter to the Durham Quarterly Meeting concerning negligence, vanity and corruption in the Society of Friends (8 September 1761).

111 T.W.A.S., 3744/233, fols. 5,7; D.C.R.O., SF/Su/2 (11 November 1713). Further examples of drunkenness concern John Bowlan of the Derwent meeting (1722) and William Wilson of the Shields meeting (1793). See T.W.A.S., Ms. 3744/1, pp. 68-9; T.W.A.S., Ms. 3744/2, p. 78.

112 T.W.A.S., 3744/233, fol. 7.

113 T.W.A.S., Ms. 3744/145 (12 December 1720); T.W.A.S., 3744/233, fol. 13. Several years later, and after a considerable degree of patience exercised by Friends, the Shields meeting also disowned his wife for her 'ceaseless and sottish way of living greatly to the shame of her sex and dishonour to her profession'. Ibid., fol. 18.

114 Ibid., fol. 32.

115 Ibid., fol. 39; T.W.A.S., Ms. 3744/4 (10 March 1736).

116 T.W.A.S., MS.3744/233, fol.96; T.W.A.S., Ms. 3744/4, 10-1-1757.

117 Cf. the conditions of work imposed by the Harford family of Monmouthshire upon prospective employees. For example, in 1796 Richard Walters was warned that he should not 'on any pretence sell Beer or other liquors to any persons whatever at any time'. If he did so, he would be fined five guineas every time he was caught. See A. Gray-Jones, 'Quaker Ironmasters in Monmouthshire, 1796-1842', *Welsh Outlook*, 12 (1925), 43.

merry night'. A more telling example perhaps was that of 13 November 1820 when he recalled that his uncle George Binns and his wife had provided him and his friends with:

> beef steaks, apple pies, tarts etc. Uncle and Aunt came down to supper, which I was very much pleased with and after supper they retired upstairs again and left us to ourselves. They sent us down two bottles of made wine and some apples, which we demolished, and after the wine glasses were removed, we had a bottle of rum, Holland's and brandy. We got about two glasses a piece, which made some of the company rather groggy. Alfred Waterfall made a complete beast of himself with his nonsense. Sutton was quite drunk. All the rest were very comfortable. We broke up about 11 o'clock after a pleasant entertainment. All the company seemed well pleased with their visit.[118]

A few months later on 26 April 1821, one of the revellers, Waterfall, was accused by his employer of 'going a whoreing and other scandalous behaviour'. Waterfall initially denied the affair, but once his guilt was established, he was confined to the house for two weeks before being dismissed and sent to his father at Coventry. There is case here for arguing that George Binns himself was in no small measure responsible for Waterfall's downfall.[119]

Northumberland and Durham Friends also made fervent appeals to members to abstain from cursing and tried to persuade neighbours to do likewise. They believed that education was the best method of affecting a reformation of manners. To achieve this end in February 1736, Newcastle Friends proposed the reprinting of Joshua Middleton's book, *A Compassionate Call to Profane Swearers.*[120] This may have been prompted by the activities of Thomas Tucker and Richard Clark, both of the Shields' meeting, who became notorious for their drunken, coarse, and blasphemous behaviour.[121] By the following January, Newcastle Friends had ordered 1200 copies for their monthly meeting, while Stockton ordered a further 750 copies, and Raby and Durham an additional 400 copies each.[122]

Gambling, racecourses, cockfighting pits and theatres became increasingly popular activities as the eighteenth century progressed, and such excessive revelry was thought, in some quarters, to encourage immoral behaviour. In 1755, the London Yearly Meeting cautioned members in England and Wales to 'avoid all vain sports, places of diversion, gaming and all unnecessary frequenting of ale houses or taverns, excess in drinking and intemperance of every kind'.[123] Equally in March 1761, the London Second Day Morning Meeting appealed to

---

[118] T.W.A.S., Ms. 1203/1.

[119] Ibid.

[120] Joshua Middleton, *A Tender and Compassionate Call to Profane Swearers, and Takers of the Holy Name of God in Vain* (London, 1708).

[121] T.W.A.S., Ms. 3744/233, fol.43.

[122] D.C.R.O., SF/Du/QM/2/2 (6 November 1735/6) (30 January 1736).

[123] Glamorgan Archive Service, D/DSF/354 (1 October 1755). For further examples, see *Extracts*, 29; R. Bauman, *Let Your Words be Few: Symbolism of Speaking and Silence among Seventeenth-Century Quakers* (Cambridge, 1983), p. 23.

Friends in the North-East to '[put] out Lights on those call'd joicing nights and the not opening of their shops on Days appointed by human authority for publick fasts, feasts, and thanksgiving'.[124] Some Friends in the region were clearly unable to resist and were pilloried by their meetings. In January 1745, John Graham of the Shields meeting was censured for his 'pernicious vice of gaming and comfort keeping'. He had been counselled by the overseers already and promised to reform, but he had continued to gamble and his extravagance was clearly having a detrimental impact upon his business.[125] The same accusation was levelled against John Newton of Sunderland who, in August 1745, was found guilty of spending too much time and money 'in sporting and in tippling and drinking'. The meeting was particularly aggrieved as they had given him so much financial support.[126] While Friends were quick to condemn delinquency and the unwelcome attention it brought in its wake, they were alive to the underlying causes of such behaviour. The idea that an indulgent or negligent upbringing was directly linked to intemperance in adulthood served to further reinforce their belief in a structured and disciplined family life. When John Hodgson of Elswick was disowned in February 1767, members restated their obligation of 'inculcating early our religious principles in to the minds of tender youth' and offering suitable advice to his parents. Hodgson, they concluded, had been exposed to 'unsuitable company', which left him 'open to the attacks of many other temptations'. They were, therefore, not entirely surprised that he had hedonistic inclinations.[127]

A Society whose moral code penalised inappropriate dress, non-attendance at meetings, and intemperance, was bound to actively condemn any sexual misconduct. A number of cases brought before the north-east meetings suggest that members struggled to resist carnal pleasures. On 2 May 1722, John Hadderington of Durham was accused of fornication and bringing the society into disrepute. Although he acknowledged his 'sinfull' behaviour, Friends were not satisfied because he would not make a written confession. They therefore recorded his misdemeanour as a warning to members.[128] This did not have the desired effect as on 6 February 1734, Iveston Friends testified against Henry Pallister of Fulford for committing 'lewd practices verry unbecoming a person professing wth us'. Pallister was disowned, but was informed that the meeting would restore him to the community if he were to 'unresignedly repent'.[129] In the same year, Newcastle Quakers were outraged by the 'scandalous life and conversation' of George Pescod of Sunderland. This was not the first time that his behaviour had caused concern. In December 1731, he had admitted that he had succumbed to the 'sinful lusts of the flesh' and married a non-member. Although on that occasion the meeting was sympathetic, his subsequent adultery in 1734 could not be condoned for he had not only damaged himself but had brought the Society into disrepute.[130] The Society's

124 T.W.A.S., Ms. 3744/9 (12 January 1761).
125 T.W.A.S., Ms. 3744/233, fol. 68.
126 Ibid., fol. 71.
127 Ibid., fol.150.
128 T.W.A.S., Ms. 3744/1, p. 68.
129 Ibid., p. 91.
130 T.W.A.S., Ms.3744/233, fols.28, 36

fears of public ridicule were sometime unfounded, but occasionally they were wholly justified as the case of Mitford Flower of Sunderland demonstrates. In March 1749, a local woman testified before a magistrate that Flower had 'carnal knowledge of her'. Despite his earlier protestations of innocence, the case had entered the public domain and it proved impossible for Friends to do anything other than to disown him.[131]

Quaker women were just as susceptible. For example, on 13 September 1731, Rachel, the wife of George Appleby of Sunderland, was testified against for her lewd behaviour,[132] while on 14 August 1732, Newcastle Friends disowned Mary, the wife of Isaac Hunter, for leading a 'scandalous life'.[133] Lastly, on 5 April 1747, Iveston Friends accused Phyllis Glenn of 'very disorderly and lewd practices'. They were prepared to welcome Glenn back if she would repent.[134] Such disownments do not appear to have been an effective deterrent as further testimonies against women members were lodged in the mid-1750s and mid-1790s. All too often scandalous behaviour was attributed to the excessive consumption of alcohol. Indeed, drunkenness was the main reason for the disownment of Hannah Maria Smith, a Sunderland Friend, in March 1756.[135]

Merry Wiesner has shown that pregnancies outside marriage were very common in the early modern period. Indeed, she has estimated that between one-fifth to one-third of brides were pregnant before the marriage ceremony in the sixteenth and seventeenth centuries, while in the eighteenth century this figure was near to one-half.[136] Nevertheless, the Quakers regarded illegitimacy as a very serious matter. In 1747, two cases of bastardy were brought before the Shields and Sunderland meetings,[137] while in September 1758, Durham Women Friends testified against Frances Mason of Brandon for her 'departure from the simplicity of ye Blessed Truth and the known ways of virtue'. Mason had not heeded the meeting's warning against indiscriminate fraternisation with the 'world's people', and 'under the Power of Darkness... betrayed [herself]... to an action of a heinous nature'.[138]

Meetings required members to confess to any misdemeanours, remain faithful, and avoid any actions likely to damage the Society. To some extent, this emphasis upon the Society's good reputation may have been an attempt to shake off the last vestiges of its earlier radical image. Michael Mullett has argued that Friends attempted to distance themselves from any association with the radical religious groups of the civil war years and that this helps to explain their inflexible

---

[131] D.C.R.O., SF/Du/Qm/2/2 (27 January 1739); T.W.A.S., Ms. 3744/4 (13 January 1749); T.W.A.S., Ms. 3744/233, fol.77. For further exclusions, see D.C.R.O., SF/Du/QM/ 2/2 (27 January 1739); Ms. 3744/233, fols. 50, 94, 137, 138, 143-4.

[132] T.W.A.S., Ms. 3744/233, fol. 25.

[133] T.W.A.S., Ms. 3744/4 (14 June 1732).

[134] T.W.A.S., Ms. 3744/1, pp. 137-8.

[135] T.W.A.S., Ms. 3744/4, 8-3-1756. For other examples, see Ibid., 13-3-1758; T.W.A.S., Ms. 3744/2, p. 153; T.W.A.S., Ms. 3744/233, fols. 95, 109, 139, 158-9.

[136] M. E. Wiesner, *Women and Gender in Early Modern Europe*, (Cambridge, 1993), pp. 49-50.

[137] T.W.A.S., Ms.3744/4 (12 November 1746, 14 July 1747); T.W.A.S., Ms. 3744/233, fols. 74, 77.

[138] T.W.A.S., Ms. 3744/35 (Mf.174). Durham Women's Preparative Meeting (1755-1789), (23 July 1758).

attitude towards sex and marriage. It was, he suggests, 'a defensive reaction to old charges of Ranter irregularity and their attempt to live down the slur of antinomianism'.[139] In effect, those who were expelled from the Society for their immoderate behaviour felt that they were social outcasts, unwelcome among those who had provided kinship and security, and unsure of their place in the wider community. In 1758, William King of Newbiggin and an elder of the Shields meeting, was testified against for fornication. The stigma of being cast out profoundly affected him. He finally confessed and sought readmission. On 4 January 1760, he concluded that 'to be abandoned by ones Friends and put in a state of separation from them... is so shocking to a human mind as not to be express'd in any words... Life at that time seemed of no further use nor value.' He was subsequently readmitted into fellowship with Friends, and a respectable marriage to Ann Purdom of the Newcastle meeting in 1760 anchored his position within the Society.[140]

Conclusion

This chapter has sought to explore the extent to which North-East Quakers constituted a separate and distinct community in the long eighteenth century. If the Society was to uphold the principles upon which it was founded, it had to construct a counter culture to the burgeoning consumer society of the eighteenth century. Although the growth of consumerism was a national phenomenon, its particular manifestation in the North-East, which stood at the forefront of progressive economic change, prompted the Society to retreat into introspection and clannish behaviour, exerting unusual control over its members. Their code of conduct ensured that all aspects of their lives were regulated, and furthermore evidence suggests that the meetings took over the normal functions of the parish, relatives and neighbours. Indeed, dependence upon the Society was not only important in times of need, but conditioned the behaviour of Quaker families throughout their lives. Apart from the enforcement of a code of conduct, there was a consciousness that as a community they should be self-reliant, conducting everyday business within the Society. They would also offer help to disadvantaged members who might otherwise become reliant upon the 'world's people'. Ruth Sansbury claims that Friends had little in common with eighteenth-century community life and that they embraced the principle of 'withdrawing from the world in order to follow the light within'.[141] This is substantiated by Elizabeth O'Donnell's view that 'the peculiarities of the Quaker community tended to set members apart'.[142] This meant that 'a surrogate form of kinship control' was used, whereby Quaker communities provided moral oversight and acted as 'large and censorious families...

[139] M. Mullett, 'The Assembly of the People of God: the Social Organisation of Lancashire Friends', in Mullett (ed.), *Early Lancaster Friends*, p. 15.
[140] T.W.A.S., Ms. 3744/4 (10 April 1758); T.W.A.S., Ms. 3744/233, fols. 107, 128.
[141] Sansbury, *Beyond the Blew Stone*, p. 55.
[142] O'Donnell, 'Woman's rights and Woman's duties', p. 10.

[safeguarding]... otherwise rootless and unsupervised individuals... from some of the typical features of early modern urban life: alcoholism, bankruptcy, prostitution and crime'.[143] Not everyone agrees. As T. A. Davies insists, the Society was not hermetically sealed. There were occasions when members co-operated with their neighbours, acting as overseers to the poor and maintaining close business links with non-Quakers.[144]

By the beginning of the nineteenth century, the Quaker code of conduct was fast becoming anachronistic. Technological advances in communications, such as railways, steam travel, printing, and the availability of new and more exotic goods, rendered their earlier isolation an impossible, impracticable vision. They had become 'as much a commercial company as a company of saints'.[145] Friends who were themselves in the vanguard of entrepreneurial enterprise and wealth generation could no longer hide from the world, but rather had to arrive at a judicious and pragmatic accommodation.

---

[143] Mullett, *Radical Religious Movements,* p. 67.
[144] Davies, *The Quakers,* pp. 201-14.
[145] Nossiter, *Influence, Opinion and Political Idiom*, p. 133.

Chapter 8

Creating Polite Space: The Organisation and Social Function of the Newcastle Assembly Rooms*

HELEN BERRY

Among the undiscovered treasures of provincial archives are repositories of eighteenth-century documents relating to the construction and maintenance of assembly rooms, detailed and informative sources which are only now beginning to receive the attention of historians.[1] One such collection relates to the Newcastle assembly rooms, which opened in 1776. An unusual amount of original documentation, such as tradesmen's and booksellers' bills, subscription lists, and legal records relating to the building itself and its managers has survived. These are supplemented by an unusually rich legacy of local newspapers,[2] which in combination with the archival sources present the opportunity to re-create a detailed picture of the planning, construction, maintenance and use of provincial assembly rooms that influenced the cultural life of an entire region at the end of the eighteenth century. The story of the Newcastle assembly rooms also sheds light upon the social and economic constraints, and hazards attendant upon public building projects in English provincial towns at this time.

There is a rare and reasonably general consensus among early modern historians that assemblies were an important feature of polite society in the eighteenth century. By the mid-1700s, assemblies had become part of the established urban scene: together with walks and gardens, they constituted the

---

*Research for this chapter was undertaken as part of the research project 'Nationalising Taste: National Identity and Cultural Value in Eighteenth-Century Britain' funded by the University of Northumbria. The author would like to thank the project's Directors, Thomas Faulkner, Jeremy Gregory, and Allan Ingram for their support and advice. Peter Borsay, Joyce Ellis and Richard Terry provided helpful comments and additional references. Mr A. G. Michaelides, the current owner of the Newcastle assembly rooms, kindly allowed me access to the building that he and his family have saved and restored. Mr Cyril Winskell generously lent his architectural drawings of the building.

[1] Peter Borsay, *The English Urban Renaissance. Culture and Society in the Provincial Town, 1660-1770* (Oxford, 1991), pp. 160-62 uses examples from the minute books of the York assembly rooms. Another example is Angela Dain, 'Assemblies and Polite Leisure in East Anglia', *Suffolk Review*, new ser., 28 (1997), 2-22.

[2] Frank Manders, 'The History of the Newspaper Press in Northeast England', in Peter Isaac (ed.) *The 'Fourth Estate' at Work in Northumberland and Durham* (Richmond, Surrey, 1999).

primary 'arenas of display' in Georgian towns.[3] Mark Girouard has described the assembly as one of the 'main manifestations of polite society, and a means of education in its ways'.[4] What, however, were the regional variations in the character of assemblies? At present in the existing historiography there is little detail about how the construction of assembly rooms was funded locally, nor how these rooms were used. The question of who funded the building of assembly rooms and patronised assemblies is crucial in judging their cultural and political significance.[5] As Kathleen Wilson has observed, the building of assembly rooms and theatres 'theoretically mobilized community support as they democratised or "commercialised" élite culture'.[6] It is therefore a paradox that subscriptions for these buildings, which facilitated a stake in the management of the venue, were opened up only to those who could afford shares, which ranged from £25 to £200. To what extent, if we take the specific example of Newcastle, did the building of new assembly rooms broaden or restrict participation in polite culture? There is also the question of whether provincial towns merely copied the metropolis or developed distinctive regional forms of urban sociability throughout England.[7] Does the concept of 'cultural emulation' adequately account for the proliferation of assembly rooms across the country, or is it a deceptive concept that masks distinct local variations on a national theme?

I

At the start of the eighteenth century, Newcastle was the fourth largest town in England, considered by contemporary observers to be second only to Bristol in its growth through trade.[8] Its prosperity was founded mainly upon the export of coal and other burgeoning local industries such as glassmaking. The accumulation of a critical mass of gentry, merchants and professionals in Newcastle during the first half of the century brought with it urban expansion and improvement, as well as the demand for entertainment, from concerts and theatrical performances to coffee

---

[3] Borsay, *English Urban Renaissance*, pp. 150-51. See also Paul Langford, *A Polite and Commercial People. England 1727-1783* (Oxford, 1992), pp. 101-102.

[4] Mark Girouard, *The English Town* (New Haven and London, 1990), p. 132. This is also of course amply illustrated in the novels of Jane Austen; see for example the first encounter between Elizabeth Bennett and Mr. Darcy, *Pride and Prejudice* (1813), Penguin edn. (1987), pp. 57-61, or Anne Elliot's meeting with Captain Wentworth in the rooms at Bath, in *Persuasion* (1818), Penguin edn. (Harmondsworth, 1985), pp. 191-9.

[5] In Langford, *A Polite and Commercial People*, pp. 59-122, for example, the subject of 'Association and Assemblies' is subsumed in a chapter about the 'middle class'.

[6] Kathleen Wilson, *The Sense of the People. Politics, Culture and Imperialism in England, 1715-1785* (Cambridge, 1998), pp. 76-7.

[7] John Brewer, *The Pleasures of the Imagination. English Culture in the Eighteenth Century* (London, 1997), pp. 494-6, describes as an 'improving tale of imitation and emulation', as a process through which 'culture travelled only one way', from London to the provinces.

[8] Joyce Ellis, '"The 'Black Indies": the Economic Development of Newcastle upon Tyne, c.1700-1840', in W. Lancaster and R. Colls (eds) *Newcastle upon Tyne. A Modern History* (Chichester, 2000).

houses.[9] Assemblies were first held in Newcastle in 1716 in a property on Westgate Street that had been the house of Sir William Creagh, where they continued until new assembly room opened in the Groat Market in 1736.[10] In this year, the composer Charles Avison started his winter subscription concerts in the town, and used the assembly rooms as one of his preferred venues.[11] We do not know where the inspiration came for these early Newcastle ventures: they may have been modelled upon those held in York, the birthplace of the assembly.[12] The York assembly rooms were less than a day's journey from Newcastle, and were one of the finest Palladian buildings in the country, much praised in *Vitruvius Britannicus*: 'The disposition of these rooms for elegance and convenience, is not surpassed by any thing of the kind in the kingdom. They were built by subscription from the designs of the late right honourable earl of Burlington; and are a lasting monument of his lordship's taste in architecture.'[13] The other formative influence, upon which even assemblies in London were modelled, was the famous assemblies overseen by Richard 'Beau' Nash at Bath. The first assembly rooms at Bath appeared in 1708; elegant new rooms in the Palladian style by John Wood opened in 1730, and were the venue for arguably the most dazzling assemblies in England.[14]

Many of the smaller assemblies throughout provincial England were held in civic buildings; the mayor's house, town hall or guildhall, or at the larger inns or 'Long Rooms'. Across the country, in towns such as Banbury and Northampton, Shrewsbury, Wakefield and Worcester, assemblies were held in the public rooms of local taverns, where existing facilities were modified or extended for the purpose. Assembly rooms available in the North East before the 1770s mostly followed this national pattern. At Tynemouth, a thriving and genteel neighbourhood, assemblies were held at the Star and Garter Inn.[15] In Morpeth, local families organised assemblies of their own at the town hall,[16] while at Alnwick, the choice was between assemblies at the town hall or the White Swan Inn.[17] The rooms of local inns were often far from modest in scale and ornamentation, but by mid-century there was a preference in many larger provincial urban centres for purpose-built assembly rooms. Bristol, which had

---

9 Joyce Ellis, 'A dynamic society: social relations in Newcastle upon Tyne, 1660-1760', in P. Clark (ed.) *The Transformation of English Provincial Towns* (London, 1984). See also R. Sweet, *The Writing of Urban Histories* (Oxford, 1997), p. 160; John Hodgson Hinde, 'Public Amusements in Newcastle', *Archaeologia Aeliana*, new series, vol. 4 (1860), 229-48.

10 S. Middlebrook, *Newcastle upon Tyne. Its Growth and Achievement* (Newcastle, 1950), pp. 126-7. Creagh, a Catholic, had been appointed Mayor of Newcastle by James II, and was ejected after 1688.

11 Tickets for the concerts cost half a guinea for the season, and went on sale at the Assembly rooms and Mr. Avison's lodgings The concerts were advertised in the local press, and ran for many years. See for example *Newcastle Courant* (12-19 September, 1741).

12 Daniel Defoe, *A Tour of the Whole Island of Great Britain* (1724-6) mentions in York 'the keeping up assemblies among the younger gentry was first set up here' (modern edition, Exeter, 1989), p. 186.

13 Colen Campbell, *Vitruvius Britannicus, or the British Architect*, IV (London, 1767), pp. 78-81.

14 Girouard, *English Towns*, pp. 138, 141; John Haddon, *Bath* (Bath, 1973), pp. 104-5; see also Peter Borsay, *The Image of Georgian Bath, 1700-2000* (Oxford, 2000).

15 *Newcastle Courant* (10 August 1771).

16 Ibid. (19 October 1771).

17 *The Diary of Nicholas Brown*, Surtees Society, 68 (1910), pp. 242, 252.

more than twice the population of Newcastle, opened its own assembly rooms in 1755; Sheffield, with less than half Newcastle's population, received new assembly rooms in 1762.[18]

In a national perspective, therefore, the citizens of Newcastle were undoubtedly slow to organise the construction of their own purpose-built assembly rooms. However, such rooms would only have been economically viable from the moment when there was a sufficiently large number of middling-sort residents and gentry to provide a market for year-round assemblies. Throughout the North-East, assemblies were customarily held according to a seasonal pattern of associational activities which brought the local gentry into the towns. The seasonal pattern of North-East assemblies is evident from their earliest appearance; in Durham during the late 1720s, they were held at a private house in Sadler Street, to coincide with the Durham assizes; in Sunderland, a Mrs Thorpe held assemblies in the High Street during race week; at Hartlepool, assemblies were held weekly during the bathing season.[19] The plan for purpose-built assembly rooms in Newcastle thus marked the growing aspirations of an expanding middle class population, permanently resident in the town.

The motto upon the foundation stone, laid in 1774, boldly staked a claim to Newcastle's participation in national society:

In an Age
When the Polite Arts,
By general Encouragement and Emulation,
Have advanced to a State of Perfection
Unknown in any former Period:
The first Stone of this Edifice,
Dedicated to the most elegant Recreation,
Was laid by William Lowes Esq.,
On the 16th day of May, 1774.

A prestigious location for the new building was chosen in Westgate Street, in what was then the smartest part of the town. The neighbourhood was the abode of clergymen and gentry, within sight of the outlying fields and high up from the coal smoke, smell and noise of the quayside and town markets.[20] The new assembly rooms were situated on a plot of land in the corner of St. John's parsonage, leased on 1 September 1774 by the vicar of Newcastle for a term of 999 years, at an annual rent of £20. The lease of church land for the purpose of building assembly rooms was unusual, but not inexplicable: Christopher Fawcett, one of the subscribers to the proposal (and another civic official appointed Recorder of Newcastle in 1778), was the brother of Revd. Richard Fawcett, vicar of Newcastle.[21]

---

[18] E. A. Wrigley, 'Urban Growth and Agricultural Change: England and the Continent in the Early Modern Period', in idem, *People, Cities and Wealth. The Transformation of Traditional Society* (Oxford, 1987), Table 7.1, p. 160.

[19] Hinde, 'Public Amusements', 243.

[20] Middlebrook, *Newcastle*, pp. 119, 148.

[21] NCL/L942.82/N5370; Welford, *Men of Mark*, II, p. 97.

The commission to design and build the new assembly rooms went to William Newton, who designed Charlotte Square, the first smart residential development of its kind in Georgian Newcastle. The choice of Newton was a mark of confidence in the capabilities of this local architect (whom several local gentlemen entrusted with improving their country houses) and was certainly a pragmatic choice: he devised a pleasing if rather conventional plan for the assembly rooms.[22] The original façade is the subject of a contemporary engraving by William Beilby (plate 4), and may be traced on the outside of the building that still survives today. No single architectural influence inspired the design of the new rooms. They were certainly not a carbon copy of any others in the country. The exterior of the building was almost austere in its classical simplicity, the only adornment being a pilastrade of six Ionic columns. A flourish was reserved for the interior, with a grand staircase leading to the first floor ballroom (similar to one at the Derby assembly rooms), 94 feet long, 36 feet wide, and 32 feet high. The floor space for dancing was bigger than at the York Assembly rooms (where cumbersome Egyptian columns hindered the dancing), and was judged to be 'more commodious than any other building of the kind in the kingdom, except the House of Assembly at Bath'.[23]

From the outset, the projected costs of this ambitious project in Newcastle were considerable, and required a large amount of capital to be raised from shareholders. The setting up of joint stock companies was still banned under the Bubble Act, but shareholders formed in effect an unincorporated association.[24] An advertisement was placed in the *Newcastle Courant* in August 1773, announcing that a subscription list had been placed in Katy's coffee house on the quayside to raise money for a 'New Assembly Room at Newcastle' after a 'General Observation' had been made at the previous Assizes that the existing facilities were 'by no means sufficient' to receive 'Gentlemen and Ladies 'at the Assizes, Guilds, Races, and other public Meetings'.[25] The original subscription book of 1776 lists the names of those who responded to this advertisement, and thus provides a means of gauging the social composition of 'polite society' in Newcastle at the time. This unpublished source supplements a printed handlist of 'Proprietors of the New Assembly rooms' printed in 1785, which gave the names of 128 individuals who bought one or more shares at £25 each, to the total value of £5840 (the duke of Portland and Lord Ravensworth's shares amounting to the irregular amount of £105 and £210 respectively).[26] The original subscription book contains five

---

[22] Thomas Faulkner, 'Conservation and Renewal in Newcastle upon Tyne', in T. E. Faulkner (ed.), *Northumbrian Panorama. Studies in the History and Culture of North-East England* (Newcastle, 1996), pp. 124-5. For further examples of Newton's work in the region, see Phoebe Lowery, 'Patronage and the Country House in Northumberland', in ibid., pp. 61, 66.

[23] Girouard, *English Town*, pp. 138-40; W. Parson and W. White, *History of Newcastle, Durham and Northumberland*, I (1827), xcvi; Lynne F. Pearson, *Northern City: An Architectural History of Newcastle upon Tyne* (Newcastle, 1996), pp. 17-18.

[24] See C. Chalkin, 'Capital Expenditure on Building for Cultural Purposes in Provincial England', *Business History*, 22 (1980), 57-62 on the financial risks of investment in projects for public cultural uses.

[25] *Newcastle Courant* (21 August 1773).

[26] Reproduced in Anon., *A Short History of the Old Assembly Rooms* (Newcastle, 1929), p. 2.

additional names: William Johnson, Andrew Robinson Stoney, Ralph Carr (the Merchant Adventurer), Benjamin Emmerson, and Thomas Maver York, bringing the total number of shareholders to 133 (see below, Table 8.1).

Table 8.1 Subscribers to the new assembly rooms, Newcastle (1776) by social/occupational status

		Number of Subscribers	As % of total
Nobility/greater gentry		17	13
Lesser gentry		39	29
Merchants/bankers		23	17
Professions		17	13
Lawyers	10		
Physicians	4		
Army officers	2		
Other	1		
Tradesmen		7	5
Unknown		29	22
Corporation of Newcastle		1	<1
TOTAL		133	100

Source: 'The Proprietors of the New Assembly rooms, 1776', Newcastle City Library, L942.82/N5370.

Table 8.1 shows how the assembly rooms were built through the combined investment of the social and political élite of Newcastle and its neighbouring counties. Of the known subscribers, 42% came from the nobility and greater or lesser gentry, evidence of the continuing influence of powerful local families which offsets the all-too-frequent impression that urban polite society was dominated by the new middling sort. The social profile of shareholders is of course no indication of who actually used the rooms once they were built, but it does indicate the importance of harnessing the wealth and patronage of the highest echelons of local society. The rooms' titled patrons included two dukes, one earl, four lords and eight baronets. The duke of Northumberland and his son Lord Algernon Percy, were the largest single investors in the project, contributing £700 between them. Lord Ravensworth gave £200. The baronets, who included Sir Matthew White Ridley MP, Sir William Loraine, Sir Thomas Blackett and Sir John Trevelyan, invested between £50 and £200 each. Among the subscribers were the wealthier gentry families of Northumberland and county Durham, such as the

Allgoods, Bowes, Blacketts, Ellisons, Liddells and Ridleys. A further 30% of investors whose status has been identified were drawn from the wealthier section of Newcastle's civic élite (the bankers, merchants and professional men). These included half a dozen of Newcastle's richest merchants (such as Ralph Atkinson, Ralph Carr, and William Monkhouse of the Side); the bankers Aubone Surtees and George Burdon; no fewer than ten attorneys, two army officers, and four medical men connected with the Newcastle Infirmary.

The social profile of members belonging to one of the earliest Assembly Room Committees confirms the primary role that merchants and professional men took in organising and running the Rooms, even though they were in the minority of shareholders. Out of the six members, half were well-to-do Newcastle merchants (Ralph Atkinson, Edward Anderson and Isaac Cookson), while Richard Bryan Abbs was a surgeon of Pudding Lane, Newcastle.[27] Another member, William Cramlington, was a roper by trade, and a partner in Blagdon & Cramlington, hostmen and coalfitters. He later married the mayor's widow, and was himself elevated to that office in 1796.[28] The final member was Richard Chambers, a saddler, who held local office as a member of the Common Council, and was Secretary to the assembly rooms in the early 1780s.[29] Such men were used to sitting on committees as experienced corporation members, and their names are associated with other cultural activities in late Georgian Newcastle. One of the earliest Proprietors of the assembly rooms was Nathaniel Clayton, an attorney at the Turk's Head opposite the Bigg Market in Newcastle, who became Town Clerk in 1785 (a position he held for thirty seven years) and was later Chairman to the Committee of the Theatre Royal.[30] Five Proprietors of the assembly rooms were also on the Theatre Royal Committee under Clayton's chairmanship: William Cramlington, George Waldie, Thomas Fenwick, Joseph Lamb, and John Stephenson.[31]

Attempting to distinguish between country gentry and urban professional groups is in many respects an artificial exercise, since many individuals had business or family ties with both interests. The initiative for opening a subscription list to raise money for the project, for example, came from William Lowes, a retired Newcastle attorney who was also squire of Ridley Hall, and was appointed High Sheriff of Northumberland in 1773.[32] The corporation of Newcastle collectively purchased eight shares, less than a one per cent share in the rooms, but this statistic under-represents the vested interests of the corporation, since nearly all of the members of the common council bought shares on an individual basis. For example, to take a 'snapshot' of the year in which Newcastle's first town directory was produced (1778) the Mayor, Recorder, seven aldermen, nine

[27] Whitehead, *Directory* (1782), *passim*.

[28] Welford, *Men of Mark*, I, pp. 656-8.

[29] TWRO/160/1/58.

[30] Whitehead, *Directory* (1778); John Fenwick, *Obituaries of Eminent Persons* (Newcastle, 1840) contains a cutting from the *Newcastle Courant* (20 February 1823) regarding a fatal accident at the Theatre Royal. It is subscribed 'Nath. Clayton, Chairman', who announced the resignation of his chair.

[31] Ibid. See also NCL/L942.82/N5370 'Proprietors of the New Assembly rooms, 1776'.

[32] Richard Welford, *Men of Mark 'Twixt Tyne and Tweed*, III (London and Newcastle, 1895), 108-9.

members of the Common Council, and the Town Clerk, were also Proprietors of the Newcastle Assembly rooms.[33] The way in which certain local families dominated public office and exerted dynastic influence is also in evidence through their pattern of investment in the assembly rooms. Four members of the Fenwick family, for example, were shareholders in the rooms: William Fenwick of Bywell, MP for Northumberland in 1774; his son, William junior; John Fenwick, an attorney of Pilgrim Street; and Thomas Fenwick, a landowner from the Earsden branch of the family.[34] It is also notable that the assembly rooms galvanised the investment of local men of national standing. One investor, the Newcastle attorney Matthew Duane, for example, was a Fellow of the Royal Society and trustee of the British Museum, and was described posthumously as 'a polite scholar, a man of high culture, of acknowledged taste in painting and music'.[35]

The 22% of subscribers whose status is recorded as 'unknown' in Table 8.1 were unlikely to come from any single social or occupational grouping, but were more likely to be of a lower status than their more eminent and easily identifiable counterparts among the gentry and nobility. It is impossible to conjecture the change that would be effected to the overall social profile of subscribers were their identity to be traced. Certain social parameters are suggested, however, by the fact that all of these shareholders bought just one or two shares each, a minimal investment compared to the hundreds of pounds invested by Lord Ravensworth or the duke of Northumberland. On the other hand, £25 or £50 represented a considerable sum of money to the majority of people in the Newcastle area, and would have been beyond the means even of most middling-sort incomes. Some of the more obscure shareholders have been traced, and their backgrounds suggest at least some of these 'unknown' subscribers would have gained an income from trade. Among the 7% of subscribers known to have come from a trading background was George Anderson, a self-made bricklayer and house builder who claimed a rather spurious descent from a gentry family of the same name. Anderson's entry into polite society was facilitated by his fortune. Not only did he buy shares in the assembly rooms, but he succeeded in purchasing Anderson Place, one of the finest houses in the town, from Sir Thomas Blackett in 1782.[36] The land surveyor and bookseller John Bell also subscribed to the assembly rooms, a figure in Newcastle's literary scene who was manager to Solomon Hodgson, the proprietor of the *Newcastle Chronicle*.[37]

Among the subscribers, there is little evidence of exclusion on the basis of religion, although the vast majority was Anglican. One exception was John Silvertop, a member of an ancient Catholic family whose estates were at Minsteracres and Ponteland, was a shareholder in the Rooms, which reflected the

---

[33] William Whitehead, *Whitehead's Newcastle Directory for 1778* (Newcastle, 1778), facsimile edition edited by J. R. Boyle (Newcastle, 1889).

[34] NCL/1942.82/N5370.

[35] Welford, *Men of Mark*, II, pp. 122-4.

[36] Welford, *Men of Mark*, II, pp. 59-60.

[37] Peter Isaac, 'The Earliest Proprietors of the *Newcastle Chronicle*', in Isaac, *Newspapers in the Northeast*, pp. 153-6.

presence of a number of important Catholic families in the North East.[38] There are, however, no nonconformists among the subscribers to the assembly rooms, but perhaps we would not expect to find them celebrating a new monument to pleasure. The contemporary attitude of nonconformists towards assemblies was well illustrated by the Baptist John Stutterd of Colne in Lancashire, in a letter to his brother, Thomas. In his correspondence, John described how a married couple in his congregation, the Adamsons, had caused a stir by going to an assembly at an inn, the 'Red Lyon' in Colne. Mrs Adamson had gone so far as to take part in the dancing, in spite of the fact that her husband had sought the deliberation of the dissenting ministers as to whether 'there would be any Harm in his going to the Assembly, if it was only for Half an Hour'.[39] The reply he received was unequivocal, 'They Answered – there would'.

Assemblies caused similar controversy among nonconformists in Newcastle. Church land was being appropriated for the construction of what some construed to be a heathen temple of pleasure: a special act of parliament was required to permit the lease of church land.[40] The assembly rooms were seen as the preserve of the 'gentlemen of Newcastle', a monument to the governing élite whose collusion in the vogue for polite culture was condemned as luxury and dissipation.[41] Newton's design seemed to confirm their worst fears, evoking for some the decadence of ancient Greece and Rome. Similar concerns were voiced in Newcastle over David Stephenson's design for All Saints' church during the 1780s, which supporters thought displayed 'a tasteful combination of architectural design, selected from the purest models of antiquity, and... a graceful and finished appearance'.[42] As at the assembly rooms, critics of All Saints' classical features 'disputed the propriety of their application' on sacred turf. The corporation of Newcastle's investment in the assembly rooms seemed particularly galling to those who believed there were more pressing and practical concerns, such as replacing

[38] Revd. William Turner described in 1801 how the Society of Protestant Dissenters in Hanover-square had thrived in Newcastle for more than a century. There were six congregations of Presbyterians in the town, a congregation of Independents, and another of 'Particular' Baptists: two large societies of the old Wesleyan Methodists, and one of the new 'Kilhamites'. There were also two Roman Catholic Chapels, and a group of Quakers – 'All these live together, on the whole, very peaceably; and while they maintain, with sufficient zeal, their respective tenets and modes, they can often, with great harmony, join with each other in plans for the public benefit, either in a charitable or a literary way.' Revd. William Turner, *Monthly Magazine* (May and June, 1801). See also the chapter on Quakers by Richard C. Allen in this collection.

[39] Stutterd Papers, Huntington Library, San Marino, California; John Stutterd to Thomas Stutterd (21 February 1785), uncatalogued.

[40] Act of Parliament (14 Geo. III) reproduced in Brand, *History of Newcastle*, I, Appendix, p. 595.

[41] John Sekora, in *Luxury. The Concept in Western Thought, Eden to Smollett* (Baltimore, 1977), pp. 1-9, 40-42, 66-67 and *passim*, argues that the eighteenth century was a turning point, a moment when classical ideas about luxury were challenged, with writers such as Mandeville, Smollett and Fielding identifying luxury as the root cause of the nation's ills. Neo-classicism evoked not only the decadence of ancient Rome, but suggested that the British Empire could meet a similar fate. Contrary to this position was the opinion that the exercise of taste could 'serve to moralize pleasure and legitimize leisure and luxury expenditure'. See Stephen Copley, 'The Fine Arts in Eighteenth-Century Polite Culture', in John Barrell (ed.) *Painting and the Politics of Culture. New Essays on British Art, 1700-1850* (Oxford, 1992), p. 16.

[42] Sopwith, *Historical and Descriptive Account*, p. 72.

the bridges across the Tyne that had been swept away in the storms of 1771.[43] James Murray, minister of the High Bridge Presbyterian congregation, and political activist against the enclosure movement, denounced the assembly rooms as a sign that 'Luxury had advanced to/ A state of perfection/ Unknown in any former period', with his own version of the founders' inscription:

When a stagnation
Of trade, and the high price of provisions,
Had reduced the poor to the greatest extremity;
When the bridge, once over Tyne,
At Newcastle, remained
Entomb'd in the depths of the river,
A heap of ruins,
A chaos of disorder;
To their everlasting disgrace, the gentlemen of Newcastle
Continue to waste their time,
And spend their substance,
In celebrating the rites of *Venus*, and the ceremonies of *Bacchus*.
Five thousand
Pounds were rais'd by subscription,
Through a vicious emulation to excel in politeness;
And land, devoted to pious purposes,
Was sold by the Vicar, a thing
Unknown in any former period;
And this fabric
was raised
On the ruins of religion, and the morals of mankind.
The pious sanction of William L—s, Esq.,
Engraved on brass, continues to show the profligacy of this age.[44]

Also notable by their absence from the subscription list were the Anglican clergy, whose modest incomes may have prevented them from buying shares in the new building even if it had met with their approval. Once the rooms had been built, however, many clergymen paid to join the Subscription Coffee Room, housed within the Westgate Street building, and there is evidence that some attended assemblies.[45]

While there is some evidence that nonconformist religion divided Newcastle society, preventing dissenters from participating in this important aspect of public life, other evidence suggests that the new assembly rooms fostered a broad political appeal. Proposals for building the assembly rooms spanned the politically sensitive period of the 1774 general election; it is therefore noteworthy

---

[43] The only bridge across the Tyne following the floods of that year was at Corbridge. John Talbot White, *The Scottish Border and Northumberland* (London, 1973), p. 133.

[44] James Murray, *Freemen's Magazine* [n.d.], reproduced in Welford, *Men of Mark*, III, 109. For an account of Murray's political activism in the elections of 1774 and campaign against the Newcastle Town Moor enclosures, see Jeffrey Smith, 'James Murray (1732-1782): Radical and Dissenter', *North East History*, 32 (1998), 55-79.

[45] One example was Louis Dutens, rector of Elsdon (see below).

that the assembly rooms project drew support regardless of political differences. In the subscription book, George Grieve, a radical with republican sympathies and friend of Marat, joined his political enemy, Lord Algernon Percy, whom he helped to defeat in the Northumberland elections of that year.[46] Notably, there were also several female shareholders: Lady Allgood (wife of Sir Lancelot), Lady Erroll, Miss Clennell (whose share quickly passed to her nephew Percival), Mrs Dixon, Mrs Charleton and Mrs Atlee. The latter was a wealthy widow, who patronised several building projects in the town: in 1787, she paid for the expensive mahogany interior of the newly built All Saints' Church.[47] While it would be rash to suggest that the assembly rooms fostered a new social and political consensus in Newcastle, it is evident that certain individuals who were excluded from institutionalised politics (with the exception of nonconformists) found, through their patronage of the rooms, a means of participating in the public life of the town. The Newcastle assemblies contrasted sharply with those in Durham, which were divided according to whether or not the party supported the bishop's candidate in contested elections.[48] This suggests that, even between neighbouring towns, assemblies had a highly localised character, and could either reflect local power struggles, or provide a space in which the imperative of polite association overcame political disagreement. Here, the size of the venue was likely to be a highly influential factor; the assemblies at Newcastle, especially at the high points of the social calendar, were simply too large to be dominated by any one political faction. This brings us to a closer examination of how the assembly rooms were managed, and the effect they had upon the crowds that passed through their doors.

II

There are conflicting reports over the total cost of building and furnishing the Newcastle assembly rooms and the amount raised to pay for them by subscription. Newcastle's historian John Brand quoted accounts for 1776/7, which gave a figure of £6701 for the total cost of the Rooms.[49] This was considerably more than the £5840 quoted as being raised by subscription in the 1785 handlist. The problem seems to have been one of capital rather than income, brought on mainly by the cost of completing the building and furnishing its lavish interior. The total cost of building and furnishing the Newcastle assembly rooms was more than double the

---

46 Welford, *Men of Mark*, II, pp. 398-402.

47 The status of these women, apart from that of Lady Erroll and Lady Allgood, is unknown. See also T. Sopwith, *A Historical and Descriptive Account of All Saints' Church in Newcastle upon Tyne, Illustrated with Plans, Views, & Architectural Details* (Newcastle, 1824), pp. 61-2. Deliberation over whether pews should be mahogany or oak was resolved by Mrs Atlee in a letter addressed to Alderman H. Hornby, one of the trustees (dated 16 February 1787), observing 'that as mahogany was both more durable and ornamental than oak, and understanding that the difference of price only amounted to about £100, she proposed to give the sum as soon as the woodwork was begun'.

48 Palace Green Library, University of Durham, Baker Baker [sic] Papers/14/86a, Judith Baker, chronology of 'Memorable Events' (1746 to 1776).

49 John Brand, *History and Antiquities of the Town and County of Newcastle upon Tyne* (London, 1789), I, pp. 121-2 quotes 'Printed state of the accounts for June 24th 1776, and ending June 17th, 1777'.

cost of many other provincial rooms; those in Bristol, for example, had cost £3600, the rooms in Sheffield, £3000.[50] At the outset, the financial position of the project was uncertain. In the first year of opening, the Trustees of the Newcastle assembly rooms borrowed £300 from Aubone Surtees the banker, and £150 from John Graham Clarke Esq. A meeting of the Assembly Rooms Council resolved that the only way out of the difficulty was to borrow more money. There followed several years of financial wrangling, as Surtees called in his loan for an unknown reason. The Proprietors were forced to advertise in the Newcastle papers in March 1777 for a creditor, and were saved through the intervention of a wealthy spinster of the town, Dorothy Cresswell, who agreed to lend them £500 upon the payment of an annuity of £50 per year.[51] Witnesses to this agreement, on 23 April 1787, were: the physician Dr John Hall; William Blakeney Esq.; Alderman William Cramlington; Richard Chambers, Sheriff of Newcastle; Thomas Gaull and Miles Monkhouse, wine merchants; and Ralph Heron, an attorney of Pilgrim Street, Newcastle.[52] The reputation and popularity of the assembly rooms does not seem to have been harmed by this temporary financial hitch, although the necessity of raising a loan to cover a shortfall of approximately 12-15% of the capital cost illustrates the financial risk that was incurred in undertaking what was effectively a joint-stock building project.[53]

The Newcastle assembly rooms took just over two years to complete from the laying of the foundation stone. The last assembly at the old rooms in Groat Market was held on 8 April 1776, following which the entire stock of goods and furniture was sold by auction, including several dozen tea spoons, a 'great quantity of tea table china'; two large boilers, kettles, tea trays, tables, chairs and looking glasses, together with thirty benches or seats covered with red cloth.[54] Newcastle's assemblies were about to move into a different league. On entering the new building, the visitor was confronted by the magnificent sweeping staircase. In the upstairs ballroom, seven enormous glass chandeliers (two more than in most other public ballrooms) provided glittering illumination. Original tradesmen's receipts for decoration and repair to the assembly rooms during the 1780s give some idea of the opulent appearance of the interior. The original colour scheme was green and gold, with green silk curtains, gilt-edged woodwork and brass door fittings.[55] All the rooms contained brand new furniture, including oval card tables and chairs in fashionable mahogany, which (as Adrian Green reminds us in his chapter on Betty Bowes) were physical embodiments of provincial gentility.[56] The table covers were made of green cloth and decorated with lace and silk, and even the bell handles for

---

[50] Borsay, *English Urban Renaissance*, pp. 158-9.

[51] TWRO/160/1/1.

[52] Ibid. See also Whitehead, *Directory* (1778), passim.

[53] Chalkin, 'Capital Expenditure', 57-62.

[54] *Newcastle Courant* (6 April 1776).

[55] TWRO/160/1/88. Bartholomew Kent charged the Committee of the New Subscription Rooms £10/16s for recovering chairs, £2 10s for covering two doors 'with fine Green frize brass Nails &c/', and green silk for curtains.

[56] TWRO/160/1/90. In November 1788, a joiner spent 17 days mending mahogany furniture after the wear and tear of the summer season.

summoning servants were made of ivory.[57] The rooms were a stimulus for the local economy: journeymen craftsmen maintained the fabric of the building and its décor, grocers supplied tea, coffee and other refreshments, chandlers procured hundreds of candles to light the rooms, which were heated with plentiful local coal, and Newcastle musicians provided the music for the minuets and country dances. Other luxuries were added after the rooms had opened, such as a large 'Scotch Carpet' seven by five yards in size that cost nearly seven pounds, a backgammon table, and a portrait of the late Sir Walter Blackett by a local artist, William Hilton, which cost a further £6 6s.[58]

The opening of the new assembly rooms during Newcastle race week in June, 1776 was announced in the *Newcastle Courant*, with three assemblies held in the first week. Ladies and gentlemen were requested to order their carriages to set them down at the gate next to the vicarage, to avoid collision with those arriving in sedan chairs.[59] A reasonably modest report followed in the local press one week later:

> Monday night the new Assembly rooms were opened, when there was a very numerous and brilliant company, who expressed great pleasure at the elegance of the rooms. The assembly was opened by Sir William Loraine, Bart. with Mrs Bell, jun. and Sir Matthew White Ridley, Bart. with Miss Allgood.[60]

The first assize week assemblies in August also met with general satisfaction ('This week there has been a great company in town, and the assemblies and concert very numerous and brilliant').[61]

The assembly room accounts for 1796/7 indicate the volume of people attending, and the wide seasonal variation in the size of assemblies. Race week in June 1796 drew 150 people to an assembly, while one month later, a total of 655 tickets was sold for the two assize week assemblies. In the same financial year, 181 and 118 tickets were sold for the October and January Guild assemblies, whereas the more usual figure for a subscription assembly between October and April was 40 to 50 people.[62] The usual price of three shillings for a ticket to an off-season assembly was raised in the summer to five shillings, presumably to capitalise upon the influx of summer visitors. Subscription assemblies varied in price: by the turn of the century, ladies paid ten shillings for a subscription to the entire season of winter assemblies, gentlemen fourteen shillings, and non-subscribers five shillings per assembly.[63] The rooms could also be hired for a fee of £2 2s. In 1780/1, for example, a musical concert was staged at the assembly

[57] TWRO/160/1/94.

[58] TWRO/160/1/58, 92, 94. The backgammon table, purchased in November 1793, cost £1 7s 6d.

[59] *Newcastle Courant* (22 June 1776).

[60] Ibid. (29 June 1776).

[61] Ibid. (10 August 1776).

[62] TWRO/160/1/29. Assembly Room General Accounts 1796/7.

[63] TWRO/160/56 'Subscription Card and Quadrille Assemblies' [n.d.].

rooms by Miss Harwood; Mr Hawdon the organist held a subscription concert, and the band of the 10th Regiment provided an entertainment.[64]

Surviving accounts indicate that the Assembly Rooms Committee, elected by shareholders to oversee financial management and decision making, was able to balance annual income and expenditure in the years 1776-1800. In the year from June 1780 to June 1781, for example, the total income balanced the outgoings of £418 5s. Just under one half of the expenditure was due to ground rent, land tax, 'contribution tax', and miscellaneous other charges such as the water rent.[65] The greatest single expense in the running of the Newcastle assembly rooms was lighting: over £115 was spent on candles in this year alone, with an additional £23 on coals for heating. Unsurprisingly, the rooms were also insured against fire, at an annual premium of just over six pounds.[66] These bills were offset against an income from the subscription assemblies, and from renting out the rooms. In 1780/1, £64 10s was taken in race week, £165 5s in assize week, and £48 6s for miscellaneous 'Dancing Assemblies' paid by subscription. The considerable sum of £111 6s was raised from non-subscribers.[67] Small sums of money were occasionally raised by the sale of odd pieces of furniture and candle ends, an indication of cautious housekeeping. It is unlikely that dividends were paid annually to the proprietors, although an account of the state of the Rooms was sent to them each year.[68] Elsewhere, for example, at the assembly rooms in Beccles, a share of £25 initially yielded a 5% return, although it is evident that the profits to be made from such a venture fell towards the end of the eighteenth century.[69] It is doubtful that shareholders regarded investment in the Newcastle assembly rooms as primarily a commercial venture, but rather as a form of social investment that increased their standing in their local town and region. Like those shareholders in the York assembly rooms who did not bother to collect their dividends, their main interest 'was in contributing to the establishment of a cultural activity from which they were expected to benefit'.[70]

Overall, contemporary sources indicate the success and popularity of the Newcastle assembly rooms in the first two decades of the building's existence, and the degree to which local élites capitalised upon their investment in the rooms through the annual rituals of public display. The detail of managing this extravagant capital building project, and raising funds to cover the unusually large deficit, was left up to a select group of experienced businessmen. This was of little

---

64 TWRO/160/221.

65 The average expenditure for the period 1776 to 1800 remained at approximately £400 per ann. In 1799, the Assembly rooms were charged £49 8s 8d for land tax, poor cess, land cess &c., £99 4s 6d in Contribution tax, £21 Ground rent, £2 in water rent, which accounted for approximately £172 out of £393 total outgoings. See TWRO/160/1/16, Annual Account, June 1798 to June 1799.

66 TWRO Misc Letters 160/203.

67 TWRO/160/221; 'Annual Account of Receipts and Payments on Account of Assembly rooms commencing 23 June 1780 and Ending 18 June 1781'.

68 Letter from Cuthbert Shafto to Richard Fisher, Hexham (27 October 1784). Shafto was George Delaval's executor, and requested that he should receive Mr. Delaval's copy of the assembly rooms' annual report. TWRO Misc Letters 160/203.

69 Dain, 'Assemblies and Polite Leisure', 15.

70 Chalkin, 'Building for Culture', 66.

concern to the gentry and civic élites, one-off investors for whom the building was a decorous new space in which the rituals of courtship could be performed and local ties of mutual allegiance reinforced. It is to the social uses of this space in its brief heyday that we now turn our attention.

III

It is through the eyes of visitors to Newcastle from London that we gain a sense that the town's cultural life surpassed expectations, which if nothing else is an indictment of long-standing metropolitan prejudices about the North. Contrary to her expectations, Elizabeth Montagu found that in Newcastle 'The desire of pleasure and love of dissipation rages here as much as in London'. She attended concerts, assemblies and balls, and reflected that if 'remote' provincial towns had become centres of such activity: 'in a little while if one would enjoy retired leisure one must dwell amidst inaccessible mountains and unnavigable rivers'.[71] Elizabeth revelled in the freedom she found in Newcastle to engage fully in the social life of the town and, in reference to the ceremony for creating a Freeman of the city (a ritual debarred to women) she explained that she was 'taking my freedom, not out of a gold box, but by entering into all the diversions of the place.'[72] Other visitors and residents remarked upon the number of women who took part in public social occasions in Newcastle. Earlier in the century, the rector of Elsdon, Louis Dutens, commended the range of eligible young women at Newcastle assemblies to his cousin: 'you find there 40, 50, 60 women, of whom 20 will be Beauties whom one would admire in London'.[73] The gentlewoman Elizabeth Cotesworth remarked in a letter to her brother Robert (heir to Park House in Gateshead): 'ye lasses have been at ye assembly, Kate bid me tell you she had a great loss of you for there was not a man asked her to dance, tho my sister had four to her share.'[74] Assemblies were an important source of news and gossip among networks of female correspondents. Rhoda Astley of Seaton Delaval wrote to her sister-in-law Lady Delaval in Lincolnshire: 'Yesterday sennight we were all of us at Newcastle Assembly. There was a great deal of good company. It was the day of the Mayor's Feast. Ridley is Mayor. My Lady Blackett was there, and made many inquiries after you.'[75] The mixed-sex character of the assembly was in contrast to other all-male forms of sociability: in Newcastle, the representatives of the landed gentry, wealthy merchants and civic officials traditionally removed from the all-male environment of their Guild meeting to the assembly rooms for their evening

---

[71] Elizabeth Montagu to Miss Carter, Newcastle (24 October 1760). In Emily J. Climenson (ed.) *Elizabeth Montagu: the Queen of the Bluestockings. Her Correspondence from 1720-1761*, pp. 207-8.

[72] Ibid.; *Elizabeth Montagu*, p. 205.

[73] '...vous y trouver 40, 50, 60 Femmes, don't 20 seront des Beautés qu'on admirent à Londres'. NCL/L920/B817.

[74] TWRO/CP/3/75, Elizabeth Cotesworth to Robert Cotesworth (30 October 1724).

[75] N[orthumberland] R[ecord] O[ffice]/ 650/D12, Rhoda Astley to Lady Delaval, Seaton Delaval (15 October 1751).

entertainment.[76] Courtship intrigues and dancing were an inextricable feature of assemblies, and were mainly of interest to young people and their chaperones. The middle aged coal magnate George Liddell told his friend William Cotesworth that he preferred to go drinking with the aldermen of Newcastle 'whilst the Young women were at ye Assembly'.[77]

The Newcastle assembly rooms were a significant fixture for 'coming out' in polite society for the sixteen-year-old Annabella Carr, the daughter of a wealthy Newcastle merchant. Her letter to her brother John describes her choice of dancing partners at an Election Ball:

> I danced with (to use Papa's expression) the Baronet Williamson who I also dined with last Monday, so that I should not be greatly surprised if you should hear a former report circulated you... This particular attention to your humble servant was noticed by the whole room and people are apt to put wrong constructions on behaviour so public... I forgot to tell you that Bowes very politely asked me to dance with him at the last Guild Assembly as did Lord Lindores and Baron Norton [son of Lord Grantley] but I was engaged to Williamson – this is ostentation but it is to let you know I'm in fashion with the Beaux at present.[78]

Annabella also met Lord Lumley, heir to Lord Scarborough's considerable fortune, at a Newcastle assembly, but the unfortunate young man put Annabella off by his lack of dancing skills: 'On Wed. we went to the assemblies and I danced with Lord Lumley. He dined with us twice in the course of the week, but is amazingly worse in his dancing, much more ridiculous than ever – tho his attentive polite behaviour makes up for every deficiency'.[79] Lord Lumley's opinion of Annabella is not recorded.

A Master of Ceremonies presided over the dancing at the Newcastle assembly rooms, which was similar to the custom started at Bath.[80] A gentleman intending to participate in the country dances drew a number before entering the Rooms, which determined his place for the entire evening. A different etiquette applied for the minuets. Ladies 'entitled to Precedency' were placed in descending order of rank at the head of the sets, while the rest had to take their chances 'in the Order in which she shall happen to fit'. Country dances consisted of sets of not

---

[76] For example, Sir Walter Blackett and Sir Thomas Clavering presided over the Michaelmas Guild of 1762 before proceeding to another 'brilliant Assembly' at the Old Assembly rooms, sponsored by the Duke of Portland. See *Newcastle Courant* (16 October 1762).

[77] TWRO/CP/1/80, George Liddell to William Cotesworth, Ravensworth Castle (28 May 1725).

[78] Arabella Carr to John Carr, October 1780. Quoted in A. W. Purdue, *Merchants and Gentry in North-East England, 1650-1830* (Sunderland, 1999), p. 195. 'Baronet' Williamson was probably Robert Hopper Williamson, Recorder of Newcastle 1794-1825, who seems to have lived up to his reputation for pretension when he claimed that he had 'never walked Newcastle streets for pleasure in his lifetime.' In Harbottle, *William Turner*, p. 54; Anon., *Collectanea Curiosa: Northumberland, Durham and Newcastle*, I (n.d.), pp. xlvi-xlvii.

[79] Arabella Carr to John Carr (10 August 1781). Quoted in Purdue, *Gentry*, p. 195.

[80] Reproduced in *Short History of the Old Assembly rooms*, p. 13. The Assembly rooms' Subscription book records that one of the Proprietors, Mr Charles Williams, at one time undertook this role. See NCL/L942.82/N5370.

more than fifteen couples, and strict rules were laid down so that none could monopolise the dance floor. No couple was permitted to leave the dance floor until the end of the dance, except 'in Case of Illness'. Minuets started at eight o'clock in the evening, with a break for tea at the discretion of the Master of Ceremonies. Caroline Twistleton recorded in her memoirs that in January, 1782, her grandfather Ralph Carr and his party stayed dancing at a Guild assembly until two o'clock in the morning.[81] Another prerequisite was that strangers should be introduced to the Master of Ceremonies 'that proper attention may be paid to them'. Jane Austen's portrayal of Mr Darcy's discomfort at being the newcomer at an assembly under close scrutiny seems to have been an accurate portrayal of the interest and singular attention that was shown to strangers at provincial assemblies.[82] The *Gentleman's Magazine* satirised this phenomenon in 'A letter from Hull to a Leeds Merchant': 'No sooner entered in the room,/But whispers fly – whence does he come?/Who or what is he? Can you guess?/Or what estate may he possess?'[83]

The 'Orders and Regulations' for the Newcastle assemblies express a conventional concern with correct dress and deportment, but indicate no difficulties over the mixing of rank, which was not universally the case throughout England. At the county assembly rooms in Lincoln, by contrast, subscriptions were open only to those 'whose quality and relation to the county should make it proper', while in Knutsford in 1790, a visitor was told that 'none but gentility' were admitted to the assemblies there 'but *on no account* any tradesmen'.[84] The diarist John Marsh recalled an episode in his youth when, as Master of Ceremonies in Romsey, he invoked the anger of his guardian, Mrs Daman, for inviting a shoemaker's son to subscribe to the assemblies there.[85] A comparative lack of social discrimination at assemblies in Newcastle was indicative of the town's commercial character, which fostered greater acceptability of 'new money' than elsewhere. Elizabeth Montagu was impressed by the size and splendour of social occasions in Newcastle, but commented that conversation was 'less polite' than in London, since the subject of discussion always turned upon money: 'the moment you name a man, you are told what he is worth, the losses he has had, or the profit he has made by coal mines'. Every gentleman, she observed, was 'as solicitous in the pursuit of gain as a tradesman'.[86] Certainly a remarkable range of social ranks could be present at the larger assemblies during the summer season: Lord Tankerville scandalised Newcastle society when he eloped with Miss Colville, a butcher's daughter whom he met at an assize ball.[87]

The survival of an (undated) original subscription list to the card and quadrille assemblies at Newcastle provides an insight into the social and familial groupings of assembly-goers during the quieter winter months. It suggests that the

---

81 Purdue, *Gentry*, p. 195.
82 Austen, *Pride and Prejudice*, pp. 58-9.
83 Jackson, *Hull in the Eighteenth Century*, p. 268.
84 Hill, *Georgian Lincoln*, 15; Girouard, *English Town*, p. 134.
85 John Marsh, 'History of my Private Life', Huntington Library, San Marino, California, HM54457, vol. 3 (January 1770), pp. 8-10.
86 Climenson, *Elizabeth Montagu*, pp. 149, 207-8.
87 Dain, 'Assemblies and Polite Leisure', 6.

range of backgrounds of assembly-goers on these occasions was more limited than at the larger 'landmark' assemblies.[88] Seventy-eight people subscribed to the winter season with an exactly 50:50 male/female ratio, although this may have been altered by the appearance of non-subscribers on the night.[89] The subscribers included nine married couples, six married women without their husbands (who may also have been widows) nineteen lone men, and twenty-one single women, who were usually accompanied by one or both parents, or another close relative. One example of such a grouping was Mrs Alice Losh, wife of William Losh, an entrepreneurial businessman who founded the Walker Iron Works. She was accompanied by her unmarried nieces Miss Sara Losh and Miss Margaret Losh, the daughters of William's brother John. They were well connected in Newcastle: their origin was among the Cumberland gentry and they were related to the Liddells, Lord Ravensworth's family. John Losh had business connections with the banker Aubone Surtees, and another brother, James, was one of the founder members of the Newcastle Literary and Philosophical Society.[90] There was only one titled couple subscribing to these assemblies, Sir Hugh and Lady Gough, and the Sheriff of Newcastle was the highest civic dignitary present. There was notably a strong military presence at these assemblies: thirteen officers from the 22nd Regiment and 4th Dragoon Guards, bringing a show of uniforms. The potential for courtship on this occasion, given the equal ratio of men and women, and the high proportion of unmarried people, is evident, as is the general social parity between the subscribers. Newcastle's élite may have been less inhibited about discussing trade than 'polite' company elsewhere, but there is scant evidence that tradesmen below the rank of merchants were a substantial presence at many public social gatherings at the assembly rooms. On the contrary, the presence of families such as the Loshes among the 'core' group of assembly-goers in Newcastle at the end of the eighteenth century, is a reminder of the continuing influence of local gentry, who neither had qualms about enriching themselves through commercial enterprise, or apparently about discussing their profits in public.

Overall, in an era when it was customary for county gentry to spend part of the year away from the North-East (in London, Bath, or in northern spa towns and resorts such as Harrogate or Scarborough) the provision of splendid new assembly rooms on their doorsteps in Newcastle provided an extra venue for polite sociability that was embraced enthusiastically, particularly by younger unmarried men and women. The early diversification of the assembly rooms in Newcastle as a venue for a variety of concerts, musical evenings, civic occasions and private functions ensured that the building continued to be a popular venue the nineteenth century even though assemblies themselves went out of fashion. In a long term perspective, the assembly rooms project marked the beginning of the architectural development of Newcastle in earnest in the last quarter of the eighteenth century,

---

[88] TWRO/1650/56, 'Subscription Card & Quadrille Assemblies'. The list probably dates from the early nineteenth century, when the quadrille succeeded the minuet as a more fashionable dance.
[89] Ibid.
[90] Harbottle, *William Turner*, pp. 64-5; Welford, *Men of Mark*, III, pp. 92-3. For further information on the influence of the Losh family, see Paul Usherwood's chapter in this collection.

just before the era of Dobson and Grainger.[91] Another local architect, David Stephenson, was inspired by plans of a Birmingham theatre built in 1774 to design a 'delicate brick façade' for the new 1,350-capacity Theatre Royal that opened in Newcastle in 1788. By 1801, the Unitarian minister William Turner recorded in the *Monthly Magazine* that the members of the musical society in Newcastle were 'at present exerting themselves to procure subscriptions for building a music-hall, upon the plan of those at Manchester and Liverpool'.[92] His proposals for the Literary and Philosophical society at Newcastle, which had its inaugural meetings at the Newcastle assembly rooms, were based upon a similar society in Manchester.[93]

In the early nineteenth century, amid a growing number of monumental buildings in Newcastle, the assembly rooms were still a popular though increasingly sporadic venue for important local events, playing host, for example, to a grand ball held in honour of a visit by the duke of Wellington in 1827, and a subsequent dinner commemorating the opening of the Newcastle and Darlington railway. The middle classes gradually withdrew into new forms of private sociability, and though the ancient ruling families of the North-East maintained a stranglehold upon property and civic government, faced with social change and economic challenges from new commercial interests in the great era of industrial expansion, the commingling of different classes in ritualised forms of public leisure was replaced by a retreat into increasingly stratified and domestic sociability.[94]

IV

This chapter has illustrated how the cultural life of Newcastle expanded in the last quarter of the eighteenth century through the construction of new assembly rooms. It was not enough simply to build new premises: the scale of the building and its rich furnishings were outward signs of Newcastle's cultural ambition. The rooms were in keeping with the national taste for polite sociability, but were designed by a local architect, funded according to local initiative, and (unlike resorts such as Bath and Brighton) patronised for most of the year by local families. The assembly rooms project was by no means dominated either by ancient landed interests or the civic élite, but was a powerful synthesis of the two, with the former contributing a large amount of capital, and the latter dedicating their money and their

---

[91] Thomas Faulkner and Andrew Greg, *John Dobson, Architect of the North East* (Newcastle, 2001), pp. 121-2.

[92] 'V.F.' [Revd. William Turner], *Monthly Magazine* (March-June 1801).

[93] Ibid.

[94] On the rise of bourgeois family values, see Leonore Davidoff and Catherine Hall, *Family Fortunes. Men and Women of the English Middle Class, 1780-1850* (London, 1987); *Short History*, pp. 6-7. By the beginning of the twentieth century, the rooms had passed into private hands. Faced with indifference from the city council, the building was threatened with demolition, but (thanks to the current owners) was saved and restored, the original façade altered by the later addition of a portico and a sign proclaiming 'The Old Assembly Rooms'.

administrative expertise to organising and running the rooms. This pattern was repeated in many of the philanthropic ventures that were a common feature of the social and cultural development of towns throughout Georgian England. A parallel example is to be found in the foundation of eighteenth-century infirmaries, which were often favoured with the prestige of titled patrons, while day to day administration was overseen by a board of local professionals and other men of middling status.[95]

The project appealed to influential members of society in the town and its three neighbouring counties. William Lowes took pains, for example, to ensure that the county nobility and greater gentry were kept informed of how the money they had invested in the project was being spent, even though they did not attend shareholders' meetings in Newcastle. The minutes of a 'numerous Meeting of the Subscribers for building the New Assembly-Rooms', held at the Turk's Head Inn on 7 February 1774, recorded an order 'That the Secretaries shall transmit to the several Noblemen of Northumberland and Durham, the Resolutions of this Meeting.'[96] The duke of Northumberland, earl Percy, Lord Algernon Percy, Sir John Hussey Delaval, and Sir Walter Blackett were thus kept informed of developments, and could give their seal of approval at a distance, without having to involve themselves in the decision-making process. Jonathan Barry has argued that development in the cultural life of eighteenth-century provincial towns witnessed the 'partisan exploitation of culture', as witnessed in the popular press. There is no doubt that cultural developments had a political dimension, as the satirical verse of James Murray illustrates. Certain assemblies in England took on a partisan character, with (for example) separate assemblies for Whigs and Tories, but there is little evidence that the Newcastle assemblies manifested any such divisions, and the diverse political loyalties of subscribers is positive evidence to the contrary.[97] This lack of partisan division reflected the continuing concentration of power in the hands of the corporation of Newcastle, with strong traditional and familial ties to the town's hinterland via the gentry of three counties frequently overriding party concerns, at least before 1800.

We have seen how the social limits of polite culture in Newcastle varied at different times of the year, and according to the occasion. In the 'leisure cycle'[98] of the town, there were seasonal fluctuations in the size and social composition of Newcastle assemblies, involving a greater participation of the nobility and county gentry of North-East England at the guild, assize and race assemblies in July, August and October, than in the programme of regular smaller assemblies that took place during the quieter winter months. The 'landmark' Newcastle assemblies in the summer months were also characterised by an unusually broad selection of varying 'degrees' of people, including the middling sort of tradesmen, a feature that was remarkable to visitors from southern towns where more rigid rules of

---

95 See A. Borsay, *Medicine and Charity in Georgian Bath* (New York and London, 1999).

96 TWRO, Cotesworth Ms., CT/6/11.

97 See Barry, 'The Press and the Politics of Culture in Bristol, 1660-1775', in Jeremy Black and Jeremy Gregory (eds), *Culture, Politics and Society in Britain, 1660-1800* (Manchester, 1997), pp. 50-52.

98 A term suggested by Peter Borsay, *pers. com.*

social segregation were often applied. The son of a nobleman could meet and marry the daughter of a Newcastle tradesman at an assize ball, but the smaller subscription assemblies were characterised by a more socially homogeneous company, drawn from Newcastle's professional groups, who often had close familial ties with the neighbouring county gentry.

The Newcastle assembly rooms had an impact that extended beyond the town to a regional level. The grandeur of the rooms, and the prestigious events that were held there at regular intervals, elevated Newcastle's cultural status in relation to other urban centres in the North-East. The cultural development of Newcastle as a 'polite' town thus contained an element of bravado. The building programmes and improvements that were made during the last quarter of the eighteenth century certainly lent a new glamour to the smarter parts of town, but this should not be seen as reflective of Newcastle's inevitable progress towards predominance in the region. From a cultural perspective, Newcastle undoubtedly became the preferred venue for the annual round of socially prestigious occasions, endorsed by the nobility and greater gentry and funded from the collective coffers of the landed and civic élite. The town's status was enhanced by the success of the new assembly rooms, even if the outward self-confidence of Newton's neo-classical building masked the financial difficulties in realising such a project, and an inflation of the town's status that was temporarily at odds with economic reality.

Chapter 9

Newcastle's First Art Exhibitions and the Language of Civic Humanism

PAUL USHERWOOD

Is it the purpose of the fine arts to make people more virtuous and more polite? Should fine artists think of their careers solely in terms of making money and getting on in society? As John Barrell and other scholars have shown, such questions were of concern to artists, patrons and institutions in eighteenth-century London.[1] But not only London. They also preoccupied artists, patrons and institutions outside the capital. Indeed, how to reconcile a civic humanist and a consumer-oriented approach to art was very much an issue for the new art institutions – miniature Royal Academies – which as Trevor Fawcett and Andrew Hemingway have shown sprang up in towns and cities throughout Britain at the turn of the nineteenth century.[2] In this chapter I will be looking in detail at art institutions in one of these provincial towns: Newcastle. As has been noted elsewhere, in the 1820s and 1830s the appearance of public art exhibitions in the town saw a prolonged and at times bitter struggle between, on the one hand, resident painters and, on the other, a number of Newcastle's middle-class élite who, in as much as they prized intellectual endeavour, pursued political and social reform and functioned as a distinct and self-conscious group, can appropriately be described as the town's intelligentsia.[3] What has not been noted,

---

[1] John Barrell, *The Political Theory of Painting from Reynolds to Hazlitt* (New Haven and London, 1986); Stephen Copley, 'The Fine Arts in Eighteenth-century Polite Culture', in John Barrell (ed.), *Painting and the Politics of Culture: New Essays on British Art 1700-1850* (Oxford and New York, 1992), pp. 13-38; Andrew Hemingway, 'Genius, Gender and Progress: Benthamism and the Arts in the 1820s', *Art History*, 16, 4 (1993); David Solkin, *Painting for Money: The Visual Arts and the Public Sphere in Eighteenth-century England* (New Haven and London, 1992).

[2] Trevor Fawcett, *The Rise of English Provincial Art: Artists, Patrons and Institutions Outside London, 1800-1830* (Oxford, 1974); Andrew Hemingway, *Landscape Imagery and Urban Culture in Early Nineteenth-Century Britain* (Cambridge and New York, 1992). It is worth noting that with the opening in July 2002 of BALTIC, Gateshead, the largest venue for contemporary art outside London, the purpose and role of art institutions in the provinces is once again very much an issue. See Paul Usherwood, 'Getting Off At Gateshead', *Art Monthly* (September 2002), pp. 1-4.

[3] See Paul Usherwood, *Art for Newcastle: Thomas Miles Richardson and the Newcastle Exhibitions, 1822-1843* (Newcastle upon Tyne, 1984). It is true the Russian-derived term 'intelligentsia' was not in use in England until the early twentieth century. However, it seems to me appropriate here: see Raymond Williams, *Keywords: A Vocabulary of Culture and Society* (Glasgow, 1976). It should be noted that as regards Newcastle in the early nineteenth century, as with Russia in the same period, it describes a state of mind rather than a social class: see Orlando Figes, *A People's Tragedy: the Russian Revolution, 1891-1924* (London, 1996), p. 125.

however, is the extent to which each side in this struggle used the language of civic humanism to present its case. Both painters and intelligentsia, it will be argued, felt obliged to pay at least lip-service to the idea that art exhibitions should aspire to the promotion of public virtues within a republic of equal, active and independent citizens in more or less the way that had been advocated by the third earl of Shaftesbury and by other theorists in the early eighteenth century.

Newcastle's painters, for their part, invoked civic humanist terms of value by choosing to call the two institutions that successively ran – or, as we shall see, gave the impression of running – these exhibitions: 'The Northumberland Institution for the Promotion of the Fine Arts in the North of England' and 'The Northern Academy of Art'. No doubt the main reason they did so was simply fashion; it was just the kind of impressive-sounding title that provincial art institutions throughout Britain tended to give themselves at the time. Those in Hull and East Riding, Bath, Brighton, Manchester and Gloucester, for instance, all incorporated the actual phrase, 'Institution for the Promotion of the Fine Arts' in their titles. However, there was surely more to it than this. These names were also chosen because they would, it was hoped, suggest certain things. In the first place a genuine addition to the public sphere. The Northumberland Institution, for instance, may in reality have been nothing more than a series of annual exhibitions staged in a gallery room which the most energetic and ambitious Newcastle artist of the day, the landscape and marine painter, Thomas Miles Richardson senior, had had built onto the side of his house in Brunswick Place off Northumberland Street to serve as a showcase for his own work and that of his painter friends. However, the name 'Northumberland Institution', coupled with the fact that the exhibitions boasted a committee composed of an impressive array of local artists, amateurs, and businessmen, gave the illusion of something altogether more substantial: an organisation that was civic and disinterested in character run by and for a select, Shaftesburian public composed of men possessing the autonomy necessary to pursue the general good free from partiality or prejudice.

Nevertheless there was no disguising the true nature of the new body for long. A few years later, in 1828, we find Richardson more or less acknowledging the private, commercial nature of the Northumberland Institution when he boasted to an audience of notables and artists about everything that it had achieved up till then; '...when [in 1813] I took up the duties of his profession' he declared, using a combatively self-important phrase to describe his decision to chance his arm as an artist, 'there was not one stationary artist in Newcastle [an exaggeration: there were in fact five artists at that time], but they [the assembled company] had only to look around to find the most gratifying increase.'[4] And the following year J. W. Carmichael, a marine and landscape painter resident in the town and Richardson's leading pupil, made a similar point. The great achievement of the Northumberland Institution, he said, was that it had allowed practitioners like himself to make a living; 'I attribute the advance I have made

[4] *Newcastle Courant* (25 July 1828).

in the Fine Arts with... the opportunity of offering my own productions for sale... at Mr Richardson's Gallery'.[5]

A second hoped-for benefit of the portentous names chosen by the painters was that they would encourage London artists to submit work. Neither Newcastle artists nor commentators put it quite this way. In fact, in 1828 the reviewer of the *Newcastle Courant* went out of his way to pour scorn on a couple of watercolours by J. M. W. Turner, one of the undoubted stars of the London art world, which the local landowner and amateur artist, Edward Swinburne, had lent to the first Northern Academy exhibition:

> I question that even the name of Turner will procure admirers for these pictures. Indeed without his name they would not be noted at all... this sort of painting may be called freedom, or spirit, or magic, but it is not nature.[6]

Nevertheless, provincial touchiness aside, there was, as the Newcastle painters well knew, no escaping the fact that the long-term commercial success of any exhibition outside London in this period depended to a considerable degree on its being able to attract submissions from recognised metropolitan names.

Unfortunately, though, the Newcastle exhibitions seldom succeeded in wooing London artists, the problem being that there was no disguising the fact that Newcastle sales figures were distinctly poor. Only four pictures were sold out of the ninety-eight on display at the first exhibition and only eleven at the second. Indeed, during the first seven years of their existence the Newcastle exhibitions took just £1,690, a quarter of the sales figure for the comparable exhibitions at Leeds in the same period.[7] Inevitably therefore one finds London artists soon deciding to give Newcastle a miss. For sure, a number of well-known London names, Benjamin Robert Haydon, Thomas Uwins, John Martin and James Ward, for example, did submit work to the first exhibition in 1822. Significantly, though, none of them sent anything to the third in 1824. There was a moment a few years later when it looked as though they might be prepared to give Newcastle another go. This was in 1828 and 1829 when the Northern Academy, the institution which as we will see replaced the Northumberland Institution, staged its first exhibitions and large dramatic pictures by two of the most acclaimed London artists of the day, Thomas Danby and John Martin, were exhibited. In the event, however, their appearance on the Northern Academy walls was not enough. The new institution did not achieve the hoped-for pick-up in sales and as a result word soon got around that metropolitan painters would have to look elsewhere if they wished to find buyers for work they could not sell in London.

A third benefit that Richardson and the other Newcastle painters probably hoped the choice of the names 'Northumberland Institution' and 'Northern Academy' would bring was enhanced social status for themselves. That is to say, it

---

[5] It is also worth noting that Carmichael revealingly refers to the Northumberland Institution not by its official title but as 'Mr Richardson's Gallery': William Carey, *Observations on the Primary Object of the British Institution and of the Provincial Institutions for the Promotion of the Fine Arts* (London, 1829), p. 52.

[6] *Newcastle Courant* (21 June 1828).

[7] Carey quoted in Fawcett, *Rise of Provincial Art*, p. 137.

would help to distinguish local artists like themselves from the various other kinds of 'artist' practising in the town: engravers, coach-painters, monumental masons and the like. Richardson and his painter friends would have seen this as important because they were doubtless only too aware how lacking they were as regards the kind of theory-based, status-giving artistic education which so many of their counterparts in London were able to boast. Typically, for instance, Richardson's own route to becoming an artist had been humdrum in the extreme. He had started out apprenticed first to an engraver and then, following the death of his master, been bound to a cabinet-maker. Then, having served his time (seven years) as a cabinet-maker, he had turned to school teaching when his father's position as a school master at St. Andrew's in the town fell vacant. When therefore he had eventually taken the plunge and turned to drawing lessons and the production of art as his sole source of income it was relatively late in life, when he was already twenty-nine years old.[8]

More particularly, it is likely the names 'Northumberland Institution' and 'Northern Academy' were chosen partly in order to affirm the Newcastle painters' professional status in the face of the extraordinary commercial and critical success being enjoyed at the time by Thomas Bewick. Painters like Richardson, we can be sure, had an ambivalent attitude towards the renowned Newcastle wood-engraver. That is to say, they would probably have been only too happy to bask in his reflected glory, for at the end of his life Bewick was not just a national, but an international figure.[9] And indeed it is noticeable that portraits of Bewick (usually by the London-born painter, James Ramsay) appeared in several of the exhibitions in the 1820s, as did E. H. Baily's bust of him (collection: the Newcastle Literary and Philosophical Society) and one of the most remarked-upon works in any of the early exhibitions, Ramsay's *The Lost Child* (plate 6), a scene of local worthies gathered in the Corn Market by St Nicholas's that gives prominence to the by-then-elderly engraver. It is worth noting also that Bewick and his engraver-son, Robert, were members of the original eleven-man committee of the Northumberland Institution. However, significantly, when it came to actually selecting Bewick's works for the exhibitions it was a different matter; Bewick's engravings were never included in any of the exhibitions. This though, it should be pointed out, would not have necessarily seemed odd at the time for the distinction between painting and engraving was one element of civic humanist art discourse which art institutions everywhere in these years were keen to uphold. Engraving was considered too narrow, menial and mechanical an occupation to take its place alongside painting because it did not give practitioners the necessary independence to qualify as professional artists; engravers had to work for others, print-sellers or publishers and thus were not fully in control of their own production. Also, engraving was seen as concerned with material objects, with particulars rather than with the

[8] Usherwood, *Art for Newcastle*, pp. 13-17.

[9] The American painter-naturalist travelled across the Atlantic especially to visit Bewick in April 1827; John Brewer, *The Pleasures of the Imagination: English Culture in the Eighteenth Century* (London, 1997), p. 519.

abstract and formal relations existing among particulars, as was the case, supposedly, with painting.[10]

What though of the other group involved in the struggle for control of Newcastle's first exhibitions, the educated middle-class businessmen and professionals whom I referred to earlier as Newcastle's intelligentsia? Politically these men were Whigs (a little earlier, during the French Revolution, they would have been 'Radicals') enthusiasts for general Progress and Reform in the universalist manner of the French Enlightenment and Benthamite Utilitarianism, in religion Unitarians. That is to say, they were members of the Revd. William Turner's congregation in Hanover Square, behind where the present-day Central Station stands. In the context of the development of art exhibitions this meant they tended to be wedded to the idea of practical, rationalist ethics of which the development of a secular public sphere in the town in the form of a variety of philanthropic and/or educational institutions was the obvious expression. The Newcastle Literary and Philosophical Society, founded in 1793, was their earliest and most important stamping ground but they were also deeply involved in setting up and running the town's Society of Antiquaries, Natural History Society, Mechanics' Institute, School of Medicine and Surgery, Society for Promoting the Gradual Abolition of Slavery throughout the British Dominions, Savings Bank, and Society for the Diffusion of Useful Knowledge.

As one might expect therefore, as regards art exhibitions, these men (and they were all men) were markedly more inclined to invoke civic humanist values when they turned their attention to art exhibitions than were Richardson and his painter friends. When, for instance, one of their number, William Mitchell (editor of the *Tyne Mercury*) reviewed the first exhibition of the Northumberland Institution in 1822, he was typically reluctant to acknowledge the works on show as a potential source of aesthetic pleasure, preferring to see them, rather, in educational terms. 'The religious, and scientific institutions; the theatre and exhibitions of fine arts', he declared, 'we conceive to be united in their object, which is the moral and intellectual improvement of the human mind.'[11]

And initially the intelligentsia seem to have assumed that the establishment of art exhibitions did simply mean the appearance of a useful addition to the town's stock of philanthropic institutions, one which would soon, within a short space of time, like all the others take its place under their control.[12] Thus we find Mitchell congratulating Richardson on not letting his personal interests prevent him from establishing an 'independent institution', one which would show up 'the unwise and almost barbarous narrow-mindedness' of London, while at the same time producing a beneficial 'effect upon the taste, habits and character of the district'.[13] Indeed in 1823 this was still his view. He was greatly

---

[10] When it was founded in 1768, the Royal Academy included no engravers, much to the annoyance of some: ibid., p. 250.

[11] *Tyne Mercury* (1 October 1822).

[12] Stephen Harbottle, *The Reverend William Turner: Dissent and Reform in Georgian Newcastle Upon Tyne* (Newcastle upon Tyne, 1997), pp. 101-24.

[13] *Tyne Mercury* (1 October 1822).

encouraged, he wrote, by the fact that James Losh, barrister and coal-owner, Edward Bulman, physician, the Revd. John Hodgson, historian, Emmerson Charnley, bookseller, and T. W. Keenlyside, solicitor, all of them leading members of the intelligentsia group, had been recruited onto the committee of the new institution.[14]

By 1825, however, Mitchell was less sanguine. In his literary monthly, the *Newcastle Magazine*, he expressed puzzlement at the fact that, whereas Carlisle's institution had somehow managed to provide art classes as well as an annual exhibition, this mysteriously seemed to be beyond the powers of the Northumberland Institution which, by contrast, seemed content to be nothing more than 'a mere show of pictures'. This was a fair point and it had the effect of goading Richardson into a response. Although we do not have a record of quite what this was, we can infer more or less what was said from the fact that two years later Mitchell felt obliged to offer an explanation:

> We had no vengeance to wreak, no spleen to gratify – though our motives are misrepresented and our critical character maligned, not only by interested parties, and their sycophantic allies but by some of our contemporary journals [probably a reference to the more conservative *Durham County Advertiser* and the *Newcastle Courant* which tended to take Richardson's side] who through ignorance or malice stoop to receive personal attacks from men whose names and histories we have only to mention to hold them up to the scorn and derision of the people.[15]

Relations between the two parties had now all but broken down and the intelligentsia seem to have decided that the only way forward was for them to take over the running of the exhibitions themselves. This anyway is how I read a report in 1827 of a scheme to rent the Institution's Brunswick Place room from Richardson which was put forward by the Northumberland Institution committee, a body which as we have seen was very much dominated by intelligentsia figures.[16] Predictably, Richardson said 'no', which in turn duly prompted the committee to announce their intention to stage exhibitions of their own on entirely new, purpose-built premises.[17] If they had actually proceeded with this, it would surely have put paid to Richardson's position as an exhibitions organiser. However, luckily for him, he had an important ally, the genre painter Henry Perlee Parker (a major contributor to the exhibitions as well as secretary of the Northumberland Institution) and Parker decided at this point to side publicly with him. Having Parker supporting him was enough to ensure that the new-look exhibitions did not go ahead, for although it would (as we shall see) be different later, at this date there was no question of the intelligentsia being able

[14] In the previous year, 1822 Mitchell had expressed some concern that Richardson had allowed the committee to become 'an unnatural hotch-potch of artists, amateurs and gentlemen' rather than of a group of appropriately disinterested gentlemen of the kind who, he believed, were guiding the exhibitions in Leeds and Manchester.

[15] *Tyne Mercury* (5 June 1827).

[16] *Newcastle Magazine* (December, 1827), p. 569.

[17] A further reason for building new premises was that although the Brunswick Place room had a new entrance and staircase it was regarded as cramped and unsatisfactory: *Tyne Mercury* (23 May 1825).

to stage exhibitions on their own without the co-operation and involvement of the town's leading artists.

Richardson, however, knew that he had only won a temporary reprieve and now resolved to set up an entirely new institution of his own, the Northern Academy of Arts which would have its own purpose-built premises but, significantly, no committee. And in September 1827 Parker and he bought a plot of land in Blackett Street, opposite the south-east corner of the newly-completed Eldon Square, and contracted the up-and-coming Newcastle developer, Richard Grainger, to proceed with a building. In architectural terms their new institution was a big advance on the Northumberland Institution with its rooms in Brunswick Place. Designed by the local architect, John Dobson, it had a stone façade and giant recessed columns outside and inside there were two top-lit octagonal rooms, which could, if necessary, be turned into a single, large exhibition space. In the words of the first catalogue in 1828, the Northern Academy offered 'much more elegance of finish and beauty of design than many edifices usually allotted to the display of works of art in England'. However, financially it was a disaster. Faced with a bill of £2000 for the construction work, the two 'Directors', as they termed themselves, were badly out of pocket from the start and even before the first exhibition we find Parker begging his friend, the Newcastle-born painter, William Nicholson, secretary of the newly-founded Scottish Academy, to use whatever influence he had to persuade London artists to submit work.[18] Luckily Nicholson was able to help out and in 1828 Thomas Danby's vast and sensational picture, *The Valley of the Upas Tree, or the Poison Tree on the Island of Java* (collection: Victoria and Albert Museum) appeared on their walls. As a result they were able to count the new institution's first exhibition something of a success; it took between £500 and £600 in sales, double the sum for any of the exhibitions of the Northumberland Institution. Indeed, as Parker reported in a letter to Nicholson, it 'would have been equal to our expectations had it not been visited with a very wet season, which we think has prevented the attendance of many visitors, as well as purchases; but from certain circumstances we have yet much hopes'.[19]

After this, however, things started to go badly wrong. In September 1828, as soon as the inaugural exhibition came down, the two painters put on a loan exhibition of works by 'the most celebrated Ancient and Deceased Masters, selected from the best collections', mostly in fact paintings from the collections of members of local landowners, Ralph Carr and Sir Thomas and C. J. Clavering. Presumably their hope was that this would win over their various critics amongst the intelligentsia and at the same time attract interest from the local gentry, always their best hope as regards selling their own work. Unfortunately though, it was a dismal failure on both counts. In the words of the *Newcastle Chronicle*, many of the works on display were 'palpable copies', and the local gentry proved to be no more inclined to buy the work of living artists than they had previously.[20] Parker was moved to complain to his friend Nicholson,

---

[18] Royal Scottish Academy archive, Edinburgh, Letters from Parker to Nicholson (6 and 12 May 1822).

[19] Ibid. (2 September and 31 August 1828).

[20] *Newcastle Chronicle* (15 November 1828).

> I am half inclined to think that nine cases out of ten the domination of the Antients to be either from fashion's sake or an affectation on account of the names of some of the painters. I might have liked the Old Masters a little more had they been the means of sending us a little more cash.[21]

Thus, by the end of 1828, Richardson and Parker found that their debts had doubled, and the only way of keeping the Academy afloat was to accept contributions from the Newcastle Corporation and members of the local gentry (such as Sir John Swinburne and Sir Matthew White Ridley) and to put on fund-raising events, such as a subscription dinner, a diorama and evening viewings of the exhibition by gaslight at 7s 6d a head. [22]

Seeing the Academy obviously floundering in this way, *The Northern John Bull*, a new, short-lived pro-intelligentsia magazine, now made a concerted attempt to end artist-run exhibitions in Newcastle for once and for all by accusing the new institution of being not just nakedly commercial but corrupt as well. 'The Academy', the magazine asserted, 'originated with, and has continued to be the private speculation of two local painters and [...] sums of money received as donations, subscriptions and admissions, flow into the pockets of the speculators untithed and untouched.' Such allegations could not be ignored, and Richardson and Parker duly attempted to defend themselves by declaring in the catalogue of the 1830 exhibition that; 'We have been assailed with a degree of virulent malignity which nothing short of personal hostility could supply or the most rancorous enmity sustain'.[23] They also enlisted the support of William Carey, a prominent London art dealer and critic who for the previous thirty years had been tirelessly championing the cause of art exhibitions in the provinces.[24]

Carey's sixty-eight page pamphlet, *Observations on the Primary Object of the British Institution and of the Provincial Institutions for the promotion of the Fine Arts; and showing the necessity, the wisdom, and the moral glory of cherishing a national spirit and the patronage of the British School, and the national pride and excellence of the British School* can, I think, be read as point by point rejoinder to the charges that the *Northern John Bull* had made. 'I am not inclined,' the author says, 'to take arms against a public benefit merely because it is connected with a private interest.'[25] After all, the most important art institution in

---

[21] Royal Scottish Academy archive, Edinburgh, letter from Parker to Nicholson (13 November 1828).

[22] The diorama was painted by Richardson and Parker and seems to have been a major enterprise. It depicted 'The Entrance to the Shrine of Henry V in Westminster abbey', 'The Interior of of the Hermitage, Warkworth', 'Melrose Abbey by Moonlight' and 'Majuri, from a Cavern in Salerno', covered 1,350 feet of canvas and, unusually for the time, was displayed in such a way that spectators were carried past rather than vice versa. There are no records of other dioramas being exhibited in Newcastle in the 1820s and 1830s although it is known that a number of panoramas were staged in the Long Room of the Turk's Head in Grey Street.

[23] *Catalogue of the Northern Academy* (1830).

[24] Fawcett, *Rise of English Provincial Art*, p. 194.

[25] Carey, *Observations*, p. 28.

the country, the Royal Academy, started out as a 'private concern only'.[26] Indeed, it was precisely because, unlike the Northern Academy, other provincial institutions elsewhere in the country lacked 'intelligent and zealous individuals... one or two able and influential "working men" at the helm' that so many of them had gone under. Nor should a provincial institution feel obliged to run a school for even the very grand and respected British Institution in London, it should be remembered, did not have a school.[27] Besides, what do schools produce? They produce artists, and surely Britain had enough of those already. What the country needed were patrons, and the best way of finding those was to put on public art exhibitions. Public art exhibitions (and this was Carey's central point) are the 'Best Mode of Creating Maecenases'.[28]

For a while, this consumer-focused argument seemed to do the trick. The intelligentsia attacks came to a halt, and the Northern Academy staggered on. However, with their debts steadily increasing, Richardson and Parker felt beleaguered. Indeed, we learn from private correspondence that Parker had been feeling under pressure long before this. In fact, even before the first exhibition opened, he was complaining to Nicholson in Edinburgh of 'anxieties and fatigues' which were 'quite disarranging my digestive organs', so much so that his physician Dr Headlam was having to prescribe a long sea voyage as a rest-cure. 'I wonder how in the world', he mused, 'you have stood it so well as my labours must have been nothing to yours – the prospect of fame however is full of compensation of these topics and an artist who will not be a martyr to his profession scarcely deserves the name of Artist'.[29]

Inevitably, the Academy eventually folded. The *coup-de-grâce* when it came in 1831 was an announcement by Richard Grainger, the Newcastle developer, of his intention to erect a music hall close by. This proved fatal, because it at once dashed any hopes that the two entrepreneurs may have had that they could soldier on by staging musical soirées and the like. So, for the moment, artist-run exhibitions in Newcastle were at an end and the way lay open for the intelligentsia to set up an art institution of their own, something which in the event they spared little time in doing. The Newcastle Institution for the General Promotion of Fine Arts was inaugurated at a meeting at the Eldon Coffee House in Blackett Street on 31 December 1831, attended by James Losh, T. W. Keenlyside, Mitchell, and various other intelligentsia figures.

Predictably, what chiefly distinguished the Newcastle Institution as well as its successor, the North of England Society for the Promotion of the Fine Arts, from the artist-run bodies of the 1820s, was an emphasis on education. They provided formal training as well as regular exhibitions. Specifically, Peter Nicholson taught 'Architectural Drawing, Geometry and perspective' to 'young and intelligent builders and engineers' and Francis Oliphant gave lessons in

---

[26] Ibid., p.17.

[27] Ibid., p. 32.

[28] That Carey's pamphlet was intended as a rejoinder to intelligentsia attacks is indicated by the fact that following its publication Richardson and Parker wrote a letter of thanks which appeared in the *Northern Courant* (2 September 1829).

[29] Royal Scottish Academy archive, Edinburgh, letter from Parker to Nicholson (28 June 1828).

'ornamental and decorative drawing and design' to 'artisans'. In addition, ten days were set aside at the end of the annual exhibition for the 'working classes' to visit 'Gratis admission', an innovation probably inspired by a similar arrangement that had been tried successfully at the Natural History Society Museum.

So does this mean that the intelligentsia's involvement in art exhibitions was genuinely disinterested and compatible with civic humanist values in a way that the painters' was not? To some extent, yes. The emphasis on education, especially the education of the working classes, can be seen as a Christian, specifically Unitarian, version of Shaftesbury's attempt to attach a traditional civic notion of virtue to a patrician, aestheticised model of social relations. When, for instance, the intelligentsia publicly discussed art exhibitions they tended to do so not as places of pleasure and aesthetic delight, but as settings for a kind of civilising ritual in which Newcastle inhabitants had the opportunity to practise being good citizens.[30] Thus, one finds that newspapers such as the *Tyne Mercury* were willing to give exhaustive coverage to individual exhibitions (one hundred and sixty-two column inches in 1827 alone). However, the comments they made on individual works tended to be platitudinous and perfunctory, and always gave the impression that what really mattered was not the work on the walls but by whom and for whom the exhibitions were being staged. When, for instance, Losh and his fellow 'Friends of the Arts' (as they called themselves) set up the Newcastle Institution, typically they made a special point of stipulating that although professional artists were allowed to be shareholders, they could be members of the management committee.[31]

In many ways, then, one can say the intelligentsia's involvement in art exhibitions was marked by the kind of unselfish dedication to public service that was fundamental to civic humanism. However, closer examination, it seems to me, shows their motives were far from completely disinterested. In the first place, the emphasis they put on education can be seen as helping to create a docile and malleable workforce, by which they as a group (many of them were employers) stood to gain. Similarly, to be seen to be in charge of art exhibitions in the town served their interests in that it gave them cultural capital, something which in the 1820s, when the Whigs were out of office and dissenters like themselves were still subject to legal constraints, they greatly appreciated. That is, membership of the managing committees of the various local bodies responsible for art, science, philanthropy and the spread of knowledge in the town provided a way, perhaps the only way, by which they could promote themselves as potential leaders of the local community. It also helped to shape

[30] This was also, it should be noted, true of eighteenth-century humanism. As Ronald Paulson observes, something that 'characterized the tradition of civic humanist aesthetics was the absence of material art objects. The position of the actually made object was usurped in this tradition by ideal hypotheses...' In *Breaking and Remaking: Aesthetic Practice in England, 1700-1820* (New Brunswick, N.J. 1989), p. 3.

[31] Interestingly, when James Losh mentioned the Literary and Philosophical Society in a speech at the Northern Academy banquet in 1829 he referred to it as the 'parent' of the Academy and this was quite inaccurate. As noted earlier, the Literary and Philosophical Society was the parent of a whole string of institutions, but not of the Northern Academy.

Newcastle's public life in their own image. Newcastle's public life was in effect redefined as being whatever sphere of activity fell (and there were few seemingly that did not) within the remit of the various secular institutions over which they presided.

Lastly, to illustrate this seemingly, but in truth not altogether selfless, stance let me turn to a particular work of art from the period I have been discussing: the twice-life-size statue by John Graham Lough of James Losh, a key intelligentsia figure whose name I have mentioned several times in this chapter, on the main staircase of the Literary and Philosophical Society of Newcastle upon Tyne. From one perspective, as the lengthy inscription on the plinth states, this is the effigy of a successful lawyer who eventually succeeded in becoming Newcastle's Recorder. This at least would seem to be the implication of the pile of books at Losh's feet, the oratorical pose and the way the toga is wound round one shoulder, as on the statue of Demosthenes in the Vatican Museum. Clearly though it is not just this. The statue is also an assertion of power. The upright yet relaxed stance, starkly simple classical attire and calm, dignified gaze combined with the location, the intelligentsia's main political and intellectual base, can be seen as classifying Losh and his fellow intelligentsia members as new, middle-class versions of Shaftesbury's ideal of the landed gentleman-philosopher-citizen. It is through the benevolent, disinterested efforts of men like these, we seem to be told, that 'the moral and intellectual improvement of the human mind' (to quote William Mitchell once again) could be, and indeed was being, achieved.

Index

Please note that numbers in bold refer to illustrations included in the book.